# Driving Over a Cliff?

*Business Lessons from the World's Car Industry*

# The EIU Series

This innovative series of books is the result of a publishing collaboration between Addison-Wesley and the Economist Intelligence Unit. Our authors draw on the results of original research by the EIU's skilled research and editorial staff to provide a range of topical, information-rich and incisive business titles. They are specifically tailored to the needs of international executives and business education worldwide.

## Titles in the Series

# Driving Over a Cliff?

## Business Lessons from the World's Car Industry

Graeme P. Maxton

John Wormald

The Economist
Intelligence Unit

**ADDISON-WESLEY PUBLISHING COMPANY**

Wokingham, England • Reading, Massachusetts • Menlo Park, California • New York
Don Mills, Ontario • Amsterdam • Bonn • Sydney • Singapore
Tokyo • Madrid • San Juan • Milan • Paris • Mexico City • Seoul • Taipei

Cover designed by Viva Design Ltd, Henley-on-Thames
incorporating photograph by Kerry Lawrence
and printed by The Riverside Printing Co. (Reading) Ltd.
Text designed by Valerie O'Donnell.
Line diagrams drawn by Margaret Macknelly Design, Tadley.
Typeset by Meridian Phototypesetting Limited, Pangbourne.
Printed in Great Britain at the University Press, Cambridge.

First printed 1994.

ISBN 0-201-59392-0

**British Library Cataloguing in Publication Data**
A catalogue record for this book is available from the British Library

**Library of Congress Cataloging in Publication Data** applied for.

*For Robin, Edward, Lucy and Julian*

There is nothing more difficult to carry out, nor more doubtful to success, nor more dangerous to handle, than to initiate a new order of things. For the reformer has enemies in all who profit by the old order and only lukewarm defenders in all those who would profit by the new order. This lukewarmness arises partly from fear of their adversaries, who have the law in their favour; and partly from the incredulity of mankind, who do not truly believe in anything new until they have had actual experience of it.

*Niccolò Machiavelli, 1513*

# Preface

Why another book about the automotive industry? Is the world not deluged with books and magazines about cars? Has it not all been said before? We think not. Much has been written and continues to be written. But it is often done from a partial or biased point of view. Looking at products only, usually in an adulatory way. Attacking the industry in a one-sided fashion. Concentrating on its admittedly fascinating personalities, or its troubles. On the whole concerned much more with the supply side of the sector and the competitive wars within it than with the demand side, the influence of the automobile on our lives, or the social and economic compromises we make to adapt to it.

We had another motivation. Both of us work with and in this industry and daily learn to understand and respect its complexity, diversity and significance. It has been described as the industry of industries. Which led us back to it through a completely different route. For some years, we have taught part of the initial residential weekend of the Evening MBA Course at the City University Business School in London. Our task has been to introduce the participants to first notions of industry and strategic analysis. Wisely or unwisely, we have chosen the automotive industry and firms within it to illustrate these principles. This has forced us both to try to look at the industry as a complete phenomenon and to seek to reduce the description of its structures and dynamics to simple principles. This book is in many ways the outcome of that process.

Few can have complete, in-depth, first-hand experience of this immense industry in all its aspects. We certainly do not claim this. Much of the evidence we put forward is in the public domain. What we have tried to add is a framework of thinking and analysis which will hopefully enable the reader to cut through at least some of the complexity and mystique. Many in the industry seem to believe that it follows its own laws. Our fundamental thesis is that, in the last analysis, this is in fact an industry like any other, subject to the same ageing process – the lifecycle – the same economic phenomena, the same market and competitive dynamics, and the same environmental and political pressures.

This book is therefore aimed at several categories of readers. It is meant to be an example of industry analysis for MBA students – not to instruct them especially about the automotive industry, but rather to have them use it as a life-size case example. We hope it will also be of value to those who work in the industry itself and on its periphery, some of whom occasionally find it difficult to step back and up, and take a more all-encompassing view of the phenomenon in which they are involved. We also offer it to the more general public, business or otherwise, for the fascinating story and challenge that the automotive industry offers.

The views expressed in it are obviously our own and our responsibility. Clearly, though, we have not invented them in a vacuum. We owe profound thanks to the many friends in and around the industry with and for whom we have worked in the course of the last several years. We particularly hope they will find interest and stimulation in it – and perhaps a partial return for all we have learned from them.

Some of the material and several of the illustrations are reproduced from articles in the EIU Motor Quarterlies contributed by authors from Booz, Allen & Hamilton, including ourselves.

*Graeme Maxton*
*John Wormald*
London, October 1994

# Contents

# Introduction

## The universal concept of the lifecycle

Like people, products and industries emerge into the world, grow, reach maturity and eventually decline. They follow a lifecycle. Like people, the opportunities for products change as they get older. Like people, producers need to understand and exploit this change if they are to prosper. This book is about the exploitation of change.

The product lifecycle has four distinct stages, as shown in Figure 0.1. *Introduction*, when the product is launched; *growth,* when the product becomes accepted and its penetration rises rapidly; *maturity,* when the growth slows; and, finally, *decline.* Each stage can last days, weeks, years,

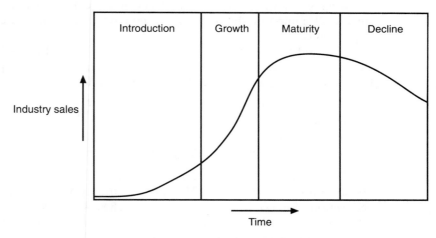

**Figure 0.1**  The stages of the lifecycle.

or even decades. Interactive media, virtual reality and genetic engineering are all industries in the introductory phase, for example. They have still to prove their value to most potential consumers. Similarly, compact discs, personal computers and mobile telecommunications are all industries in their growth phase. They are much more established in terms of their technology and product development and are in high demand. The ubiquitous Mars Bar is a common example of a mature product with relatively stable demand. Finally, in the developed world at least, shipbuilding, steel production and coal mining are all examples of industries in decline.

One of the most critical phases in the lifecycle is the transformation from growth to maturity. Competitors move from high growth, fast-moving markets to ones where penetration is high and there are few new growth opportunities. In the growth stage, the level of competition is often not particularly intense. It doesn't need to be, because growth comes from the ever-expanding market-place. In the mature phase, competition becomes much more intense as suppliers struggle to maintain their profitability. Industrial consolidation and rationalization are much more likely as competitors make acquisitions or drive others out of business to increase their market share.

An additional problem for an industry approaching maturity is that often those who work in that industry refuse to acknowledge the position until it is too late. Managers who have become used to an expanding market tend to believe that any slowing of demand is temporary. It is the result of economic conditions, of a recession, they say. Such short-sightedness can be very damaging.

It is essential to understand the effects of maturity on an industry. Failure to do so can be expensive. Thirty years ago, few governments or managers in staple industries would accept that these sectors were maturing or that they would eventually decline. Yet those who worked in steel, coal mining or shipbuilding are now only too well aware of the implications.

To avoid the same mistakes in the future, we need to understand what happens when major industrial segments reach a plateau. Competitors need to be able to answer several questions:

- When will maturity end and decline set in?
- How will other competitors and suppliers behave?
- How can future growth be maximized for the enterprise?
- How can profitability and dividends be maintained?

They need to identify strategies that will put them in the strongest possible position in the future. They need to know whether or not to seek acquisitions for economies of scale or niches with opportunities for differentiation. If these options do not exist, they need to know whether diversification is realistic. One thing seems clear: the strategy that was most appropriate during the period of high growth is unlikely to be optimal during the phases of maturity and eventual decline.

# The implications of the lifecycle for the automotive industry

For most of us alive today, certainly in the developed world, the car is an accepted and apparently permanent part of our lives. The influence of the motor industry has also grown steadily since cars first emerged at the end of the 19th century. It is now one of the largest and most important industrial sectors in the world. It accounts for around 13% of the GDP of most developed nations, and employs one in seven people, directly or indirectly. The increase in mobility that cars have allowed is a one-way street: we cannot conceive of this new liberty being taken away, or limits being placed upon it. Similarly, few people working in the industry can conceive of a world where the number of cars in use will not continue to grow. And, who can blame them? The industry has experienced an average compound annual growth rate of more than 8% over the last 90 years, even if it has slowed down of late. A glance at most predictions for the car industry show a never ending upward trend, an extrapolation of the past. More people, more wealth, more cars, more roads.

Yet there is a conflict. We know products have lives, that they mature, that growth rates decline. There are considerable pressures for change in the car industry today. They are not about new competitors, or cleaner engines or more structured supplier networks. They are not about improved manufacturing methods, shorter model cycle times and the integration of components into subsystems. These new pressures are not incremental, as they have been in the last 30 years. They are structural and, what's more, fundamental. They affect the very future of the industry because they are the result of its maturity.

The industry has grown very rapidly, has brought us a revolution in terms of production processes, is now one of the most important industrial segments on the globe, will remain focused on the wealthiest nations for many years to come – and is running out of major new opportunities for growth. What then makes it worthy of study? The answer is that this is an exceptionally interesting case of a complex global industry facing maturity. Slowing growth and intensifying competition are driving a fundamental change in its economics that will force rationalization and consolidation on the suppliers.

This in itself would be worthy of analysis, particularly given the influence the motor industry has on other business sectors. However, other fundamental changes are also taking place. Not for the first time in its history, there is a growing rebellion against the motor car. This time it seems serious. There are demands for lower emissions, greater safety and less congestion, which are creating new and difficult challenges for vehicle producers, component suppliers and governments. Other changes are also taking place. In much of the developed world, real disposable income levels are expected to fall in the next decade because of rising social costs. This is likely to affect the fundamental characteristics of demand – it may shift buyers from expensive high-speed, executive saloons to more basic, low-cost, utilitarian runabouts.

The motor industry, at the very broadest level, faces a difficult future – a period in which there will be low growth, firms will be forced to consolidate, there will be increasing environmental pressure and fundamental changes in the nature of demand. This is an unstable mixture and a potentially explosive mixture, full of both threats and opportunities. This book identifies what maturity will mean for the world's automotive industry. It reviews the pressures for change and offers suggestions for competitors. How they can act now, to win tomorrow. How they can ensure that they continue to survive.

The book has far more to offer, however. Many of the forces for change in the car industry will affect a great many other sectors. The effects of these pressures on the oil industry, the railways and the airlines are perhaps most obvious. But the pressures will also affect the telecommunications sector, the plastics industry and many other chemicals and materials suppliers. More importantly, the lessons for the automotive sector should be equally valuable to suppliers of computers, fast foods and even financial services. Indeed, businesses in most sectors would, we believe, find the lessons in this book useful in developing their longer-term strategies. There are also lessons to be learned from the sometimes fraught relationships between the industry and governments.

There have been many books on the automotive industry in the past. We believe this one is fundamentally different. Many other books just look at the 'supply side' of the industry – the manufacturing processes, the technologies being applied to new cars, and the companies and individuals responsible for them. These books often only give a passing acknowledgment to the other side of the equation, the 'demand side' – the market and how it has evolved, the level of vehicle penetration that has been achieved and the impact that cars have had on society. A typical example is Bricnet and Mangolte's interesting book, *L'Europe automobile*[1], whose introduction opens with these words: 'This book is written in a town invaded by the automobile ... but in it we shall examine the production and selling of cars.'

Clearly, as any student of economics will tell you, to look at one side of a market without the other is to have a one-sided view. To study the determinants of supply without understanding the needs of the market is simply misleading. It can also lead to poor investment decisions. After all, to take a topical example, what is the point of investing in electric cars if no one wants to buy them?

This book tries to redress the balance. While it discusses the supply side – the technologies, and engineering and manufacturing resources and organizations required to produce world-class motor vehicles and the future development of cars themselves – it also puts a great deal of emphasis on the market and on forces external to the industry:

- What are the factors that will determine the demand for cars in the future?
- How are environmental and social pressures likely to affect demand?
- What sort of vehicles will consumers want?
- What influence will legislators have?
- How many cars will be sold in different parts of the world over the next decade?

By understanding these issues, car producers will be in a much stronger position to determine how vehicles should be produced. They will also have a much better understanding of where to manufacture cars, what type of cars they should design and how they might approach the market.

Most importantly of all, this book should give those with an interest in the car industry an insight into the strategic alternatives open to them and their competitors. As we shall see, for many companies involved in the car industry today, the options are limited. Many vehicle and component suppliers face a stagnant market, tougher competition and intense pressure to consolidate. Without overstating the case, if the strategic priority that characterized the industry in the past was growth, that of the future will almost certainly be survival. And, simply put, those companies that act decisively and with foresight today will almost certainly have a better chance of making it in the future. This book aims to provide a little of that foresight.

Part One deals with society and the demand for automobiles, covering the social impact of road vehicles, the durability of demand for them, and the changing nature of that demand, as seen from the perspective of the end-customer.

Part Two covers the supply side today: changes in product structures and offerings; the roles played by the car manufacturers; the growing global power of the Japanese vehicle manufacturers; the restructuring of the components industry; the continuing imperfections in distribution, retailing and aftermarket structures; the restrictions on the entry of new players into the industry; and the overall state of the industry today.

Part Three examines the outlook for the industry, globally and region by region, in terms of market and competitive dynamics.

Part Four explores the options for the future use and design of cars; for individual car manufacturers; and for the other players in the industry.

Part Five summarizes the lessons to be learned from the lifecycle changes that pervade the industry and their applicability across other sectors.

# Note

1.  Bricnet and Mangolte. *L'Europe automobile: Virages d'une industrie en mutation.* Nathan

# Society and the demand for automobiles

# 1

# From blessing to curse? The societal impact of road vehicles

## From horse to horsepower

In the time it takes to read this sentence, five new motor vehicles will have been produced somewhere in the world. The rate of production and consumption of motor vehicles is little short of astounding. Every minute, 95 new cars are manufactured and sold – 24 hours a day, 365 days a year. The production for one day alone would generate a line of vehicles nearly 400 miles long.

Most of us in the developed world take the car for granted. We use it to travel to work, to visit friends and to carry out essential tasks such as shopping or taking children to school. The car is now a basic element in our lives. Even those who do not own cars make the majority of their journeys in them. Compared with 100 years ago, the car has given us undreamed of levels of mobility and freedom. Yet, given its effect on our lives, it is easy for us to forget that the motor vehicle is a comparatively recent phenomenon.

Although the car was introduced at the end of the last century, the market for passenger cars only really took off in the United States after the First World War (see Figure 1.1) and in Europe after the Second World War, 50 years ago. Even then, its major impact has been concentrated on a few select regions of the world – the economic Triad of North America, Europe and Japan. The Triad may account for most of the world's wealth, but it only accounts for 14% of the global population. The car is therefore a relatively recent and a highly exclusive commodity.

9

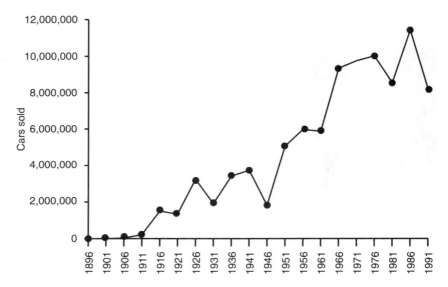

**Figure 1.1**    Growth of car sales from 1896–1991 in the United States. (*Source*: *Automotive News*, Polk, and others)

The impact the car has had on our lives in the developed world is huge. Just 100 years ago more than 70% of prime mover horsepower came from the railroads and work animals – mainly horses themselves (see Figure 1.2). In just over 30 years after the introduction of the automobile, the influence of traditional sources of horsepower declined dramatically. By 1920, 70% of prime mover horsepower in the US was installed in road vehicles. By 1970, more than 90% of it was generated by cars, buses and trucks.

Will this impact continue to grow? Or will it wane? What are the prospects for the world's automotive industry? Is it a special case, or is it subject to the general laws of business?

# If you were sitting in 1890, would you do this?

With the benefits of hindsight, has the automobile been good for mankind during its first 100 years? The answer is inevitably mixed: the development of motor vehicles has clearly brought us enormous benefits but also a high degree of dependence on them and some considerable associated costs.

Our dependence on the car has increased steadily in the last hundred years. In the UK the average distance an individual travelled in 1890 was

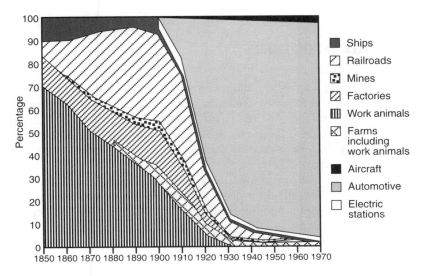

**Figure 1.2**  US automotive horsepower share of all prime movers, 1850–1970. (*Source*: Statistical abstract of the USA, reproduced from: EIU, International Motor Business, Q3, 1993)

13 miles a year. By 1990, it was 13 miles a day. As individuals we use cars for almost all (94%) of our travel requirements in the developed world. Similarly, the great majority of freight is carried by road. Oil crises demonstrate the extent to which developed societies have become automotive-dependent. They show that we cannot function normally without motor vehicles.

The motor industry has therefore given us mobility and freedom. While this is probably its single biggest benefit, it is very difficult to quantify. The car has enabled us to live and work in different places, to shop at out-of-town superstores that offer economies of scale, to visit friends in distant places and to have weekend breaks in the country. We can drive across borders to stock up on bargains, save time using drive-in restaurants and banks or simply take a tour, ensconced in warm mobile look-outs. Cars are generally reliable, low cost and practical. The marginal cost of a journey, in terms of fuel, is small compared to other forms of transport, even in Europe. Cars also offer status, prestige, something to aim for.

The motor industry brings many other benefits, some of which are explored in more detail in later chapters. They are net contributors of taxes in many countries, bring in huge export revenues and are responsible for a large proportion of employment in most developed nations. Most significantly of all, the industry has brought us mass production, which has had a radical influence on almost all manufactured goods.

# Societal problems

The car has always had its enemies. In the early years Anti Automobile Associations were common, particularly among farmers in America. Many pioneering drivers suffered verbal abuse, vandalism and ridicule, particularly if their cars broke down. Indeed, it was not uncommon for early drivers to give up their machines after a few years, such was the harassment.

It's true, of course, cars have drawbacks. They are polluting and noisy. Cars and their drivers have been responsible for millions of premature deaths and injuries in the last 100 years. The industry has brought new words like joyrider and carjacker into the language. Cars have meant that much of our land is now covered in roads, our cities reorganized into one-way systems and our yards and basements changed into parking places. These are probably the most obvious drawbacks. A few statistics illustrate some of the costs:

- According to a study done in Los Angeles, 220 cancer cases are caused every year by drivers breathing in the benzene in unleaded fuel while filling their tanks.[1]
- A US Department of Transport study showed that property values decrease by $182 for every decibel increase in noise level. Within the OECD, 110 million people are exposed to unacceptable levels of noise (> 65 decibels) due to motor vehicles.
- According to the European Commission, motor vehicles release 19 million tonnes of carbon monoxide and 4 million tonnes of nitrous oxide a year into Europe, with serious consequences for health and the region's ecology.[2]
- The OECD estimates that the environmental damage motor vehicles create is equal to 1% to 2% of an industrialized nation's GDP.[3] That is around $200 per person a year, in Europe.
- The Confederation of British Industry in the UK calculated that motor vehicle congestion cost the country nearly $23 billion a year, or roughly $1000 per vehicle.[4]

Other effects of vehicles include damage to building foundations, emissions from paint shops, leakage from abandoned batteries and air bag propellants as well as the dumping of used motor oil. More than 450 million tyres are discarded annually worldwide as are more than 550 million gallons of engine oil.

We analyse the negative influence of motor vehicles under five categories:

(1)   Pollution and waste
(2)   Accidents and deaths

(3)   Congestion
(4)   Noise
(5)   Other social effects.

It is important to remember while reading this that while the motor industry and national governments recognize these problems, they can do little to reduce their effects in the short term. It is simply not practical to limit car use, or make cars safer and less polluting overnight. Even if all new cars were as safe and as clean as technologically possible, there are hundreds of millions of cars already on the roads that will last for at least another six or seven years, on average. For the time being therefore, the problems caused by motor vehicles have to be regarded as a consequential cost of the vast increase in mobility.

Having said that, there are two factors that will stimulate change:

(1)   Increasing awareness of the problems
(2)   An increase in the level of damage vehicles cause.

First, there is a growing awareness of the problems motor vehicles cause and their effects. Many more government bodies now study the impact of air pollution, congestion and road fatalities. Universities produce more and more evidence on the damage exhaust fumes cause to our health. The Green movement, particularly in Europe, has arisen partly out of this growing awareness. Cars are one of the most visible sources of pollution, simply because so many people use them.

The second factor that is likely to stimulate change is the increasing damage that motor vehicles are causing. While road deaths are almost constant in the developed world, thanks to legislation and increased vehicle safety, the number of accidents continues to rise in proportion to the volume of vehicles. Similarly, the output of exhaust pollutants is also growing, despite the use of catalysts, because of the increased number of vehicles in use. The situation is the same for noise pollution. Difficulties with congestion are also growing rapidly as additional vehicles have a geometric rather than an arithmetic impact on it.

# Pollution and waste

The motor industry is responsible for a number of different air pollutants. Hydrocarbon (HC) compounds, or volatile organic compounds, are released from exhaust pipes, fuel systems and filling stations. Some hydrocarbons can cause unpleasant side-effects, including drowsiness, eye irritation and coughing. One of the hydrocarbons emitted is a known carcinogen. According to the World Health

Organization, the recommended concentration of benzene in the atmosphere is zero. It is always wise, therefore, to turn your head away from the filler when refuelling, particularly with unleaded fuel, unless the pump nozzle is fitted with a vapour capture system – still a rarity in most of the world, including most of Europe.

Hydrocarbons are important because they react with nitrogen oxides to form ozone at ground level. Ozone, while necessary as a shield against solar ultraviolet radiation in the upper atmosphere, is an aggressive oxidant, which attacks the lungs. It is also one of the principal causes of urban smogs.

Cars are the main source of carbon monoxide (CO) in most developed nations. Nearly 100% of the CO emissions in urban areas are caused by road traffic. CO reduces the efficiency of the bloodstream to carry blood around the body. Exposure to CO can result in impaired vision, co-ordination, judgement and drowsiness. It also affects the central nervous and cardiovascular systems. Motor vehicles also produce carbon dioxide ($CO_2$) because of the carbon basis of fuels. They account for 22% of all $CO_2$ emissions. Carbon dioxide is claimed to be a major cause of what scientists believe may be a gradual warming of the planet, the so-called Greenhouse Effect.

The third major pollutant is nitrogen oxides (NOx). This covers both nitrogen dioxide and nitric oxide. Nitrogen dioxide reduces the productivity of some crops and can irritate the lungs and respiratory tract. Nitrogen oxides are precursors to ground-level ozone and contribute a large proportion of acid rainfall – some claim as much as half.

The final pollutant from fuels and exhausts, mainly from diesel engines, is particulates or soot. According to the EU, 50% of particulates in the atmosphere in Europe come from motor vehicles. Again, these have been blamed for aggravating respiratory diseases. There has also been a debate for many years on the possible carcinogenic effects of particulates, although this remains unproved. None the less, the International Agency for Research on Cancer stated in 1989 that diesel exhaust particulates were a probable carcinogen.

Car makers claim that most of the pollutants in the atmosphere have other origins in any event and that exhaust catalyst systems will remove up to 95% of the carbon monoxide and hydrocarbon emissions, as well as up to 80% of the oxides of nitrogen produced by car engines (the US Environmental Protection Agency claims that catalysts only remove 80% of CO and HC as well as 65% of NOx). Catalysts do not remove carbon dioxide.

The problem is that catalysts need at least four minutes to warm up before they work efficiently and the great majority of journeys, particularly in Europe, are not much longer. In the UK, for example, 75% of journeys are less than five miles. The catalysts also have to be in good condition and most only last around 50,000 or so miles – less than half the life of the car. Moreover, the number of cars is rising, as is the total number of miles driven a year, which increases the total volume of emissions to be dealt with. And, while Japan and the USA have had catalysts for decades, they are comparatively recent in Europe. There is still a vast number of non-catalyst-equipped vehicles contributing to the problem.

As a result, the transport sector's share of overall emissions in Europe will increase from 22% to 24% for $CO_2$ and from 58% to 59% for NOx, offsetting the benefits of the new emissions standards. On a global scale, the problem of pollutants will rise substantially, with the growth of car use in the less developed world. To make matters worse, most of the new vehicles sold in these regions are unlikely to be fitted with catalysts or fuel injection systems. This makes their environmental impact even more serious.

In addition, serious concerns have been raised about depletion of the ozone layer by escaped chlorofluorocarbons (CFCs). These have led to the replacement of these compounds by alternative working fluids in air conditioners. Even these substitutes, however, are not entirely satisfactory, so that the gains from their use may well be offset by the increasing proportion of vehicles fitted with air conditioners.

# Legislation is getting tougher

Between 1970 and 1992, legislated limits of CO, HC and NOx in the USA and Europe have halved every six years. The legislation on particulates halves every three years. This trend is expected to continue. The battle, although hard-fought, is winnable, as the data for the Los Angeles area shows (Figure 1.3).

In 1998, any car maker wanting to sell vehicles in California will have to sell a proportion of Zero Emission Vehicles (ZEVs). The number will be low at first, at 2%, but the legislation increases the proportion steadily. It also requires car manufacturers to sell Low Emission Vehicles (LEVs) and Ultra-Low Emission Vehicles (ULEVs) in greater and greater quantities. Existing, catalyst-equipped vehicles do not meet most of these requirements and so some sort of electric vehicles are likely. The consequences of this legislation are outlined in Figure 1.4.

It has been argued that General Motors' much heralded and then abandoned 'Impact' electric vehicle, was really a cynical attempt to prove the impossibility of the task to the Californian authorities. If the legislation remains unchanged, then GM and Ford will each have to manufacture nearly 6500 electric vehicles in 1998, based on their sales in the

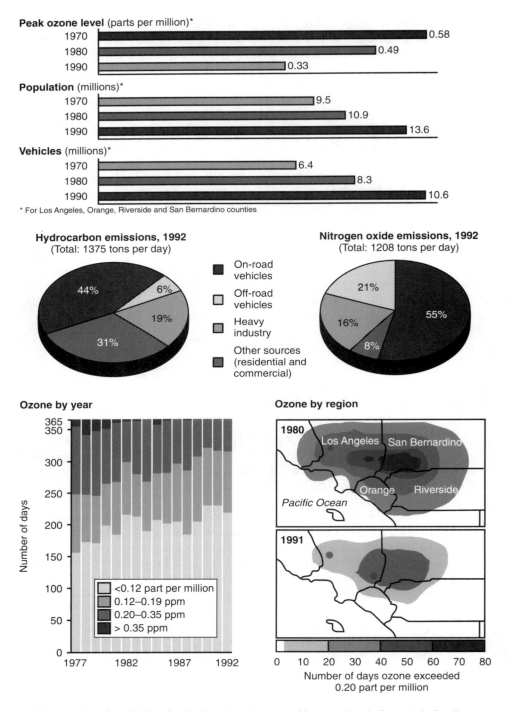

**Figure 1.3**    Air pollution in the Los Angeles area. (*Source*: South Coast Air Quality Management District, *Scientific American*, October 1993)

**Legislated limits for carbon monoxide emissions**

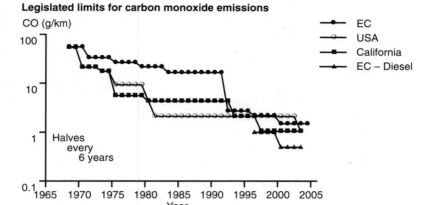

**Legislated limits for hydrocarbon and oxides of nitrogen emissions**

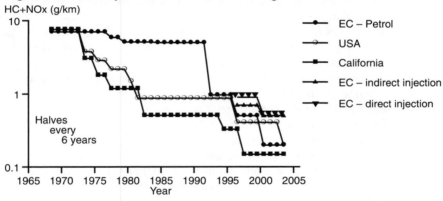

**Legislated limits for particulate matter**

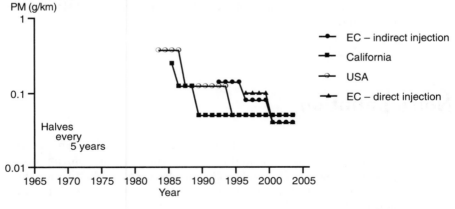

**Figure 1.4**   The impact of legislation on the fuelling of cars and light commercial vehicles.
(*Source*: Lucas Automotive Ltd with thanks to Tony Waterman)

state in 1992 – or face the prospect of having no sales in California at all. Together with Chrysler, they have been lobbying the Californian Air Resources Board (CARB) to reverse or delay the ZEV timetable. The vehicles cannot be built, they say, the technology is simply not available – just as they said with catalysts.

The fight between the CARB and the Big Three will be hard. The outcome will also be significant. If the CARB does not relent then GM, Ford and Chrysler face a huge problem. They have not developed a prototype to meet the market's requirements and so will face the loss of more than 10% of their sales. The Japanese, on the other hand, view the legislation as a market opportunity. Toyota, Honda, Nissan and Mazda have expressly stated their wishes that the 1998 legislation should remain unchanged. They are investing in the necessary technology.

In the short term, the decision will therefore be whether or not the Californian authorities are willing to let the national suppliers suffer so that they can have cleaner air. Based on the arguments presented so far and the animosity the Los Angeles authorities still feel towards GM, after it was found guilty of colluding to destroy the city's tram system in the 1950s, the answer seems clear. Just like the 1973 oil crisis, this is a major market opportunity, for those that are willing to exploit it.

Other air pollutants come from the manufacturing process. One estimate claims that the energy required to manufacture a car is equivalent to 20% of the total energy used by the vehicle during its lifecycle. The pollution that results from this process can be estimated to be of a similar proportion. There are a number of damaging chemicals involved in vehicle production. Methylene chloride and trichloroethylene are used in the paint process, while chlorofluorocarbons (CFCs) are used in seat-foam manufacture and to clean electronic circuits. CFCs are claimed to be responsible for the destruction of stratospheric ozone. The automotive industry has also had to make enormous investments in non-solvent-based paint processes in controlling industrial emissions of all kinds.

# Noise pollution

According to the *Official Journal of the European Communities* (C138), the transport sector, including air, is the biggest contributor to the problem of noise. Cars and trucks are also responsible for a great deal of noise pollution although, to be fair, the industry has done much to address this issue. If the noise made by an average car in the late 1970s equals one unit, then an average European truck generated nearly eight units of noise. While today's car produces a third of the noise it did then, the truck now produces more than 80% less. That is not to say it is adequate, it is simply much better.

## It is too easy to blame the car manufacturers

It is too easy to blame the cars and the car manufacturers for these problems. This is not strictly fair. While it is true that car manufacturers produce such polluting machines, it is the consumers who own and drive them. Although, in the past, steam and electric vehicles were popular, gasoline- and diesel-powered vehicles became dominant for a number of good reasons. First, they offered much greater range and flexibility, one of the major benefits of road transport to many. Second, the development of the fuelling infrastructure was possible thanks to the recent oil discoveries. Third, and most important, oil-derived fuels won because they became so inexpensive.

If we want to have cars that are less polluting, they are technically possible. They have drawbacks, however, certainly using today's technology. Electric vehicles still have limited range and cost considerably more. Similarly, the new emissions legislation in the US will create problems not obvious at first.

Removing much of the remaining 10% of pollutants will mean considerable additional investment. To make matters worse, vehicle manufacturers cannot pass on the investment and cost of meeting the new limits to the consumers, certainly initially, as it would mean a huge rise in the price of cars. The new catalysts might add around 5%–10% to the price of new vehicles. Not only would that deter buyers, it would encourage drivers to hang on to older, dirtier cars for longer.

For the car driver, vehicle producers and the legislators, the choice today is to continue polluting or to accept restrictions on mobility. That may mean limitations on vehicle use, the use of EVs, as in California, or increasing the cost to make motoring, as it was at the start, a luxury for the wealthy.

# Cars cause many deaths and injuries

Cars coming steadily off the assembly line make an impressive sight, an awesome demonstration of industrial scale, organization and power. There is a more depressing aspect also. 'Just think', said one car company manager to one of us as we stood by the line, 'about how many of these new cars will end up with blood on them'.

More than three million people have died in the United States in the last 90 years, directly as a result of passenger cars, according to the US National Safety Council. More than 200 million have been injured. An article in *Automotive News*, the American industry journal, stated that more Americans have died on the roads in the last 15 years than in all of the nation's wars since the American Revolution.[5] The largest proportion of the dead and injured are young, under 35. Car accidents are the number one cause of death in that age group in America. In terms of years of life expectancy lost, road deaths are equal to, or more than, those caused by cancer or cardiovascular disease.

New drivers are proportionately responsible for many more accidents than those who are experienced. In France, drivers with a licence less than a year old are three times more likely to be killed in a road accident than experienced drivers. Again, the roads are the prime cause of death among 18 to 24 year olds in France. The group accounts for 11% of the population, but 24% of the road deaths.

To be fair, it is often not the car or the industry that is at fault. Any insurance company will tell you that the number of accidents among the under 35s is so high because they are simply more reckless, statistically. A great many fatal-accident drivers, particularly in this age group, have subsequently been found to be under the influence of alcohol or drugs. These play a significant part in European accidents and fatalities. A third of pedestrians killed are under the influence of alcohol. The number of drivers killed in road accidents whose blood alcohol level exceeds the 0.80mg/ml limit varies between 15% and 45% in different EU member states. The risk factor associated with alcohol is indicated in Figure 1.5.

One of the other major factors is vehicle speed. Cars are much faster than they used to be. In France only 10% of cars sold 25 years ago could exceed 150 km/h and nearly a third had a maximum speed of less than 110 km/h. Today, nearly 80% of new cars sold can reach 150 km/h, while many can reach 200 km/h. Most of the remainder can exceed 130 km/h. As the average speed rises by 10%, the likelihood of fatalities rises by 50% and so this growth in vehicle performance is being matched by a huge rise in the seriousness of injuries. Other French evidence also shows that, while some drivers reduce their speed at night, others actually increase it – which accounts for the disproportionate gravity of night-time accidents.

Vehicle mass also has an important influence. Industry bodies often report the total number of commercial vehicle accidents that result in deaths and compare this to the figure for cars. Commercial vehicles almost always appear to be better using this measure. However, as the number of commercial vehicles is so small in proportion to the number of cars, the figure is grossly misleading. In fact, the proportion of deaths caused by commercial vehicles in accidents almost always exceeds those caused by passenger cars by a substantial margin. This is because

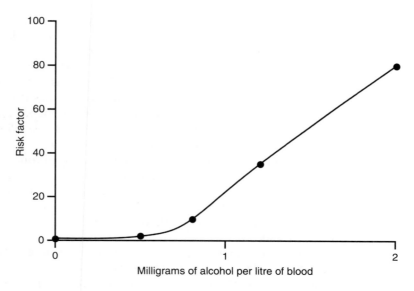

**Figure 1.5**   Alcohol and the risk of an accident. (*Source*: Direction de la
Sécurité et de la Circulation Routière, France)

they build up much greater kinetic energy and have a lesser braking
capability.

The economic cost of road deaths and injuries is huge. In the EU
alone there are 54,000 deaths and 1.7 million injuries every year. The
European Commission estimates the cost of this to be more than $90
billion a year, or $280 per citizen. This cost covers hospital treatment,
work days lost, and an estimate for the pain and suffering, but excludes
the cost of damage-only accidents, the largest number of incidents. It is a
larger sum than the gross domestic product of some of the EU's smaller
member states, such as Greece, Ireland or Portugal.

In the UK, which has the lowest proportionate incidence of vehicle
fatalities in the EU, each death is estimated by the Department
of Transport (DoT) to cost the state $1.1 million. This covers the lost
investment in education and training as well as the knock-on effects of
the individual's death in terms of lost tax revenues. The EU estimate for
the cost of deaths is similar, while it estimates the cost of injuries at
around $150,000 per casualty, on average.

There are 200 road deaths or injuries in Europe every hour. The
deaths are equivalent to a fully loaded 747 crashing, with the loss of all on
board, every three days. It is such a common occurrence that most of the
deaths rarely make the newspapers. This is probably just as well. In the
UK, for example, which has an above average safety record, the national
newspapers have 12 new road deaths to report every day. If detailed they

would use up a page of the newspaper every day of the year. Towards the end of 1993, the UK's *Independent* newspaper did devote a whole page of one edition to recent road deaths to illustrate the point.[6]

In general, roads and vehicles are much safer than they used to be. Airbags, anti-lock brakes, seatbelts and crumple zones have all increased the chances of our surviving a car accident. However, as the number of cars on the roads has risen, so has the number of accidents. As a result, the average number of deaths a year on the roads of the developed world has remained virtually the same for more than 30 years.

There is still an unresolved issue in most developed countries of how these problems should be tackled. In many countries the emphasis is on the education of the most vulnerable: children, cyclists and pedestrians. But it can be argued that it is drivers who should be educated, their machines made safer and the issue of road accidents accorded proper importance by society.

Many of the deaths and injuries could be avoided altogether. The fact that the number of accidents varies so much between European countries shows that some are much safer than others (Figure 1.6). Identifying the factors that make roads safer and legislating in favour of these could reduce the number of casualties.

There are several ways of measuring the comparative safety of roads. As a proportion of population, cars cause 100 deaths per million inhabitants in Japan. This compares with 149 in Europe and 192 in North America. As a proportion of the number of vehicles, Japan is again safest with 241 deaths per million vehicles, while North America has 259. The poorest record exists in Europe, where there are 367 deaths per million vehicles, or half as many again as the other two developed regions. The third and probably most meaningful measure is deaths per vehicle kilometres. In this case, the United States is shown to be safest with 1.4 deaths per hundred million vehicle kilometres (Figure 1.7), because of its better-constructed and generally less-crowded highways, low speed limits and disciplined drivers. Using this measure Europe has the most dangerous roads and drivers, with 2.7 deaths per hundred million vehicle kilometres. If Europe could equal the record of the United States, 20,000 lives would be saved every year.

So why do these variations exist? They are partly the result of different legislation in each country on speed limits and the use of seat-belts and air bags; but also, very significantly, because of different social values and attitudes. In Germany, for example, few pedestrians (<5%) will cross the road unless signalled to do so. In contrast, in the UK, where people appear to feel some sacred right to wander across the highways, the majority (65%) of pedestrians are happy to venture out onto the roads whatever the signal. The effects of this are obvious: the UK has the highest level of pedestrian deaths per head of population in Europe. Social values affect car drivers also. In some parts of Europe, driving

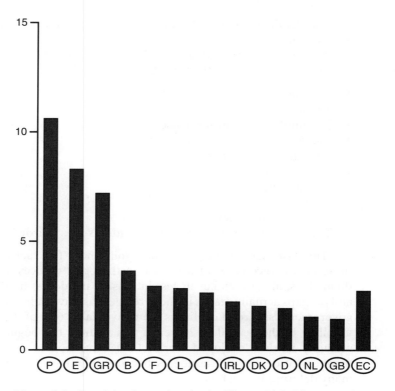

**Figure 1.6**  Road deaths per hundred million vehicle kilometres in the European Community. (*Source*: EU)

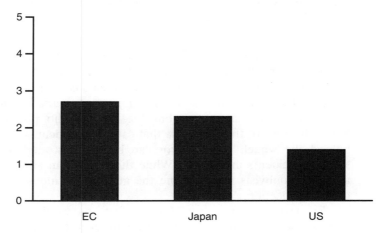

**Figure 1.7**  Road deaths per hundred million vehicle kilometres in the Triad regions.

while under the influence of alcohol or without a seat belt is still regarded lightly by many.

The variations in road accidents between countries are caused by a range of factors. A study by the EU found that these include:

- Population density
- The level of urbanization
- The number of vehicles in use
- The distances and speeds vehicles travel
- The state of the roads
- Traffic density
- Topography
- Climate
- Regional temperament
- The seriousness with which road accidents are regarded.

This last factor is of particular significance. The fact that most of these deaths receive scant attention in the press reduces awareness of them. This, in turn, makes us less interested in addressing the problem and perhaps actually makes us more reckless as drivers. In the past, many governments saw road deaths as the unavoidable cost of the increase in mobility. In the last 10 or 20 years, this attitude has begun to change, certainly in the developed world. Legislative bodies can reduce the numbers of deaths and accidents because they have responsibility for many determining factors:

(1) The road network
(2) The standards for vehicle manufacturing
(3) The laws governing vehicle use
(4) Influence over the opinions and behaviour of road users through education, training, information, regulation, enforcement and penalties.

It is important to point out that it is generally not the vehicles or the motor industry that are to blame for this appalling catalogue of deaths and injuries. While the very existence of cars can be blamed for all of these problems, it is like saying that guns cause wars. It is not the guns themselves that cause wars but the people who pull the triggers. Similarly, it is not the car *per se* that causes road deaths, it is the driver behind the wheel. Driver error can be demonstrated in more than 90% of accidents in the EU. While this may seem almost trite, many anti-road lobbyists try to blame the automotive industry, which is an oversimplification.

Even so, there are many safety products that would help protect lives if they were fitted more widely, although legislation may be needed to make them more prevalent. Air bags, anti-lock brakes, the compulsory use of safety belts and better brakes on trucks are known to reduce injuries. Other measures that governments could consider are tighter speed restrictions, particularly in built-up areas, to protect pedestrians, or for certain types of vehicles. There is clear evidence that all these measures increase the safety of our roads, yet there is little legislation, especially within Europe, to increase their use. None are legislated for in all members of the EU.

The EU is ambitious in terms of road safety research, and would like to reduce the number of deaths or serious injuries by 20% to 30% by the year 2000, according to a 1990 report by Christian Gérondeau.[7] If there is no change by then, at current rates, one in three Europeans will be injured on the roads during their lifetimes and one in a hundred will be killed.

There are a great many research programmes that should help make roads safer in the longer term. These include the development of devices to detect 'driver failure'. These identify when a driver violates a traffic regulation such as speeding or driving through a stop light. They also register the driver's state of alertness and whether or not he is suffering from fatigue or the effects of alcohol. Other programmes are working on collision avoidance by using radar, improved night vision and navigation systems, for example. European governments also fund a programme on industrial technologies and materials (BRITE/EURAM) that are likely to improve both vehicle and road safety. Other proposals include one to make vehicle designs more calming and less dangerous to pedestrians. Part of the Prometheus and Drive projects also has to do with collision avoidance.

# The future

And what of the future? In the developed world road deaths should remain relatively constant as the increasing numbers of vehicles on the roads dilutes the benefits of improved safety measures (Figure 1.8). One irony is that congestion may actually reduce deaths, although not the number of accidents, because they reduce average speeds, although the number of accidents continues to rise (Figure 1.9).

In the less-developed countries (LDCs), the prospects for road deaths are less bright. The number of car drivers is rising rapidly in these countries and the necessary legislative controls have often not been developed to cope with this growth in traffic. The cars bought in LDCs also tend to be lower cost, smaller vehicles that are more likely to result in serious injuries or fatalities when involved in an accident.

There are also social issues. When citizens of countries experience the mobility that the car can offer for the first time, a kind of madness

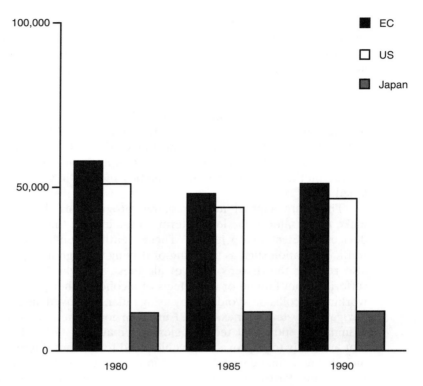

**Figure 1.8**   Numbers killed in road accidents, 1980–90. (*Source*: EC)

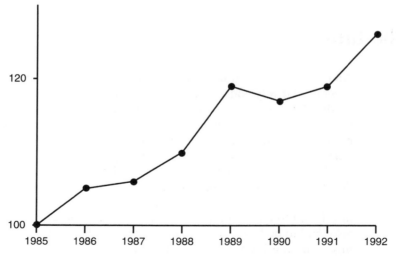

**Figure 1.9**   Index of road traffic accidents in Japan, 1985–92. (*Source*: Japanese Ministry of Transport)

seems to ensue. This can be illustrated by looking at the number of accidents in Mexico and some cities in India and China which have seen a rapid growth in car ownership in the least ten years. Even within the more regulated EU, the number of road deaths has increased in the less-developed parts of the community when the passenger car became more affordable. In Spain road deaths rose by 30% between 1975 and 1990. In Greece, they increased by 42% in the same period. At the same time, Germany managed to reduce the number of fatalities by around 40%. As one EU study found, the total experience of each country as it copes with the growth in mobility is of great importance.

# What can we do about this?

So, where does responsibility lie? How can we reduce the number of accidents and injuries? Responsibility lies in three main areas; with individuals, with car manufacturers and, most of all, with governments and legislative bodies. There are also a number of other bodies that have influence. The insurance companies and the media can have a considerable effect on the types of vehicle in use and the way they are driven.

Statistical evidence shows that mistakes and bad driving by individuals are responsible for almost all accidents. In France, small towns are statistically the most dangerous spots – there is, in fact, an inversse correlation between size and risk. Those driving at night actually speed more than those passing there during the day. The 10% increase in average speeds that this represents causes a 40% increase in average kinetic energy. The top end of the night-time distribution in particular represents exceptionally high speeds and kinetic energies, not observed during the day (Figure 1.10). This is seen as a prime explanation of why disproportionately more night-time accidents are fatal.

Yet it is misleading to attribute everything to driver error. The quality of driving also depends on the road environment, the level of congestion, the state of the roads, the behaviour of other road users and the degree of enforcement of regulations. The impact on a driver of his or her mistakes depends greatly upon these factors. An accident on a country road is four times more likely to result in a death than on a motorway, despite the higher speeds involved in motorway driving.

Similarly, car manufacturers can develop products that help drivers avoid accidents, such as ABS, or that reduce the injuries they cause, such as air bags. Vehicle manufacturers cannot, however, do all that much to reduce the likelihood of accidents occurring. But they might perhaps desist from stressing the aggressive aspects of car ownership in their

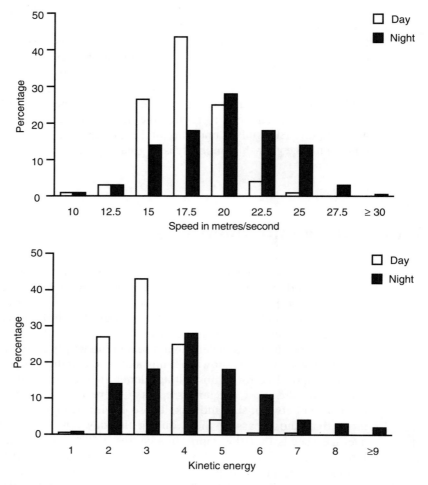

**Figure 1.10** Speed and kinetic energy distributions by day and night in a small town. (*Source*: Recherche Transports Sécurité, No. 40 – September 1993)

advertising. Similarly, they cannot be expected to fit safety-related products unless they are demanded by drivers or required by legislation. They do work extensively with governments on vehicle safety.

As a result, the greatest responsibility for reducing the number of accidents in the future must fall on governments. Only they can take action that will have a lasting impact on the entire car-driving community and significantly influence car-driving behaviour. The belief that it is the responsibility of the individual is too often used as an excuse for inaction. It is a collective, public responsibility.

While some legislative bodies, notably the EU, have adopted this approach, many others have not. They still regard the freedom of the road user as sacrosanct. The EU, on the other hand, is beginning to believe that 'road users, like consumers, must be regarded as potential victims, needing protection, regardless of their involvement in starting accidents' (report of the high level expert group for a European policy on road safety, February 1991).

So, what scope do legislators have? There are a number of factors that governments can impact:

(1)    Fitment of safety related products
(2)    Education and training
(3)    Public information
(4)    Traffic law and regulation (including speed limits)
(5)    Control and enforcement of regulations, including penalties.

The use of motor vehicles can be made considerably safer through government intervention. Reducing speeds and attaining a uniform speed has a dramatic effect on the number of fatalities. We can make massive improvements to road and vehicle safety without any radical change to the vehicles or the road infrastructure.

# Traffic congestion

In 1993, the *Journal of the European Communities* stated that 'a situation has been allowed to evolve in many parts of the Community ... wherein imbalances in terms of disproportionate mobility by road, [have] led to ... a form of rationing by congestion ... it will not be possible in the future as it was in the past, to base transport policy on the demand side of the equation.' (C138/33, section 4.3.)

Congestion is a major problem. In purely economic terms, congestion causes inefficiency and pollution. It wastes time, damages health and reduces potential economic wealth.

In Bangkok, for example, many mothers now get up to take their children to school at 4a.m. to avoid the traffic jams. The volume of traffic is so bad that it is not worth their while returning home, so they spend the day in the city shopping or at the stock exchange until they can collect their children again in the afternoon. Many will not reach their homes in the suburbs until late in the evening. Teachers and office workers often report that they do not arrive home until 11p.m., although they leave their offices at 5p.m. Garages sell portable toilets, a helicopter had to rescue a woman trapped in the gridlock when she went into labour and a book called *A Family on the Road*, about a family living entirely in a car, was a prize winner in 1993.

A new 12-mile section of elevated highway, completed in 1993, remained closed while the contractors squabbled with the government over toll charges. The government eventually had to gain an injunction to open the road while the legal wrangles continued, on the grounds that there was a threat of public violence if it remained closed. Drivers charged up the entry ramps as soon as the court made its ruling, frustrating the country's Deputy Interior Minister who was to have performed the opening ceremony.

The problems in Thailand are particularly severe because the road network has not developed as rapidly as the volume of traffic. Only 9% of Bangkok is turned over to roads, while for most cities it is 25%. Bangkok is symbolic of what may yet happen in the developed world and what is likely to happen in many other less-developed countries as car ownership rises.

The Thais estimate that the costs of their traffic chaos, in terms of lost time and wasted fuel, is between $2 billion and $6 billion year. Citizens have called for 'draconian' changes and asked the government to declare a state of emergency. The government has even considered moving the capital. Letters to the Bangkok *Post* demand vehicle restrictions, so that cars can only enter the city every second day. Such a solution has already been tried in Athens and Lagos, with little success, however.

Congestion is now a major problem in many countries. The average speed of rush-hour traffic in the centre of Seattle is down to 4 mph. In London, average speeds at peak period are no better than the days of the horse and carriage.

A 1988 study by Bouladon estimated the costs of congestion in Western Europe to be 2.5% to 3% of GNP, or around $115 billion a year. Similarly, the OECD estimates the costs of congestion at 3% of GNP. In the UK, the Chartered Institute of Transport estimates the cost at around $750 per person per year and that 112 million person hours are wasted annually in traffic jams. This results in lost productivity, higher distribution costs and 'congestion induced stress', according to the Confederation of British Industry.

There are 44 cars per kilometre of road in the European Community, with some countries such as Germany with more than 63 per kilometre. Parking those cars reduces mobility by taking up valuable road space.

The conclusion, certainly from a European perspective, is that, once again, government intervention will be required if the problems of congestion are to be addressed.

# Other social factors

There are many more, less obvious, aspects of our lives that have been affected by the automobile. Pedestrians have almost disappeared in many towns, especially in the United States. Those that remain are more exposed to street crime – because of the rarity of pedestrians. Children have lost much of their freedom to play on the streets, are shepherded to and from school and spend much more of their youth indoors watching television or playing computer games. These changes have been found to result in less fit and healthy children, obesity and poorer social skills.

Cars have contributed to the decline of village economies and latterly of city centres as consumers go to out-of-town shopping centres. The village store has become almost obsolete. Without the car, the upper-middle-class suburb would never have been feasible. According to Stephen Sears' book, *The Automobile in America*, suburban communities grew dramatically during the 1920s and 1930s, principally because of the increasing use of cars. Beverly Hills grew by 2500%, Shaker Heights in Cleveland grew by 1000% and Grosse Pointe Park in Detroit grew by 725%, for example. According to a study commissioned by the Hoover administration in the 1930s, *Recent Social Trends in the United States*, the city centres of New York, Chicago and Cleveland lost 24% of their populations. This contributed to the divisions within society, as it was typically the poor, the minorities and the elderly that stayed behind.

As the number of people with cars has grown, demand for public transport has fallen, particularly in rural areas. It is no longer economic to run bus and train services to remote villages in many parts of Europe. This means governments are faced with a difficult choice. They can either subsidise local transport to ensure that those unable, for whatever reason, to run their own car are still able to travel or allow free-market economics to resolve the problem. In this case, it means that the poor and elderly often cannot afford to stay in rural areas. Without a car they have no access to facilities such as Post Offices, shops, schools or medical treatment.

If the poor and elderly cannot afford to remain in rural areas these regions either face decline or become the exclusive preserve of the young and wealthy. This, in turn, changes the demographic structure of the region, creating a distorted social group. The impact of this varies enormously, but it is a little like interfering with the food chain – changing one part often has unpredictable and unexpected consequences on the remainder.

Some of these effects are very visible. Village stores have become a thing of the past in many areas. As an example, Blockley, a village of around 8000 people in England's Cotswolds region, had 22 shops as recently as 1970. It had four public houses, two butchers, a wool shop and a store for photography equipment. Today, it has just two shops and two public houses, all of which face a difficult financial future. Although the nearest large town is 20 miles away, those who live in the village now prefer to travel there rather than shop closer to home.

The car has changed the way we live and expanded our horizons. It has also made us more lazy, unhealthy and lonely. The Hoover study in the US concluded that 'car ownership has created an automobile psychology; the automobile has become a dominant influence in the life of the individual, and he in a real sense has become dependent on it'. Gordon Whitnall of the Los Angeles Planning Commission wrote that 'it might almost be said that Southern Californians have had wheels added to their anatomy.' And that was in 1927.

Cars also raise massive and unfulfillable hopes in those who cannot afford them – which remains most of the world. The industry is extremely wasteful. The number of model variations, the number of vehicle manufacturers and the frequency with which models are replaced cannot be economically efficient. It wastes vast quantities of energy and resources as a result.

So the car and the automotive industry have brought many problems that offset the benefits to a large degree. They are significant. If the benefits have driven the direction of the industry in the past, the costs may threaten to gain the upper hand in the future.

# Notes

1.  Study carried out by the US Environmental Defense Fund and reported in *Automotive News*, 1993
2.  Towards sustainability. *Official Journal of the European Communities*, C138. May 1993
3.  *Transport and the Environment.* OECD, Paris, 1988
4.  *Trade routes to the future: Meeting transport infrastructure needs in the 1990s.* CBI, London, 1989
5.  America at the wheel. *Automotive News*, September 1993
6.  *The Independent.* 22 December 1993
7.  Christian Gérondeau (1990). Report of the high level expert group for European policy for road safety

# 2

# The ratchet effect: why cars are here to stay

## The emotional ratchet

It is easy to conclude from the preceding chapter that our increasing dependence on the car must and will change. We simply cannot carry on building more cars and more roads indefinitely. There are physical limits to the numbers of cars we can have. Eventually, there will be more cars on the roads than the land space can cope with, particularly in Europe. We know there is a ceiling. However, before we get to that ceiling there are pressures that are likely to bring about change. Beyond the obvious barriers of market saturation and congestion, the pollution and damage motor vehicles create are increasingly outweighing their benefits. There are therefore strong and powerful arguments to reduce our dependence on the car. Yet, because there is a ratchet, any attempts to do this in the foreseeable future will be largely futile.

The truth is that our attachment to cars is profoundly rooted – not only in the practical necessities of life but also in our emotions. Research shows that there is a deep psychic connection between freedom and movement. Babies achieve locomotion. Adults re-experience it through the motor car. Waiting for a bus or a train unleashes hidden, unconscious fears of abandonment in many. This has profound implications, not only for how cars are used, but also for how they are sold, as we shall see in Chapter 3.

# The social ratchet

The social ratchet effect makes it extremely difficult to limit the desires and aspirations of individual citizens for individual mobility. The car has changed the very way we live. This ratchet is not just about attitudes, it is structural. We may be able to limit future growth, but reversing the trend, reducing the number of cars in use, will take a very long time.

If our dependence on motor vehicles is to be reduced, there are two broad options:

(1)   We can try to limit the number of journeys people undertake, and/or,
(2)   We can try to encourage the use of alternative forms of transport.

As we shall see, neither of these is terribly practical in the short term.

## Reducing the need to travel

Before the car, people typically lived near their place of work, their friends and facilities such as shops. In the 1930s, the car allowed people to move to the suburbs or out of town; it allowed them much greater flexibility in where they chose to live and work. Over the last 50 years this flexibility has increased, so, what was a privilege of the better off at the beginning is now a common aspect of the lives of most people in the developed world. Today we take the car to work, to schools, to visit friends, to out-of-town shopping centres and to the corner shop. Shopping malls and centres are only able to exist because we can travel to them by car. The very structure of our lives has changed and we cannot conceive of this new freedom being taken away. There is therefore a structural need to travel which will be very difficult to change.

An analysis of the purpose of individuals' journeys shows that most are regarded as essential and that few can be eliminated. Today, on average, 85% of our journeys are by car, 94% are by road. In most parts of Europe, for example, nearly 80% of trips are to and from work or school, are on personal business trips or are for shopping. That is, only 20% of our journeys are seen as having been made out of 'choice'. This implies that only 20% of journeys today are for purely social, recreational or pleasure purposes; the remainder are essential to the individual and/or the economy.

The average distance travelled to work has also increased by nearly 60% in the last 20 years, making the need for transportation and travel greater than before. In Europe today around 70% of these journeys to work are by car. The percentage is higher in North America. Nearly two-thirds of business trips are by car in Europe. Even in households without a car, four times as many journeys are made in other people's cars as are made by train. Banning cars or limiting their use would therefore have a devastating effect on the developed world's lifestyle and economy. As a result, this heavy dependence on the car and road transport cannot be changed easily or quickly (Figure 2.1).

Eighty-nine per cent of freight tonnage is carried by road. Commercial vehicles distribute most of the goods we use on a day-to-day basis such as food, drink and clothing. We cannot change the places where we live and work overnight, even if the majority of the population want to. Similarly, we cannot easily find some other way for goods to get from factories to shops by legislation or market forces.

It is this practical dependence on the car and the structure of employment today that makes even radical solutions unlikely for the time being. The much-vaunted future world of virtual reality, tele-working and video conferencing is not only some years away, it is also only likely to be a real alternative for a small minority of the working population. These options possibly offer an opportunity to reduce congestion at the margin. If home-working were to become practical even for only 10% of the working population in the developed world, this could slow the growth in traffic and might even reverse it slightly. This is clearly an opportunity, although even this will need much more technological development and

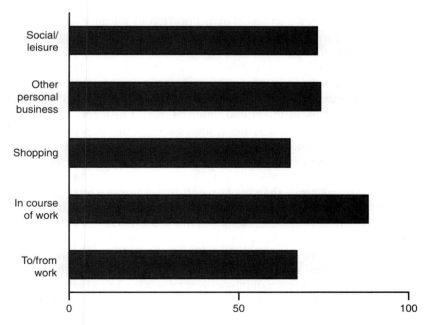

**Figure 2.1**   Percentage of journeys made by car in the UK. (*Source*: SMMT Road Facts, 1993)

significant changes in social and working patterns before it becomes a reality.

As a result, motor vehicles are here to stay, certainly for a good while yet. Without a radical change in our social and working patterns, there is little we can do to change our dependence on the industry. But could we encourage the use of alternative forms of transport to reduce the environmental damage and reduce congestion?

## Encouraging the use of alternative forms of transport

An individual selects a particular form of transport on the basis of several criteria. Although the decision is not entirely rational and most often not a conscious one, he or she will choose the mode of transport that best meets his or her needs primarily on the basis of cost, flexibility, safety, environmental impact, speed and comfort. Each journey, and each mode of transport, offers a different blend of these on each occasion.

A train, for example, offers a good blend of safety, speed and cost. It is 125 times safer than road travel. It also does much less damage to the environment than other forms of transport per passenger mile. Yet the rail industry, particularly in the USA and parts of Europe such as the UK, is a minority provider of passenger transport. Road transport accounted for 11 times the number of passenger miles in Europe in 1986 and was growing twice as fast. The proportion of journeys accounted for by rail fell sharply between 1975 and 1985 in the US and Europe, while the use of air and road transport rose.

However, the rail industry is forecast to grow in the next decade, particularly in Europe. This will partly be the result of the use of more high-speed trains in France, Germany and Italy, together with the development of an integrated, international, European, high-speed, rail network. There is a growing awareness of the benefits of rail. For every passenger mile, trains produce much less atmospheric pollution than any other form of transport. That means fewer health problems and less damage to the environment. Trains also use up much less fuel and land per passenger mile than road or air travel. They also offer greater flexibility in terms of the type of fuel used, particularly if they are powered by electricity.

It is for these reasons that many countries and cities have invested in national and light rail systems in the last few years. By the end of the 1980s more than 180 cities around the world, including 92 in the US, had announced or started to build urban rail systems. Although it will take time, and its overall impact will be small, the rail industry is expected to grow in the next 20 to 30 years, partly at the expense of road transport.

However, the overall impact of the rail industry will be limited. The train scores poorly in terms of flexibility, unless the start and end point of the journey are close to stations that have a direct service between them.

In addition, although trains offer more comfort and less stress than a car journey, they force passengers to travel together. While this may seem trivial to many, a large number of commuters choose to use their car because it allows people to be alone. They retain a sense of their individuality.

Even if a government in one of the industry's major markets decided to force personal travellers onto other forms of transport it would take many years and be extremely expensive. The development of a rail system, for example, can take 10 to 15 years. Mass transit is only cost-effective in limited circumstances and the amount of private investment in automobiles exceeds what governments could ever dream of spending on public transport. One of the additional problems is that the alternatives proposed are typically up-dates of 19th-century technologies that the car displaced more than 50 years ago. This makes them even more difficult to sell to travellers.

Flying scores well in terms of speed and safety, but less well in terms of cost, certainly in Europe. It is also not terribly flexible, can still be very uncomfortable and is polluting in terms of noise, emissions and land usage. Given the air congestion and the time taken to travel to and from airports it is also arguable how fast air travel really is today, at least over the shorter distances. The TGV (*Train à Grande Vitesse*) in France has had a dramatic impact on air traffic volumes on some routes, such as Paris–Lyon. We can probably expect the same effect on London–Paris and London–Brussels, two of Europe's busiest (and most profitable) air routes, for the same reasons.

A car journey scores well in terms of speed and some aspects of comfort. It is less safe and more expensive than rail or bus transport and is much more damaging environmentally per passenger mile. The greatest benefit that the car offers, however, is flexibility. For most journeys this is simply not tradeable against the other benefits, without accepting a great deal of inconvenience.

Travellers are willing to pay a great deal for the freedom of the car in terms of lives, pollution and fuel cost. This is made even more obvious if one considers that the flexibility cars offer is not nearly as great as it once was. In fact, it is sometimes only a perceived flexibility for many journeys today. The volume of traffic is now so great that in many cases buses, trains and even bicycles offer much faster journey times at far less cost. Even so, the cocoon of the car ranks higher than the rationality of the alternatives.

Most of the journeys taken in cars are very short, certainly in Europe. Three-quarters of those in the UK, for example, are less than five miles, and just over 6% are under one mile. Yet, it seems, few drivers would be willing to give up their cars even for short distances. A study done by General Motors in the United States, as part of its research into electric cars, found that most trips were short too. Given the present limited range of electric vehicles (EVs), it felt this showed that the EV had a market. However, further research showed that, while there was a clearly identifiable opportunity to sell EVs to rational buyers, it did not exist in practice. Buyers were not rational. Drivers felt strongly that they wanted the flexibility to get into their car, when they felt like it, and drive wherever they wanted. A weekend away, a visit to friends, a drive-in meal. The fact that these trips were rare was unimportant, the freedom to embark on them was critical. It shows that even though most journeys are short and other modes of transport make sense, the market is not rational. Car owners prefer to use their vehicles because of the perceived flexibility.

Flexibility and independence are essential components of car travel. That is why 'park and ride' systems have little impact – they reduce both the flexibility and freedom of the traveller. As a result, and despite the much greater cost involved, particularly in Europe, the car remains the preferred means of transport for the majority. It is also the primary reason why the idea of moving large numbers of passengers off the roads and into trains, planes and buses is simply not practical.

But what else can we do? Many argue that we can solve some of our problems by moving freight off the roads. Certainly, this would reduce congestion. In addition, heavy trucks are more responsible, proportionately, for road damage and serious road accidents than cars or buses. Trucks, after all, have a much more limited braking capability, when fully loaded, than cars. Trucks are actually involved in around 30% fewer accidents, but because of the momentum involved, the results tend to be much more serious. Fewer trucks would therefore mean less government expenditure on road maintenance and medical care. Fewer road deaths would also mean economic savings.

However, it is difficult to reduce our dependence on commercial vehicles when 80% of freight is moved by road. It is often suggested that commercial freight should be moved onto the rail network, particularly as rail utilization is low in most countries, other than Russia and China. Yet this is not as easy as it at first appears.

Even where an adequate rail infrastructure already exists it is rarely economically viable to move freight by rail unless the goods are transported more than 300 kilometres. Rail transport also results in a loss of flexibility, particularly for part loads or where several drops are required. There is also the problem of getting the freight to and from the railway station from its point of origin and to its final destination. These journeys are still likely to require road transport. It is for these reasons that the goods that are most carried on the railways are typically bulk commodities such as coal, cement or chemicals.

The second major problem exists if the rail infrastructure needs development. In many developed countries, particularly the USA and the UK, the rail network has been cut back. There is simply no track on many potential freight routes. To move the goods onto trains would therefore need investment in the rail infrastructure. Yet, the lead-time for planning, building and beginning to use a major new piece of track can be 15 or more years. The option of moving freight to rail, therefore, is not as simple as might be assumed.

There are a number of other means of transport for commercial traffic worth mentioning: pipelines, sea, air and inland waterways. However, all have drawbacks and limitations compared to road transportation. Pipelines can only carry particular goods while waterways are typically slow and indirect, making them inappropriate for today's just-in-time delivery expectations. As a result, pipelines and waterways are likely to continue to account for only a small minority of freight traffic.

Any significant reduction in road transport is therefore unlikely in the short term. Attempting to reduce the need to travel by car or persuading people to adopt some other form of transport is largely futile, unless there are structural changes made to the way we live.

# The industry ratchet

There are other reasons why reducing our dependence on the car will be difficult. First, there are the vested interests of governments, fuel and vehicle suppliers and others in the industry that benefit from the *status quo*. Not only do the motor industry and motor vehicles themselves bring substantial revenues to governments, they also bring vast economic activity and employment. Second, the investment in the road and vehicle infrastructure is enormous and has taken many years to develop. Few politicians would want to see that investment wasted or under-utilized. They want to see a payback, they want to be seen to have spent wisely from the national purse. There is therefore a built-in resistance to change among those that are responsible for transport policy.

The parc and the rate of technological implementation are also parts of the ratchet. There are hundreds of millions of vehicles in use today. Each will, on average, continue to be around for another six or seven years. New vehicles are being added every year, replacing and increasing the total number. These vehicles represent a huge barrier to legislators or alternative forms of transport.

A huge proportion of the developed world's population has invested hard-earned cash in these cars and they do not want to see that investment wasted. They will be reluctant to buy or accept new technologies, or use alternative forms of transport, until they have extracted the maximum value from their investments. As a result, any attempt to replace one technology or product with another takes time – even if that change is marginal. The car was first developed a hundred years ago yet it was nearly 40 years before the number of horses in use fell dramatically. Car and commercial vehicle owners have typically invested heavily in their vehicles. They are unlikely to endorse any legislation that limits the use of this investment or, worse, reduces its value.

These vehicles also represent a barrier to the rate of implementation of new technology. If, for the sake of argument, a clean, safe and energy-efficient vehicle was launched tomorrow it would be seven or eight years before it became dominant and twice that before it accounted for the bulk of the parc.

This is certainly what the industry would argue and, generally, it is true. However, when the oil crisis occurred in 1973, the motor industry showed remarkable fleetness of foot. GM in the US, for example, re-engineered the Opel Kadett from Germany to make it suitable for the American market in a startlingly short 21 months. To be fair, however, GM had to modify an existing product, not develop a new one from scratch.

Vehicles sold today use well-known and established technologies. The ideal of the safe, clean and energy-efficient car is still only a concept, if that. We are still many years from developing the ideal fuel. Similarly, although the technology exists for automatically piloted and extremely safe aircraft, it will be many, many years before such technologies can be used in motor vehicles. For a start, the levels of complexity are much greater on the roads than in the air. Even when the right fuels and technologies have been identified the development and testing of a new motor vehicle takes between three and eight years.

So, if it takes at best another eight to ten years to perfect new fuels and safer vehicles, it will be 12 to 15 years before these vehicles appear on the roads. Add to this the industry's resistance to change, the slow pace with which new technologies have been introduced in the past and the size of the existing parc and it is clear that safe, efficient and clean cars will not be prevalent until at least the second decade of the next century – despite all the well-intentioned concept cars shown at motor shows.

# The fuels ratchet

We cannot adopt alternative fuels or methods of propulsion in high volume quickly or easily. There are many reasons.

First, the network of fuel stations is vast and relatively specific in application. A change in fuels would therefore make the enormous investment in these largely worthless. Such a cost would be difficult to justify economically. Today's fuel stations are designed to use liquid fuels that offer a particular vehicle range and a limited refueling time. They are therefore not suitable for many alternative fuels or other methods of propulsion.

Today's design of electric vehicles, for example, needs a long recharge, typically at home overnight. Although some French vehicle manufacturers are looking at a more rapid recharging time of around 15 to 20 minutes, to supplement the overnight charge, this has drawbacks in terms of battery life. Whatever the method of charging, traditional fuel stations are of little use.

Of the range of alternative fuels and engines being developed, only methanol, ethanol, liquefied gas and bio-fuels would really suit the traditional supply infrastructure. All of these have other drawbacks for anything other than limited use, however.

The second major reason that we are unlikely to see any radical change to alternative fuels or engines is, again, the parc. With more than 470m vehicles on the roads already using gasoline and diesel it would take more than a decade, at current levels of production, before these could be replaced by an alternative – even if one were available tomorrow.

The third reason is that the investment by oil companies in exploration and refining is enormous and dependent on very long payback periods. It is not just a matter of the lobbying power of the oil companies – it is simply not economic to write off this colossal investment in hardware and know-how and people. Any attempt to reduce significantly our dependence on petrol and diesel would have a drastic effect on the countries, companies and workers that provide oil-derived products today. As the oil infrastructure is such a large proportion of the economic wealth of developed nations, and as petrol and diesel account for such a large percentage of their output, any radical change would be economic suicide.

The fourth main reason why we are unlikely to see any radical change in the engines or fuels in use is that there is actually no practical alternative today. Although we could change to other liquid fuels, such as ethanol or methanol, they would need to be subsidized. Both also produce different emission problems. Bio-fuels also have drawbacks, except in a number of limited applications. For a start, with today's yields there is simply not enough land space to grow crops for all the needed vehicle fuel. All of the other options, from EVs to hydrogen, flywheels and gas turbines, have major technological or cost hurdles today.

The fifth major reason is cost. Despite high levels of taxation and thanks to economies of scale in the oil industry, the cost of traditional fuels is, comparatively speaking, very low. It would take any alternative years to reach a level of cost equivalent to that of gasoline or diesel – if we could ever attain it.

As a result, although we are likely to see the emergence of some electric vehicles in parts of the United States, some hybrid vehicles in Europe and the continued use of bio-fuels in countries like Brazil, there is not likely to be any radical move away from gasoline or diesel in the foreseeable future. There is simply no magical alternative to the traditional fuels. Each of the exceptions to the above is stimulated by legislative necessity, not economics. The EVs in California are instigated by legislation caused by climactic conditions, the hybrids by taxation and the bio-fuels by a shortage of foreign currency. They are therefore exceptions, for use in minority and specific applications. They are unlikely to be adopted *en masse* for many years, if at all.

There will be some changes, however. To reduce emissions, both gasoline and diesel fuel may well be modified or reformulated, and it is possible that they may be combined with other fuels such as ethanol or methanol. These changes are not radical however, and will not result in any significant changes to the vehicles or our transport network.

# The design ratchet

There is also a ratchet in the design of motor vehicles themselves that limits any radical changes. Like the social ratchet much of this constraint is because of the perceived utility that motor vehicles bring. For example, a radical option might be to design small one-person vehicles for commuting, as these would be more energy-efficient and less polluting. After all, most of the vehicles driving into cities contain only one person, making them very inefficient. The idea of designing smaller vehicles also has other benefits, in that lanes could be narrowed to accommodate these one-person cars. This would increase road space dramatically. It would also reduce congestion – assuming we were not all on the roads at once.

However, there are drawbacks. Buyers want to have the flexibility to take their family and their possessions on a longer journey, when they choose. The fact that this accounts for a tiny percentage of their journeys seems irrelevant. Once again, the perceived flexibility is critical. Another limitation to design is, yet again, the existing parc. Although it may be possible to design a small and safe vehicle for one person, it may not feel that safe, beside existing vehicles. While new materials may make safety a possibility, the practical experience of sitting in a ten feet by three feet car alongside a 20-year-old articulated truck doing 70 miles an hour may not be too pleasant.

As a result, the traditional vehicle with a gasoline or diesel engine, a trunk and the capacity to carry four adults is likely to remain with us for the foreseeable future.

# Conclusion

There is no justification for assuming that the demand for, or supply of, personal transport will change radically in the next 20 years. There are social barriers. The car is now an essential part of our lives in the developed world. Any alternative is perceived as less attractive even though it may cost less, be less environmentally damaging or get us from A to B more quickly. There are also industry barriers. Vested interests, tax revenues, a huge parc of existing vehicles and the need to develop new technology all indicate that any radical change in this industry is many years away. As a result, neither market forces nor government intervention can change this ratchet or one-way street in the foreseeable future – and that means well into the next century.

# 3

# From conveyance to icon...and back? The changing nature of demand

## From unsatisfied demand to overcapacity

Viewed superficially, the automotive industry seems to be everlasting, although its individual products – the vehicle models – clearly have lifecycles of their own. Some are short-lived, lasting less than 10 years in production. Some go on for decades, such as the VW Beetle and the Citroen 2CV, which lasted for almost 40 years. But does the overall life-cycle curve of the industry go on for ever? Will it eventually decline?

Cars have so penetrated our lives and become part of them that we – in the developed world at least – can scarcely do without them. As more and more people have been able to have cars, our whole way of life has adapted to them. The patterns of production, employment, residence and social behaviour have all been moulded by the automobile. In turn, cars create an entrenched and virtually irreducible demand for individual transportation. With the best social conscience in the world, it's hard to rely on public transport in Los Angeles today.

At the underlying level of transportation needs, change comes fairly slowly. There may be temporary, localized blips – caused, for example, by fuel shortages, as in the 1973 oil crisis – but demand seems to bounce back to normal fairly quickly. It looks – on projection – as though the demand for road-based passenger-kilometres or ton-kilometres will continue inexorably upwards. Total US passenger-car kilometres increased by 40% between 1983 and 1990, even though annual growth rates in unit

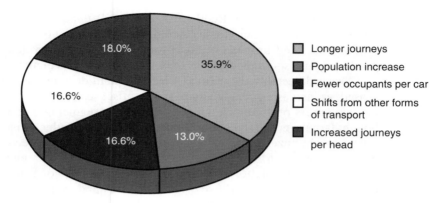

**Figure 3.1**   Origins of increased total passenger car kilometres in the US (1983–90). (*Source*: US national personal transportation survey)

volume of car sales remained modest. Figure 3.1 explains the origins of this considerable increase.

The nature of demand in the developed world has been undergoing a qualitative transition for some time. The 1973 oil shock signalled the end of the era of post-war reconstruction and industrial development. It was also, coincidentally, the point at which automotive markets in the Western developed countries began to enter the phase of maturity.

As demand growth slowed, markets shifted from being producer-dominated to customer-dominated – although it took much of the industry some time to understand this. Continued capacity investments, based on over-optimistic demand forecasts, started to result in over-capacity. In the early 1970s in Europe, for example, it was often necessary to wait a long time to receive the car one had ordered. This began to change, and customers no longer had to wait for the privilege of obtaining a vehicle. This phenomenon is by no means unique to the automotive industry: over-capacity cycles have long been a feature of the chemical industry, for example, as competitors simultaneously rushed to commission new process plants.

# A changing market segmentation pattern

In the era of mass-production – after the First World War in the United States and after the Second World War in Europe – there was a single, dominant, fast-growing market segment. This was made up of buyers of the single, standard, mass-produced product, typically the Model T in the

United States or the VW Beetle or Renault 4CV/Dauphine in Europe. Alfred Sloan and GM broke this mould, to the detriment of Ford. A generation later, the European volume producers gradually broadened their product ranges spontaneously, as their national markets matured.

This is detectably the point at which constant declines in real prices ceased, as increasing complexity began to offset scale. Nevertheless, the manufacturers pretty much defined the market segmentation. The rich bought large cars and the poorer bought small cars. Product ranges were set up to optimize supply-side economics rather than the needs of car buyers explicitly. Most volume manufacturers in Europe covered the market with four platforms and a limited range of major components, notably engines and gearboxes. The platforms and major components were kept in production as long as possible, in order to amortize their huge development costs over the largest possible volumes.

This historical product-based segmentation pattern has now broken down to a large extent. As national markets have matured, manufacturers have sought growth in exports, across regions at first and then globally. The choice available to consumers increased dramatically, particularly during the 1970s and 1980s, diminishing their brand loyalty.

A natural response of the vehicle manufacturers to the increasing difficulty of capturing the attention of consumers was to add more features. This is exactly what has happened to other consumer durables, from cameras to microwaves. In the car industry, it meant that the price difference between the most meanly and the most luxuriously equipped vehicle based on a given platform was enormous. A top-of-the-range small car could cost considerably more than a bottom-of-the-range large car. The consequences of this shift from market structures is illustrated diagrammatically in Figure 3.2.

The growth in features has meant that market segmentation has triumphed over product segmentation at last. The primary segmentation distinctions are now no longer Big Car vs Small Car but Car Lover vs Utilitarian Transportation Buyer. Today, the Car Lover may buy a large BMW or a highly-featured small Peugeot. When Mercedes launched its small car, the 190, many predicted its failure: 'no one will buy a 2-litre car at that premium price'. Yet, it and the BMW 3-series were outstanding successes. The sceptics failed to anticipate the segmentation change.

Despite these changes and the fact that they occurred 10 to 15 years ago, most discussion of the industry remains product-based. Almost all the available industry statistics relate to products – their characteristics and the volumes in which they are produced, sold and registered. A consumer-segment-based analysis requires access to proprietary databases on car buyers – syndicated by the manufacturers in the case of Europe – and extensive analysis and manipulation. It would be highly unfair to charge the automotive industry with being backward in this respect. The computer hardware industry is also almost wholly

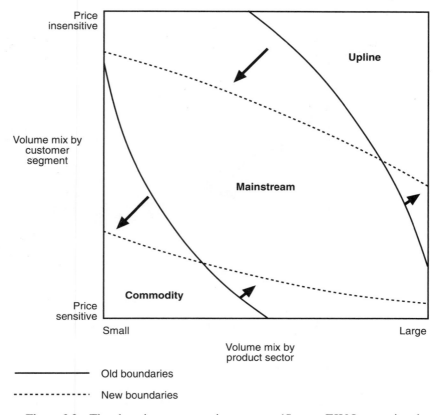

**Figure 3.2**   The changing segmentation pattern. (*Source*: EIU International
Motor Business, July 1990)

documented in terms of product features and performance, and shipment
volumes. Meaningful end-user segments – in terms of specific applications and equipment selection criteria – and distribution channels remain
obscure.

The market-driven feature race in the car industry has been reinforced by mandatory requirements, especially on emission controls, fuel
consumption and safety. This has meant that more and more features
are being fitted, some driven by demand, some by the need of vehicle
manufacturers to differentiate their products and some by legislation.
The cumulative consequences for car prices in the US are shown in
Figure 3.3. The real price of the underlying vehicle – i.e. at equivalent
feature content – has continued to fall as improvements in productivity
have been made.

A significant example of a market-driven, demand-driven feature is
air conditioning. This has become a virtually standard feature in the

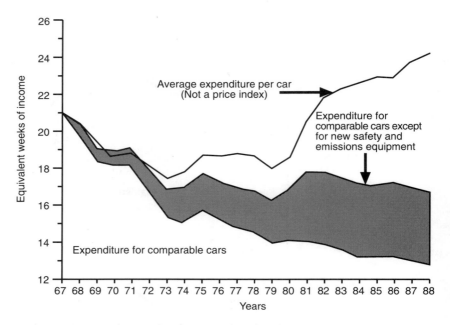

**Figure 3.3**   Components of new car expenditure in the US. (*Source:* EIU Motor Quarterlies)

United States, with a 91% fitment rate in 1992. Conversely, air conditioning remains a luxury in Europe, although efforts are being made to promote it more systematically. An obvious historical explanation is that the countries of southern Europe, where the climatic need for air conditioning is greatest, are the least wealthy, while higher-income but colder northern Europe has less need of the product. In fact, very limited fitting also raises the option price and causes lengthy delivery delays,

However, fitment is now reaching much further into the middle ranges of cars in Europe as a standard. A great many other vehicles offer it as an option – notably Japanese cars. Penetration is thought to have reached 14% or 15% in 1993, compared to 10% in 1990 – perhaps indicating an incipient breakthrough in acceptance and demand. In fact, rapid growth is forecast. Valeo, the largest supplier of such systems in Europe, believes penetration will reach 20% to 25% by 1995. Systems prices are expected to fall by 20%. The ultimate level will never equal that in the US but could reach 40% to 50%.

Gasoline (petrol) injection is another case of delayed option take-up. Initially developed for military aircraft engines by Bosch in the 1930s, it was first applied to upline cars in Europe, as a market-driven performance feature. It later became a mandatory technology for achieving government-imposed emissions standards in cars – hence its later mass application in Europe, as compared to the United States.

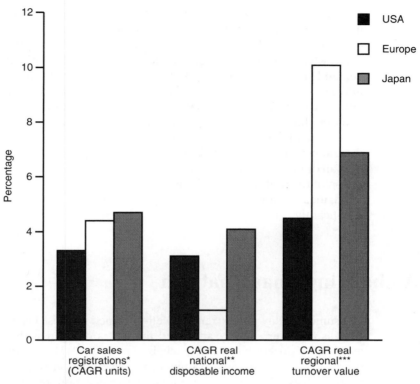

Percentage

| | USA |
| | Europe |
| | Japan |

Car sales
registrations*
(CAGR units)

CAGR real
national**
disposable income

CAGR real
regional***
turnover value

Notes:   * USA 1984-87
         ** 1984-87
         *** Based on 9 European, 3 USA, 3 Japanese manufacturers
CAGR = Compound Annual Growth Rate

**Figure 3.4**   Increase in units, national disposable income and turnover in the US, Europe and Japan (1984–88). (*Source:* EIU International Motor Business, July 1990)

Anti-lock brakes (ABS) represents an intermediate case, of a desirable safety feature which has not been officially mandated (except in Europe, for intercity buses and trucks carrying hazardous goods) but which has nevertheless penetrated the market to an increasing extent, despite a high option price at first. Initially a source of differentiation, it is now almost a qualifier to play at all. The growth in the fitment of air bags is similar.

The consequence of these changes to a more market-driven segmentation, with increased feature fitment, has been that the automotive industry's growth – in developed country markets – has progressively shifted from unit volume to value-per-unit. A historical illustration of this is given in Figure 3.4. This has worked adequately well so far, in that consumers have in general been prepared to pay more for their vehicles, in real terms, accepting that their cars would consume an increasing proportion of their disposable incomes. But it does raise some questions about what happens from here. Some care is needed in projecting future demand. The projected growth of industry turnover has to be separated into its components of unit volume and unit value, in real terms. The influence of technology, regulation, economic and social patterns, fashion and branding on both of these factors must also be distinguished.

Demand for personal mobility in the developed countries, which determines the unit volume of vehicles, is expected neither to grow nor fall dramatically, under foreseeable normal circumstances. The interaction of the motor car with living and working patterns will, in all likelihood, mean that underlying volumetric demand for cars will not decline significantly.

# A changing image pattern

Consumers today are extremely well-informed in most instances about what is on offer – every advanced market is deluged with newspaper articles, TV programmes and specialized periodicals about cars. No other product is so extensively examined, reviewed and critiqued. New and resale prices, the costs of running, insurance and repairs – all are available for public scrutiny. The car remains the most functionally complex product that most of us are likely to own. But it has lost a good deal of its technological mystique – not least because it has become so much more reliable and hassle-free. Also we are, perforce, extensively in contact with the car. In the UK, for example, the average driver spends one and a half hours a day in the car, more than 9% of his or her waking time. Based on average miles driven, the driver's average speed over this time is 18 mph.

There has to be something more to this than travelling or masochism! The car has become an icon, a symbol, a means of personal identification and differentiation. Brand strength – of the marque or of individual products – now matters enormously to vehicle manufacturers and is boosted with the help of constantly increasing advertising and promotional expenditures. It ultimately rests on the quality of products. But perceptions matter considerably also, as do market share and the size and quality of distribution presence. In some cases, there appears to be negative price elasticity for vehicles within a given class in a given market – the greater the volume the higher the price realisation – because of the image effects. The package that sells a car today is far from that which sold the utilitarian Model T or the semi-utilitarian Beetle or 2CV, with their product standardization and steadily falling real prices, based on increasing production scale and experience.

Cars are therefore sold as much on image as they are on engineering. They are not only a convenient, cost-effective form of personal travel, they are also a means of self expression.

Cars have acquired strong sexual connotations since the 1930s. Fast, attractive and powerful – even today, cars are sold with the help of partially-clad women draped across the hood. Just visit any car show, if you think that the blonde in the bikini is a thing of the past. Cars remain shapely symbols of power, influence and fertility. They evoke images of speed, exhilaration and wealth. A study conducted in the 1950s by Ernest Dichter, president of the Institute for Motivational Research, concluded that men 'saw a convertible as a symbolic mistress'.

The industry has worked hard to develop its current position in the world's psyche and was already at it in 1911. The message then was, 'Cars are so simple to use, even she could drive one'. Insulting enough. Many argue the images of today are little better – they are just as exploitative. They are often not just sexually but also environmentally outdated. With the growth in environmentalism and the pressure for recyclable, emission-free, city cars, the continued emphasis on high performance seems increasingly inappropriate. The image of the car is going to have to start to change.

For car producers this change is critical, as image is an essential element of the sales 'package'. In fact, it matters so much that many price differences between products cannot be wholly explained by an analysis of their inherent performance or features. Correcting for objective physical differences such as interior volume, engine power and various features and options still leaves large unexplained residuals – up to plus or minus 20%. These can be accounted for by looking at brand strengths in particular markets. The effects of branding and image are so strong that there is actually a negative price-volume elasticity within given product segments in a given national market – that is, the leading brand achieves a better price realization. Not news for professional marketers of consumer goods. It is hard, however, to avoid the impression that the industry's profit margins are becoming increasingly – and dangerously – dependent on marketing hype.

## Limited room for changes in unit volumes sold

There is undoubtedly room for a certain 'evening up' – some parts of Southern Europe up to Northern European levels, the more successful Eastern European countries to those of Western Europe, and so on. However, simply projecting a convergence with North American levels of penetration frankly seems unrealistic. There is a ceiling on the penetration of single and multiple car ownership that is itself the result of the physical environment. Manhattan has far lower levels of private car ownership than the US average, for good reasons. Central London is lower than the UK average. The balance of transportation needs in Europe will never be exactly the same as those in the US. Any significant further increase in car sales is unlikely.

The real constraints on the future development of the motor industry are societal and environmental. The lock-step between living styles and mass use of vehicles works both ways. There is not enough physical space left on existing roads and societies are becoming less willing to pay the price of more roads and parking facilities. The cost to the quality of life, in cities and the countryside is getting noticeable. We may have somewhat overshot the point at which the cost to the community exceeds the maximisation of the utility for individuals. Individual mobility was once an inexhaustible resource – when the roads were empty.

Driving through rural France on holiday can still be a real pleasure. The *Autoroute du Soleil* on a busy weekend is a nightmare. Mobility is a positional asset, in the terms used by Fred Hirsch in his book *Social Limits to Growth*.[1] In other words, it is a finite asset that people compete for and whose very value diminishes as more people have access to it. Average road speeds in central London are barely better now than they were 100 years ago. The demand system is to a large degree self-regulating, at the volume level. This all suggests that demand will only change marginally. This is probably realistic in volume terms.

However much technology is applied to clean up emissions from conventional vehicles, increasing vehicle mileages will eventually wipe out the gains. Major changes in the design of vehicles – zero-emission, electric cars, and so on – are likely to change the cost-benefit balance of individual vehicle ownership so much that the usage pattern could be significantly altered. Some of these possibilities are discussed later.

Short of such changes – which would have to be imposed by legislation, as in California – the pattern of the modal mix of transport is not likely to change all that much. More cities will impose road-pricing or other forms of restraint on private cars in their centres during business hours. There will be more investment in urban public transport. But it is only a credible alternative on high-density routes. A better balance can surely be found, with the right analysis, planning and control mechanisms – but it will probably not be radically different from what we know today. Technology can help: road pricing, automated toll collection, navigation and congestion-avoidance systems. But it will simply marginally improve traffic flows and vehicle utilization.

Europe seems set to invest in a new network of high-speed railways. The investments will be colossal and will certainly bring benefits. But who will be affected? Not the average commuter, shopper or parent taking children to school. More likely business people on business journeys. Probably the airlines more than road transport. Similarly, electronic communications may have a larger impact on business travel, although the need for face-to-face meetings will never disappear. There will be more home-working based on communications technologies. But the shift to a higher proportion of services in the economy cannot be managed wholly by these means: many services require face-to-face contact and therefore personal travel. A world in which we all stayed at home and communicated through electronic interfaces would be a pretty dismal one.

## But a real possibility of the hype collapsing

The discontinuities could be in the qualitative aspects. A big push for much lighter, smaller and environmentally less burdensome cars can only be achieved through major changes in their fundamental design. Only governments could cause this to happen. This may seem far-fetched and the industry, with all its huge investments in existing designs and technologies, would no doubt try to oppose it. But it has happened to some degree before: the US downsizing, forced through the CAFE regulations; and the general considerable tightening of safety, consumption and emissions standards. Under present fuel and vehicle taxation levels and policies with respect to the control of vehicle use, existing technologies and designs are pretty rational. Furthermore, they have been considerably refined, through a lengthy process of continuous improvement.

The much more significant fragility in the demand structure lies in the hype element that has become so much more important in recent years. The efforts put into sustaining it are shown in Figure 3.5. Of course the car is something special: the only means – short of piloting an aeroplane or helicopter – through which human beings can extend and multiply their physical capabilities. But there is still the underlying transportation element.

The dynamic pleasure of driving – the sports car on the country or mountain road – is an increasingly rare pleasure. The styling and image components have now been boosted perhaps well beyond rational levels of utility. What's the good of a 200 kph car with nowhere to drive it? How long will consumers go on paying substantial price premiums for brand image? The influence of brands has started to diminish in other consumer goods fields: what will happen to the motor industry if this spreads to cars?

There will always be car-lover segments in the market, people who want to pay more for a high-performance or luxury vehicle – whether 'objectively' justified or not. These have grown as the industry has systematically targeted and developed these segments, and showered them with new product offerings. But who says they will go on growing?

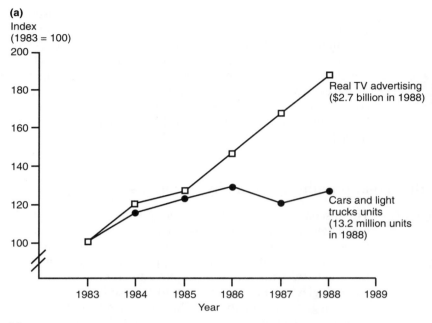

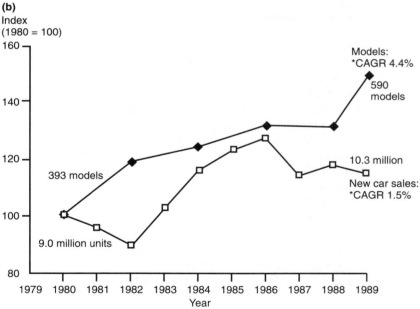

* CAGR: Compound average growth rate

**Figure 3.5**   Driving the hype: (a) TV advertising versus new car and light truck sales (*Source:* TV Bureau of Advertising; MVMA); (b) Model proliferation versus new car sales (1980-89) (*Source:* EIU European Motor Business, May 1990).

Could not this prove to be a zero-sum game? Those who try to push all of the industry to target these segments may simply be sowing the seeds of its next crisis.

There is a possibility – although not a certainty – of societal change in this respect. While most people would still like to have a car, for the freedom and convenience it offers, the age of the car as a cult object may be drawing to an end. Not in all market segments, clearly, but perhaps for significant parts of the market. Again, the phenomenon is self-regulating: as cars have ceased to be rare goods to be striven for and become simply part of the furniture of everyday life, the glamour fades. Social and technological forces create and enable 'waves of interest' that go well beyond short-term fashion cycles. The car provided vastly expanded physical mobility for the majority of the population. It is now seen almost as a right.

The individual aspirations of today's and tomorrow's teenagers and children may well be moving onto different tracks. Witness the vast growth of the video and video games industries. They have developed at a prodigious speed – far faster than the motor industry – and will continue to do so. This is because there is so much more 'stretch' in their underlying technologies. Cars can only become incrementally better means of personal transportation because physical transport cannot be micro-miniaturized. Saying that, if the automotive industry had done as well as the electronics industry a Rolls-Royce would be a centimetre long, cost a thousandth of what it does and run 50,000 km on a litre of petrol, is a conceptual nonsense. Yet it highlights the contrasts.

The potential for developing co-ordination skills, intellectual capabilities and emotional sensitivities through electronics technologies remains far from fully-exploited. It will surely be much more thoroughly exploited, to both desirable and undesirable ends, creating its own set of personal and social problems and challenges. It would surely be sad if we ended up as troglodytes, forever stuck in front of our screens or immersed in virtual reality. Kids will probably end up congregating as much as ever. They will probably still want access to individual transportation and clamour to borrow the family car. But it will become more of a means and less of an end. The spending priorities will shift, the branding and images will attach to other things, and the premiums will be spent elsewhere. The shift may initially be gradual but it could quickly accelerate with the generational change. It will also be reinforced by environmental consciousness.

# Note

1.  Hirsch (1977). *Social limits to growth*. Routledge & Kegan Paul

# Summary of Part One

The determinants of long-term demand are often much more complex than is suggested by superficial analysis and conventional wisdom. They go well beyond the simple laws of traditional market-place micro-economics.

- Major innovations can have disrupting and damaging effects, as well as benefits. The effect of a product on people and society may need legislative intervention on occasions. There are some problems that free-market economics cannot solve. Supply and demand alone cannot resolve such issues. In the case of the car industry, and most other industries, being 'clean' and producing in an environmentally friendly way, is unlikely to maximize purely economic efficiency. Green suppliers are often disadvantaged, unless supported by the law.

- Change is not always rapid or reversible. Markets are often subject to ratchet effects, irreversibilities that make change difficult. Any change that does occur can take decades. For example, when cars were first developed, it took 40 years before they had a major impact on the horse population. Ratchets are barriers – often structural – that make reversing 'progress' difficult.

- As industries move through their lifecycles, the segments structure for both markets and products can shift radically – and more than once. The nature of end demand and the basis for growth and competitive success often change considerably. This can create both opportunities and threats for existing and new players.

# The automobile industry at a turning point

# 4

# Getting what you want: the breakdown of product class barriers

## A stable pattern of products today

So, if demand is relatively fixed, certainly in volume terms, can the product itself be changed? The CAFE regulations in the US forced a partial alignment of American cars to world norms. The same has not happened in trucks because of still widely-differing construction and use regulations, and useage patterns, as well as operator needs and expectations. In cars, the result has been the emergence of fairly stable underlying product line structures. Basic car designs are now very similar throughout the world. Except for the larger car categories, cars mostly have transverse engines, driving the front wheels. Engines are mainly 4-in-line or V-6, with some other less common forms, such as 3-, 5-, or 6-in-line, or V-8.

In Europe, the typical volume producer operates with four to five platforms – the invisible part of the car, made up of floorpan, suspension layout and driveline, which give the car its fundamental operating characteristics. These are usually the B (supermini), C (small saloon), D (medium saloon) and E (large saloon) car classes, in the size categorization scheme. Some manufacturers – those with large markets in Southern Europe – make more or less permanent forays into the smaller A (mini) class.

There will also normally be two or three engine blocks, from which engine families are derived. This reflects a compromise between diversity of offering to maximize market coverage and penetration, and the considerable costs of developing and testing these major items. Similar compromises are made with gearboxes, whether manual or automatic. These are the two major, most complex and costliest to develop elements of the powertrain, the dynamic heart of the car.

This continuum of vehicle classes stretches across quite a wide range of sizes and prices, as shown in Figure 4.1, which illustrates the traditional European product segmentation pattern. Underneath these products sits – or used to sit – a category of older products. These contained classics such as the Citroen 2CV, the VW Beetle and the Renault 4.

Some cars of the previous generation had long lives and typically offered a lot of space and fun for little money. The problem was that they were engineered before today's crash testing legislation came into force. More importantly, the needs of the market have changed. These older cars have therefore disappeared because of passive safety requirements and because of their low sophistication and performance. As we will see later, this style of car may not have gone for good, however. Perhaps the day of such vehicles could come again, if hype fades and speeds are more strictly controlled.

Above the continuum of A to E class vehicles, sits the wedge-shaped area of upline, executive, luxury and speciality cars. These cars are those that deviate from the volume market norm in terms of their price to size ratio. In the upward direction, of course.

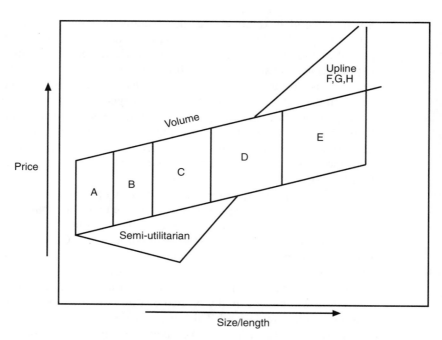

**Figure 4.1**   Size and price range of European vehicle classes.

There is nothing exceptional about the fundamental design or functionality of these vehicles. Many have rear-wheel drive but this is a packaging option that makes relatively more sense for larger cars anyway. They are distinguished from volume cars by more features, higher quality components, more investment in development to perfect their handling – and particularly strong branding and substantial price premiums.

A similar pattern used to exist in the United States before downsizing, simply sitting a few notches further to the right on the diagram. Cadillacs and Lincolns sold at a premium over other GM or Ford brands but were not fundamentally different products.

# A changing product segmentation pattern

This pattern – which became fairly homogeneous throughout the developed world following US downsizing, albeit with the US still producing somewhat larger and heavier vehicles than Europe or Japan (Figure 4.2) – has started to change significantly again. This change in the passenger car sector – and, by extension, into some light commercial vehicles and niche products such as multi-purpose vehicles and 4 × 4s – reflects the long-term transfer of power from producers to consumers already discussed in Chapter 3.

The era of initial mass motorization is long since past. Vehicle manufacturers have broadened their model ranges to address the

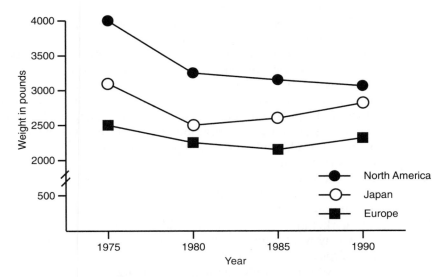

**Figure 4.2** Average vehicle weights, 1975–90.

**Table 4.1**    Illustrative automobile consumer segments.

| Segment | Descriptive statements |
|---|---|
| Economy-minded | • I like to do a lot of my own maintenance<br>• I want the cheapest, easiest-to-maintain car I can find |
| Driving enthusiast | • If money were not a problem, one of the things I'd like to have is a high-performance sports car<br>• The Japanese and the Germans make much higher quality small cars than we make in the US |
| Conspicuous consumer | • When I buy a car I like it fully equipped with all of the latest options<br>• I tend to switch brands of cars more frequently than most people I know |
| Socially aware | • I'm more concerned than most people with social issues like air pollution and energy conservation<br>• To me, cars are just basically transportation<br>• The most important thing to me in a car is good gas mileage |
| Loves cars | • I spend a lot of time washing and polishing my car<br>• I tend to buy cars more for styling than for engineering features |
| Domestic intender | • The most important thing to me in a car is the comfort it provides on long trips<br>• It's important to me to 'buy American' whenever I can |
| Transport buyer | • To me, cars are just basically transportation |

(*Source*: EIU Motor Quaterlies)

increasingly complex segmentation of the end market-place. The basis of segmentation has shifted from the A to E product class to consumers grouped as a function of common attitudes and expectations. These groups are illustrated for the US in Table 4.1.

The result is a quite new market/product segmentation pattern, shown for the US in Figure 4.3. It is based more on the common horizontal relationships between groups of consumers and their expectations than on the vertical product class structures. This is reflected in product offerings and pricing. The range of versions and variants developed from a given platform (and their prices) has increased enormously, to the point at which the price difference between the lowest and the highest specification version of the same basic model typically exceeds that between the average for adjacent models in the product range. Changes in the US price structure that reflect this are shown in Figure 4.4. Similar changes can be observed in European markets.

There is nothing at all surprising about this. It reflects a natural adaptation to the needs of an increasingly sophisticated and discriminating market-place. A wealthy individual in the 16th arrondissement of Paris may want a luxuriously equipped car but not necessarily a large one. Typical examples are 'hot' hatchbacks or GTIs. Conversely, a large family with limited income may want a large, simply-featured vehicle, such as a base version of a station wagon.

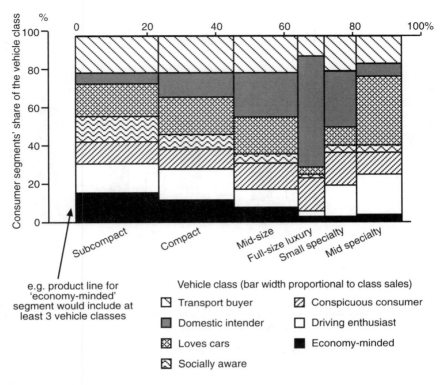

**Figure 4.3**  US market/product segmentation. (*Source*: EIU Motor Quarterlies, 1991)

## The ratchet effect on features

For vehicle manufacturers, there is a distinct ratchet effect at work on features. Once car drivers become used to them, they expect them as standard. Improved or additional functions can penetrate the market quite quickly, once demand for them passes a certain threshold and the option price falls sufficiently. Products such as radios, electric windows and central-locking are recent examples of features that were once only fitted as standard to upline cars but which are now largely expected on every car. In the future, the same could happen for power-steering, ABS, air-conditioning, automatic transmissions or air bags in Europe. Many of these functions or features, once the preserve of the luxury or high-performance market and product segments, are becoming widespread as a result of regulation, legislation and increasing disposable incomes. Yesterday's luxury option therefore becomes tomorrow's standard feature.

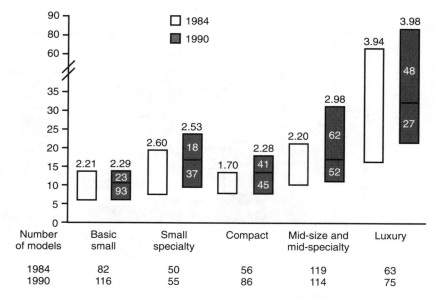

Note: Numbers above bars indicate max/min price ratio within segment. Solid line within bars indicate 1990 median transaction price. Numbers within bars indicate number of models below and above median transaction price.

**Figure 4.4**   Price ranges by market segment, 1984 vs 1990. (*Source*: EIU Motor Quarterlies, 1991)

This change in the product segmentation structure, driven by consumer demand, has had two important consequences. First, the notion of world cars – made in one place and shipped to worldwide markets – has disappeared. It existed in the age of the Model T, the Beetle and the early Corolla. Today, the underlying designs may well be common but the vehicles will be styled and adapted for local needs. This is precisely the globalization strategy that Ford Motor Company is apparently pursuing.

Second, the historical distinction between volume and upline cars is threatened with disappearance. Traditionally, upline car marques have been able to protect the distinctiveness of their brand and their premium prices by offering distinctly superior design, performance, features and finish. They occupied worldwide market niches, generally building their vehicles in one location. For a long time, the fact that Mercedes-Benz or BMW cars were made in Germany was an inherent part of their quality image and brand appeal. As the technology and feature content of volume cars continues to increase, this barrier against the entry of the volume producers into upline markets weakens. This trend is reinforced by the fact that more and more of the added technology and feature content relies on electronics, which are often not the property of the vehicle manufacturers.

In fact, upline vehicle manufacturers are likely to have increasing difficulty in maintaining their own distinctive technology edge, with their limited volumes. Two cases illustrate the potential threat to them: the gains made by Toyota's upline Lexus product and brand, especially in the US; and the success of Saab-GM in building the new Saab 900 on an Opel Vectra platform. Some niche products will probably survive, however, such as 4 × 4s or sports cars, typified by the Mazda Miata (MX5 in Europe).

Heavy commercial vehicle markets and product lines are also changing, although driven by different factors. As the volume of road freight has grown, steadily gaining at the expense of other modes, so competition has intensified and the haulage industry has consolidated and concentrated in most regions. Deregulation led to massive improvements in capacity utilization in the United States. Large and sophisticated operators emerged, who can determine their own needs and specify products with accuracy.

Europe lags behind, in that real freedom of haulage within the Union is not yet fully established, with the result that many small operators remain. But the sporadic truck drivers' blockades testify to the threat they perceive. As the historically nationally-based construction and use regulations are aligned within Europe, true pan-European demand and product segments are emerging. However, patterns of use and regulations still differ widely between Europe, North America and Japan. To talk of a world truck today is meaningless. Yet some of the future technology requirements – for diesel engine-emissions controls, for example – may well lead to world components being built into trucks.

# 5

# A battle of Titans: the achievements of the vehicle manufacturers

## The birth of the industry

Although car production started at the end of the 19th century, experiments with motorized carriages had already been going on for a long time before that. The first steam-powered vehicle was built and patented by Oliver Evans in Philadelphia in 1805. Evans even prepared a prospectus for the formation of a company, Experiment Co., to manufacture the vehicle. However, no backers were forthcoming and, sadly, the vehicle was not developed further. In 1860, Sylvester Roper of Roxbury, Massachusetts, claimed to have developed a steam car capable of 25 mph. The vehicle produced two horsepower, was fuelled by coal and could carry two passengers. Again, this venture failed to attract any support.

Various other, mainly steam-driven, vehicles were developed during the last quarter of the 19th century with similar results. It was not until Nikolaus Otto produced the first four-stroke gasoline engine in Germany in 1876 that the car as we understand it today could become a reality. Within nine years of Otto's development, fellow Germans Karl Benz and Gottlieb Daimler had constructed a marketable vehicle. Their breakthrough came because they were able to design an engine that had high power and low weight, essential for automotive applications.

Although Europe can be credited with having invented the gasoline-powered car which dominates the field today, it was the United States that developed the industry into its present form. The first US company to manufacture vehicles, Duryea, began production in 1896. By 1899, just three years later, 800 cars had been registered. Two years after that there were ten times that number and by 1910 the number of cars had risen a further 57 fold to 458,000, a compound annual growth rate of nearly 50%. The number of car suppliers also grew rapidly. Between 1900 and 1910, more than 300 companies began manufacturing cars in North America alone.

By 1920, sales in the US were 2 million vehicles a year, while the number of cars registered was 8 million, a 1000 fold increase in just 20 years. Yet, even then, Americans still owned twice as many horses as cars. Within another ten years, the reverse was true. By 1930, 80% of all cars in the world were in America. It led the world in terms of productivity. The best American factories took 70 man days to produce a car. In Europe it still took 300 man days. The growth of the global industry, in its first 75 years of production, is shown in Figure 5.1.

In the US, the parc – or stock of registered cars – grew by four orders of magnitude in 22 years: from 800 in 1898, to 8000 in 1900, 458,000 in 1910 and 8 million in 1920. Unit sales went up forty-fold: from 49,000 in 1901 to 1904, to 166,000 in 1905 to 1908, 864,000 in 1909 to 1912, and 2 million in 1920. The price of cars fell rapidly, as the sales volume grew. A Locomobile steam car cost $1000 in 1901, an Olds Curved Dash $650 in 1901, and a Sears Auto Buggy $395 in 1905. The effect on the horse-drawn carriage industry was devastating: while car sales went up, its sales crashed from 2 million units in 1909 to 10,000 in 1923.

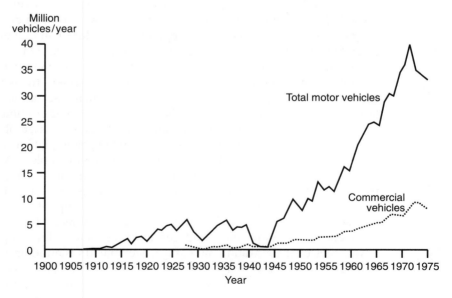

**Figure: 5.1**   The first 75 years of motor vehicle production. (*Source*: World motor vehicle data)

# Mass production and the birth of the corporation

A major step forward took place in 1908 when three Cadillac cars were shipped to England and dismantled. The parts were then mixed and the vehicles reassembled. Importantly, this demonstrated interchangeability. This was the basis of the 'American' approach to manufacturing, pioneered for weapons production during the Civil War. It contrasted sharply with the 'English' approach, based on the craft-fitting of individual parts.

The same year, the Model T was introduced by Ford. Within a few years Ford combined the idea of interchangeability with a continuously moving assembly line and an extreme division of labour. This made possible the economical mass-production of highly-complex, multi-functional objects – such as automobiles. Note that this was different from the, already well-established, mechanized mass production of standardized commodities, such as textiles. The process was first adopted fully at the new Highland Park facility in 1913. By 1919 the Model T held 42% of the US market.

Until the development of mass production, components were individually produced and fitted by skilled craftsmen, with each operation different. The key to mass production, the element which distinguished it so fundamentally from the craft production which preceded it, is repetitiveness. Complex products were broken down into their components which could be repetitively produced and repetitively assembled together, because they were interchangeable. Hand adjustment and fitment became a thing of the past. Much of the margin of error was taken out of operations. This allowed two critical steps to take place: the automation of parts production, using equipment such as automatic lathes and later numerically controlled (NC) and computer numerically controlled (CNC) machine tools; and the sub-division of assembly tasks.

It was not only parts that became interchangeable, labour did too because the skills required for each task were less complex. A minor example of this in the industry today is the use of modular components to make up exhaust systems in the aftermarket. These are typically fitted in specialized, high through-put, fast-fit outlets, by simply-trained fitters instead of by highly-qualified automotive mechanics. This is mass production at the product and service level and offers huge cost advantages over the traditional garage. McDonald's is another example of a business that has emerged thanks to the benefits of mass production. Again, the process has affected both its products and its approach to service.

Mass production was a total revolution, in terms of the product, the production process and the organisation that made it work. It radically changed the determinants of cost. It made the automotive industry scale-driven – a factor that Henry Ford made unhesitating use of. Interchangeability and repetitiveness meant standardization to high tolerances, which is difficult without automation. As a result, multi-skilled employees were replaced by unskilled machine tenders and assembly-line workers, who required less training and could be paid lower wages. The resulting huge gains in productivity made it possible for Ford to increase the hourly rate for the line workers to ensure he attracted the best. This also made life more difficult for his competitors, who had to match the wage rates without the benefit of large volumes.

It is difficult to overstate the importance of mass production. Its development was by no means evolutionary. Ford, together with Charles Sorensen and Charles Lewis, approached the whole production process in an entirely new way. Until then, cars, like other complex products, were assembled like houses. The foundation, or chassis, was constructed first and then all of the components were brought to it and attached. Mass production turned this on its head. Instead of components being carried to the chassis, the chassis was carried to the components, on a continuously moving line. While this may seem obvious today, it was a fundamental and visionary change when it was conceived in 1908. Output was increased from just over seven cars an hour to 146 – which terrified competitors. Prices plummeted. The Model T cost $825 in 1908. It cost $290 in 1926. There is no better illustration of sustained cost reduction, driven by growing scale and cumulative experience of production.

Technological developments were also important. Why did Ford originally offer the car 'in any colour, as long as it's black' ? Because black paint dried faster than any other colour, which meant Ford could produce more vehicles. Even then, the paint process took 30 days. At the time, Ford was producing 1000 cars a day, which meant the company had to set aside 20 acres of covered space to store cars as they went through the different stages. Yet this process was used largely until 1924, creating a major barrier to the development of production capacity in the industry. DuPont then introduced a paint that cut the paint process to two days. Shortly after, Ford began using ovens that cut the time down to a matter of minutes.

It is rare to be able to visualize the different eras of production at the same time. An opportunity for this was provided in an exhibition on the history of the automobile, staged by Fiat at the Science Museum in London in the 1980s. The company provided four videos, showing assembly operations being conducted in its first plant in the 1910s; then in their first purpose-built assembly plant, Rivalta, in the 1930s; at the giant Mirafiori complex in the 1940s; and in the highly-automated Cassino plant in the 1980s. The contrast between the first and the last is as of two different worlds.

The car was also largely responsible for the birth of the corporation. Mass production was only one means of achieving economies of scale. William Durant discovered that the combination of suppliers and different vehicle manufacturers into a conglomerate, General Motors, was another. The creation of GM not only produced an integrated supplier network that could maximize revenues, it also allowed the car manufacturer much more control of the entire sequence of operations.

The social role model pioneered by Ford was also extremely significant and durable. It was much studied and imitated. Despite, or perhaps because of the paternalistic approach inherent to the $5 day and as a result of the Taylorian fine control of work and employees, Ford was involved in some very bitter disputes with labour. The emphasis on control of a whole value-added chain has a very corporatist flavour. This endured for decades. Even with progressive vertical deintegration, with vehicle manufacturers contracting-out increasing proportions of the chain to suppliers and dealers, the determination to control – in detail – remained (and remains) very strong. Much of the flavour endures today: the 'industry of industries', male-dominated, macho in its relationships, presuming to know 'what's good for America', oligopolistic and often introverted. But also immensely resourceful, creative, endowed with talented people, vital to many economies, a continuing pioneer in industrial organisation and one of the first global industries.

Perhaps it is not surprising that the whole concept of motorization appealed so strongly to the fascist regimes: a model of industrial and social discipline and control; a means of satisfying individual aspirations without political concessions; opportunities for spectacular demonstrations of technical prowess through racing; and for grandiose public works projects, such as the *autostrade* or the *Autobahnen*. 'A powerful and delicate machine, which brings together titanic rhythms in its steel heart', as Mussolini described the automobile, had an immense emotional appeal in that period. The appeal of the automotive industry as a national showcase industry is still alive today in some developing countries – and in some developed ones also.

# The change to lean production

Lean production was the next major change on the supply side. It combines the advantages of mass and craft production while avoiding the problems. Craft production is typically expensive, while mass production is very inflexible. Lean production extracts the best from each approach and actually increases flexibility and reduces cost in the process. It is 'lean' because it cuts the human effort required, as well as the assembly space and the investment in plant. Products can also be developed much more quickly. There are other benefits, such as lower inventory requirements. There are also fewer defects, which reduces cost further.

Lean production involves a fundamental change in emphasis: in the way people work but also in the way they think and act. Shopfloor jobs become more challenging but they are also more demanding of involvement and initiative. Lean production often means that product designs need some adaptations for the process to work well. Yet the ideas of 'design for manufacture' or 'simultaneous engineering' have also been applied in traditional mass production environments. There are examples of this, often forced by the exigencies and resource shortages of wartime, such as the mass-produced Liberty ship, built in sections and welded together, or the Sten gun, the Kalashnikov and its ancestor the German G-44 assault rifle, all of which used stamped steel parts to replace more complex and costly machined components.

The lean production approach can also be taken much further. Beyond the initial concept, which is closely linked to just-in-time supply, there are structural implications. It is not just about what should be done better, but who should be doing it. For example, just-in-time has moved from a concept of delivery, sometimes buffered by inventories, to one of production. No manufacturing step is started until a demand signal is received from the market. A further step is to have the supplier of the component not only produce and deliver the part, but fit it as well, a 'store-within-a-store' concept which gives the supplier total responsibility for the fitted performance and design of its product. The potential implications of this for the structure of the automotive industry are far reaching indeed.

Lean production is a means of optimizing the use of assets, including human assets, by acting on the determinants of cost at the systemic and operational levels. This is not a trivial issue in an industry with such a long development and supply chain and is why the pioneering work by the Japanese has brought them such a great competitive advantage.

The change involved in going from mass to lean production is different from that pioneered by Ford in 1908. It is more evolutionary and less revolutionary, less imposed from above than led, more dependent on organizational behaviour than on methods engineering and technocracy. Again, it is hard to understand without seeing it in operation: the quality of a lean-production shopfloor, compared to the traditional industrial approach, is hard to describe without resort to platitudes – but very evident in the attitudes and behaviour of those involved.

Whereas the automotive industry made a leap ahead of the times with mass production, it is in effect catching up with social realities in instituting lean production: co-operation in place of conflict, leadership by demonstration rather than imposition, multi-skilling and appealing to individual creativity instead of reducing tasks to their lowest common denominator, relying on the 'pull' of individual commitment, responsibility and enthusiasm rather than on the 'push' of dictated instructions. It is, in another context, as paradoxical as Alexander Dubĉek's 'socialism with a human face' – with the difference that it works. It is not easy to institute, precisely because it calls for such a change in behaviour and in the nature of power relationships – between individuals and enterprises, and suppliers and customers, at all levels through the complex innovation and delivery chains of the industry.

# The growth of the Japanese

The car and the truck as products were originally developed, with their underlying technologies, in Europe. Germany and France were the earliest main centres of production. France arguably remains the most enjoyable country in the world for leisure motoring, at least away from the main highways and conurbations. The battle of Verdun, on the French side, was the first example of mass supply logistics executed by trucks. World car architectures have to a considerable extent crystallized around European design concepts since the downsizing of US cars in the 1980s. Several fundamental technologies, such as the pneumatic tyre, petrol and diesel injection, and disc brakes originated in Europe. The first origins of the industry fit closely with the traditional European 'rich patron' approach to innovation in both the arts and the sciences. But the huge step forward to mass production and mass availability was distinctly a product of American genius, which was subsequently emulated worldwide. The third, behavioural transformation is Asian in origin – but has also begun to be replicated across the globe. Thus the industry has become a unique cultural melting-pot, incorporating major innovations from each of its three main regions in turn.

If the industry has only really taken off outside the US since the Second World War, the influence of the Japanese is even more recent. It was the oil crisis of 1973 that gave the Japanese the opportunity to enter the market in North America and begin exporting seriously for the first time. Now, as shown in Figure 5.2, they control nearly 30% of that market, as well as nearly 14% of sales in Western Europe and 96% of their home market in Japan. In 1993, five of the world's top 12 car producers were Japanese. Japan now sets the standards for productivity in the industry.

The assault by the Japanese has affected Western competitors dramatically. In the US, American Motors, Renault, Peugeot and Rover have all been driven from the market. Others, such as Alfa Romeo, Saab

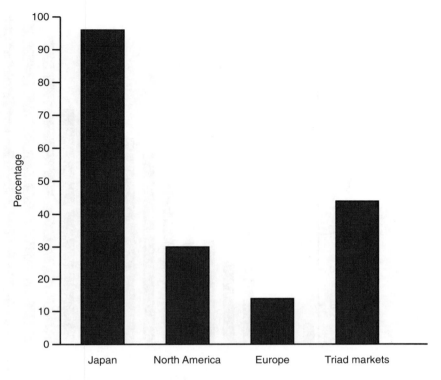

**Figure 5.2**    Market share of Japanese vehicle manufacturers in the largest markets.

and even Volkswagen have been marginalized. Of those that remain, General Motor's market share has fallen by nearly a third, Ford went through years of losses and Chrysler was almost driven to bankruptcy. Conversely, in just 13 years, Honda's Accord became the best selling car in the US.

The competitive impact of the Japanese in Europe so far has been less dramatic than in the US. Even there, however, Sweden's Saab and the UK's Rover have been absorbed by larger suppliers. The failure of the Renault/Volvo merger in 1994 has left both parties and particularly Volvo in a weak position. Part of Volvo, in the Netherlands, is now closely linked with Mitsubishi. While the Japanese manufacturers have made large inroads into unprotected European markets – those with no major national vehicle manufacturers – their share has been limited by protectionist measures in four of the five largest markets, France, Italy, the UK and Spain (see Figure 5.3).

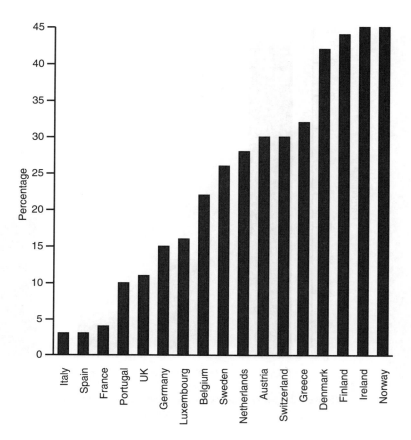

**Figure 5.3** Passenger car market shares of Japanese manufacturers in Western Europe, 1991. (*Source*: EIU)

The influence of the Japanese in Europe is growing, however, as they have now set up 'transplant' assembly and manufacturing operations onshore. Despite strong historical protectionist policies within the European Union, the Japanese will be able to manufacture around a million cars locally by the end of the century, roughly equivalent to 8% of the market demand today. In 1993, Nissan became the largest exporter of cars from the UK, beating Ford, Rover, General Motors and Peugeot for the first time. At the time, the UK was the only significant market in Europe to experience any growth. New car sales in the rest of the region fell by an average of 12% that year, yet Nissan managed to export 80% of its production (196,000 cars) to other parts of the region.

The share of Japanese manufacturers in Europe is expected to continue to rise. First, the quotas for Japanese imports are being phased

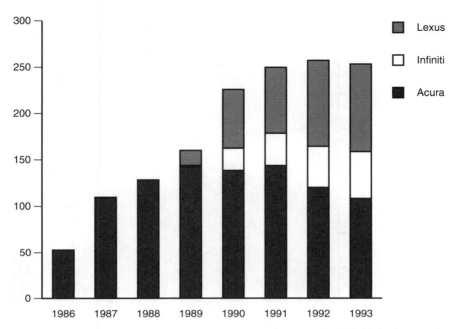

**Figure 5.4**    Sales of luxury Japanese marques in the US, 1986–93, in thousands of units.

out and second, vehicles made within the EU are not restricted. As we shall see later, Europe is the next real competitive battleground for the Japanese. Given that Europe is the largest car buying region in the world in terms of annual sales, the battle promises to be hard.

The Japanese have also been successful throughout the model range. It may seem difficult to remember today, but the original Japanese cars were small, noisy and had a tendency to rust. The first cars imported into the US and Europe were not seen as a threat to local producers. Local manufacturers were fooled into a false sense of security. Many stuck their heads in the sand as the Japanese vehicles improved. By the early 1990s, they not only had a formidable share, they had also captured the top end of the market. The growth of sales of luxury Japanese marques in the US is shown in Figure 5.4.

The success of Lexus, Acura and Infiniti in the United States has been astounding. After launching in 1989, against formidable European competitors like Mercedes-Benz and BMW, Lexus took only a few years to dominate the sector. The Europeans claimed that their reputations were enough to maintain their positions for years. Yet in 1993, Lexus was already selling twice as many cars as Mercedes. The impact on the positions of the Europeans is shown in Figure 5.5.

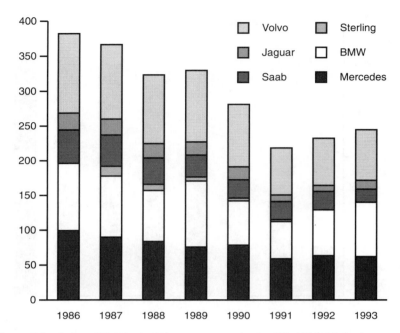

**Figure 5.5**   Sales of European luxury marques in the US, 1986–93, in thousands of units.

When the Japanese began to export vehicles they targeted the number of model variations on offer by the US suppliers. In the US, in particular, some vehicles were made in hundreds of thousands of different variations. Different colours, different engine sizes, various trim options and a choice of features were offered to consumers. It meant that each vehicle was almost unique as each car buyer selected the features, colour, trim and engine sizes they wanted. This was what the manufacturers thought consumers wanted.

When it was launched, the Honda Accord offered only 16 variations, mainly different colour options. Almost all of the features such as air conditioning, power steering and radio, were fitted as standard. On the one hand, this offered less choice, on the other, it offered almost everything the consumer wanted. More importantly, because there were fewer variations, the cost of manufacturing the car was lower. That meant the retail price was lower. The Japanese therefore achieved greater penetration by offering fully equipped vehicles in a limited range of colours at lower prices. The consumer, at the time, placed more importance on the price than any desire to create his own unique car. As a result, the Japanese managed to use the choice offered by US vehicle manufacturers as a weapon against them. Choice meant complexity in manufacturing, which meant added cost. Less choice meant less complexity and less cost, and they could still afford to fit all the added features consumers wanted.

Twenty years later the Japanese reversed the process. They offered the consumer increased choice and more product variations. At the time, the American and European manufacturers were attempting to standardize, to reduce the costs of complexity. This time, however, the Japanese had improved their production technology so that they could produce a wider variation of vehicles on the same production line at the same time. Once again this matched the emerging needs of consumers. While in the 1970s cost and features were important, in the 1980s and early 1990s there was a growing sense of individualism. Greater wealth meant that more people could afford to select cars that better matched their individual needs. The Japanese manufacturers were better placed to meet this consumer need without huge complexity costs.

Strengths and weaknesses are what you make of them. What one company or industry sees as a strength can be viewed by another as a weakness. While the US vehicle manufacturers thought choice was a major strength, the Japanese turned it into a liability. Similarly, when the US and European manufacturers had adopted the new economics of the industry and standardized their products, the Japanese turned the tables again. As before, what the traditional manufacturers thought was a strength became a weakness.

The examples also illustrate the changing nature of marketing in the vehicle industry, or any consumer goods sector for that matter. In the last 20 years the car industry has been largely characterized by product-push. The vehicle manufacturers strandardized and pushed the products at the car buyers, they knew best what the consumer needed. This has changed and is still changing. The industry is now much more characterized by demand-pull. Competition is more intense and customers more difficult to find. Consumers are also wiser. They know much more about what they want, about the products on offer and about how to make their feelings known. Pushing products out to them without taking this into account is very short-sighted and, as we will show, will ultimately prove fatal.

# The motor industry today

The motor industry is now the world's largest single manufacturing activity. In 1990, the industry's most recent peak, it produced more than 50m vehicles worldwide. At the end of 1993, there were estimated to be more then 470m cars in use worldwide. Seventy-five per cent of these are in the US and Western Europe. In the US there are 600 cars per 1000 people, while in Europe there will be 500 per 1000 by the end of the 1990s. The growth rate of the parc, the number of vehicles in use, has been equally spectacular. In the UK there were 108 cars for every 1000 people in 1960. By 1991, there were nearly four times that many.

Three-quarters of the vehicles produced are cars, the remainder vans, trucks and buses. Of the 50m vehicles produced in 1990, each contains at least 5000 individual parts of widely varying materials. These are made by highly specialized factories throughout the world. There are therefore 250 billion parts of original equipment needed every year, just to manufacture new vehicles. There is also a massive industry dedicated to the production of replacement parts (the aftermarket), needed when the originally-fitted equipment wears out or is damaged. There is also a range of businesses that focus on vehicle distribution and sales as well as a massive network of industries involved in the supply of fuel, finance and insurance, without which the car parc itself could not function. The automotive industry is a huge consumer of energy and raw materials. It is also a vast source of employment.

At an average cost of $20,000 a car, the value of the new vehicle industry alone is $1000 billion a year, roughly equivalent to the economies of France, the UK or Italy in 1990. It is twice the size of the Spanish or Brazilian economies, four times the size of South Korea's or Mexico's and nearly 20 times the size of Russia's. Even then, this estimate only accounts for the original equipment or new vehicle market – the part of the industry directly served by the vehicle manufacturers themselves. It ignores the aftermarket and the parts and accessories sector. Adding these in broadly doubles the total. It also ignores the used-car sector, the dealers, the distributors and the service and repairs businesses. There are many other sectors that benefit directly from vehicle production that are not included either – the insurance companies that cover drivers in the event of theft or accident, the oil producers that generate the fuels and lubricants, the banks that finance the sales and investments and the hospitals that deal with those injured in motor vehicle accidents. All directly depend on the production and use of motor vehicles in one way or another.

When all of these and other relevant sectors are included, it becomes clear that this is one of the largest and most important industrial segments in the developed world. Like an engine itself, the motor industry is directly responsible for turning the wheels of many other business sectors. It is therefore one of the world's largest generators of wealth and employment.

This wealth and employment is almost exclusively concentrated in a small part of the globe. Throughout its history, the motor vehicle market has been dominated by the US, Europe and latterly, Japan. Even today, more than 80% of the world's motor vehicle production and sales come from these Triad markets.

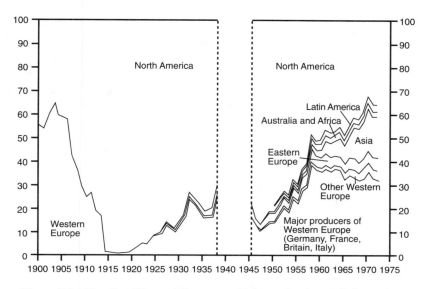

**Figure 5.6**    The first 75 years of motor vehicle production, split by region.
(*Source*: World motor vehicle data)

This dependence on the Triad is not likely to change for many years. While there are manufacturing satellites in less-developed countries, their total impact is small. Similarly, although sales of cars are increasing rapidly in hugely populated countries like India and China their weight relative to the Triad is also minimal. Because of their size and potential, these countries are frequently cited examples of how the motor industry is becoming less dependent on the Triad. Yet, as we shall see, this is simply not true. The size of the largest markets is simply so much greater than that of the new ones that the industry's dependence on these will continue for very many years to come. The car will essentially remain a product for the affluent. Figure 5.6 shows the regional breakdown of production over the first 75 years of the industry.

Market saturation and low growth are perhaps the most obvious challenges for the industry in the future. In the main markets today, the comparatively slow pace of economic development, and market saturation, are limiting further growth in sales. Some forecast regional economic growth rates are given in Figure 5.7. Although in most of the developed markets the numbers of vehicles in use will continue to rise for some time, the period when annual sales continued to grow rapidly has gone.

The forecast for the next decade is for annual growth of only 2.4% worldwide. While some regions will clearly grow more quickly, the

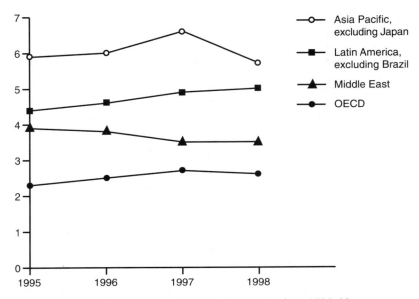

**Figure 5.7** Forecast of economic growth rates, 1995–98.

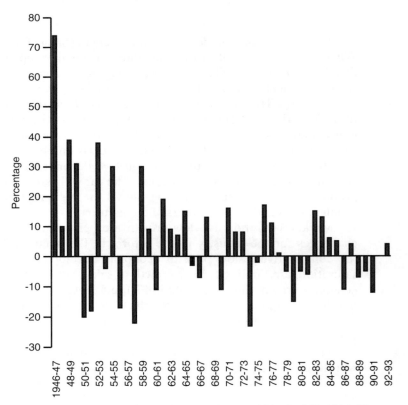

**Figure 5.8:** Annual growth rates of cars sold in the US, 1946–93.

largest markets are expected to experience very low growth rates indeed – 1.2% a year in Europe, 1% a year in Japan. Although the growth rate may be slightly higher in the US, this is driven by short-term recovery. The US market is already saturated and mature – it has been so for many years. Figure 5.8 shows the pattern in growth rates over the last 47 years.

One of the most serious problems is that vehicle manufacturers have become used to long-term growth. Their shareholders certainly have. The changes in market growth rates mean that suppliers will have to find new ways of meeting the needs of their shareholders – they must find some means of continuing to grow, even though the market is virtually stagnant.

# 6

# Sweeping the globe: a still incomplete Japanese dominance

## An industry in transition

Despite the growing degree of overall market maturity – or perhaps because of it – the passenger car industry is undergoing far-reaching, fundamental changes at the competitive level. The industry has become more open and dynamic, not less so. The supply side of the industry is still a long way from having achieved equilibrium or stability. Many changes are still under way. The shifts are not just from mass to lean production – itself far from fully accomplished – but also an accompanying shift from supply-driven to market-driven – at least in the first and second worlds, and from national or regional to global competitive structures. While there may be no world cars in the sense that they are designed and built globally, outside some specific niche segments, there is effectively a set of world technologies and standards, in both products and production.

Competition therefore has to change from a war of position to a war of movement. Again, this is characteristic of the onset of maturity in an industry – a final great burst of competitive activity before positions become frozen. This is typically a time of segment upheaval and redefinition, of jostling for position within an industry, of alliances and consolidation. It is absolutely vital to recognize where the industry is in the lifecycle in this respect. These changes require a deep-seated alteration in the behaviour of vehicle manufacturers, their internal organizations, their suppliers, and in the nature of their relationships with their suppliers.

A key distinction must also be made in all strategic thinking between assets – the legacy of past activities and successes – and capabilities, the means of controlling one's future destiny. Capabilities are a combination of know-how – which can be transferred or acquired relatively easily – and business processes, which are usually proprietary and hard to duplicate. In any period of major and rapid change, the future-oriented capabilities of a competitor are far more important than its historically-derived positional assets.

One must also be very careful to distinguish between qualifying capabilities and differentiating capabilities. The former are required to play in the game at all: there is not much to be gained by trying to be better than others. The differentiating capabilities are the ones that provide the basis for sustainable competitive advantages. That does not mean that they are everlasting: they eventually mature into qualifiers, as the competitors start to catch up. Again, this is a reflection of the universal phenomenon of segmentation structures and of barriers evolving or even dissolving as industries go through their lifecycles.

# The Japanese wave: moving the crossover point

Many of the changes in the more recent past have been competitively driven by the Japanese vehicle manufacturers. They have become extremely powerful because of their capabilities. These are based on perfected business processes. These were first developed and applied in the delivery chain, i.e. manufacturing and supply, but later extended to the innovation chain, i.e. product development. The Japanese did not really change the individual activities through which cars are planned, designed, developed and delivered to end customers. But they did redesign the chains of activities, simplifying them, shortening them, and eliminating redundancies and waste. By doing so, they executed a ju-jitsu throw on their Western competitors. In effect, they moved the cross-over point in both the delivery and innovation chains radically upstream. The traditional approach of building cars to some demand forecast and then matching customers' orders to the available finished goods has been turned upside down. This was first seen through the secondary effects of the just-in-time production system in the delivery chain: lower cost and better quality.

The ability to react virtually instantaneously to real customer orders was initially masked by the length of the shipping chain from Japan. It has not yet been fully exploited by the Japanese, as they have adopted fairly conventional distribution strategies in export markets. Nevertheless, the initial impression that the Japanese made cheap, nasty products was rapidly and dramatically dispelled, as they invaded a series of open markets, i.e. those not subject to import restrictions, as was shown earlier in Figure 5.4.

Traditionally, vehicle manufacturers handled the innovation chain by 'reading' demand, designing a product in a process lasting up to six years, and thrusting it at the market – 'push' selling something necessarily out of date by the time it appeared. This worked all right as long as the market and its expectations did not move too much during the development process. But it fatally exposed traditional competitors to the Japanese newcomers, who not only could respond quicker to the market but even drive it in the direction that suited them.

# The attack on the US market

The battle for global dominance by a handful of vehicle manufacturers is arguably more advanced in the United States than elsewhere. The Japanese manufacturers have been particularly successful there, taking market share from traditional vehicle manufacturers over a period of 20 or more years. While this has hurt, the competitive positions of manufacturers in the US are now increasingly stable. The market is approaching equilibrium. Six vehicle manufacturers now control nearly 90% of the market, while more than 22 smaller competitors fight over the other 10%. Five of the top six suppliers have a global presence, while the sixth, Chrysler, offers valuable lessons in survival within one regional market.

Among the remaining 22 competitors, there are a number of well-known names that face the prospect of becoming sub-scale in this, the world's largest single vehicle market. They include famous European marques such as Alfa Romeo, Saab, Mercedes-Benz, BMW, and even Volkswagen. Many once had a substantial and growing share of the US market, yet today they face the prospect of having to pull out. Others – Rover, Fiat, Peugeot and Renault – have already left. Why?

The position of the European car manufacturers in the US is perhaps easier to understand in military terms. Imagine a battleground. Imagine too, that in the 1960s the troops from Europe, mainly from Germany, France and Italy, decide to advance into new territory, the US. This is what the car manufacturers based in these countries did. For a while, the advance is successful. Fiat, Alfa Romeo and Lancia from Italy, Renault and Peugeot from France, Volkswagen, Mercedes-Benz and BMW from Germany and others such as MG, Triumph and Volvo were all extremely successful in the USA in the 1960s and 1970s. In the mid-1960s almost all imports into the US came from Europe, mainly from these suppliers. In

1970, for example, Volkswagen alone sold 569,000 cars in the US, accounting for nearly 7% of the market that year. Other Europeans accounted for an additional 3% of sales.

However, after years of success things began to change. Troops from another country, Japan, began to invade the US too. Their smaller, lower-cost vehicles were initially disregarded by US and European suppliers alike. Indeed, they were almost treated with derision in some quarters. Most of the Japanese models were tiny, were badly designed and built, and had a tendency to rust. The suppliers were certainly no threat to the makers of gas guzzlers in Detroit and the manufacturers of traditional European sports and luxury cars. Or so they thought.

This over-confidence on the part of the US and European manufacturers has become one of the great lessons in business strategy. By ignoring the threat the Japanese posed, they gave them a massive strategic advantage. Although the oil crisis and resulting fuel shortages of 1973 helped the Japanese sell their small, more fuel-efficient cars more easily, their task of penetrating the market had already been made simple by the behaviour of the importers and traditional manufacturers.

The Japanese manufacturers developed their cars and their market position gradually, increasing their penetration by stealth rather than directly. Even in the early 1980s, with a market share of more than 20%, there were many car industry employees in Detroit who still said that the Japanese vehicle manufacturers were not a threat. This is almost a tribute to the success of their strategy; a silent, steady and relentless advancement concealed under the loftiness of the traditional competitors.

The impact of the Japanese imports as they grew in the 1970s and 1980s was much more serious than that of the European assault a decade before. The Europeans had entered the US market during a period of rapid growth. The car market grew by 44% between 1960 and 1969. That meant that there was room for new suppliers. Why should the local manufacturers worry about a few new competitors? They had enough trouble meeting the growing demand themselves.

In contrast, in the 1980s, when the Japanese entered the market, growth was slowing. The market was maturing, stabilising. Between 1970 and 1980, it grew by only 7%. So, while the Europeans were taking crumbs from an ever bigger cake, the Japanese had to fight for their share. The Europeans were given a false sense of success because winning sales in a growing market is so much easier. As a result, they thought that their push into the US had been a success, a victory. But all the Europeans had shown was that their troops could run downhill. The Japanese, on the other hand, had climbed a cliff. As a result, it was the Japanese that built on their success and the Europeans that lost it. The Japanese had taken share from the huge, complacent domestic manufacturers. They had also begun to eradicate the smug, over-confident European entrants.

In 1965, General Motors held 50% of the US car market. At the end of the 1970s, after the European wave, its share had fallen to only 46%, but its sales had increased by 15%. Its share had fallen, but it was still growing, it was still the biggest car supplier in America, by a long way.

By the end of the 1980s, after the Japanese wave, GM's share was only 35%. Worse, its sales were down by more than a third compared with a decade before. While it was still the world's biggest vehicle manufacturer, GM had been hurt badly. Its image, like its advancement of the last 50 years, was in tatters. The positions of Ford and Chrysler were little better. Chrysler was almost driven to bankruptcy, requiring government help, while Ford had suffered years of losses.

For the Japanese it was a different story. Their share of the US car market had reached nearly 28% by 1991, approaching one car in three sold. Toyota had become the third largest vehicle manufacturer in the world, not far behind and catching up on Ford. Nissan was the fifth largest, while Honda, Mitsubishi and Mazda were all among the top 12.

The Japanese led the world in terms of productivity, designed new vehicles in half the time it took traditional manufacturers, and were still able to produce cars with more features at a lower cost than their US and European competitors. They had even set up transplants within the USA, to prove that they could work their magic using US labour. By 1991, the Japanese onshore assembly capacity in the United States was equivalent to 30% of the entire US market. This has displaced less competitive US capacity and triggered large numbers of plant closures. They also brought in their component suppliers to increase their total share of the added value. Japanese vehicle manufacturers also started to supply unbadged engines and vehicles to traditional US competitors to increase their share of the total market further still.

Their effect on the European manufacturers in the USA was even more serious. In 1980, the European suppliers controlled just under 7% of the US car market. By 1993, their share had been halved. Some suppliers were hurt particularly badly. Volkswagen's sales fell by 83% between 1980 and 1993, from 268,000 cars to under 44,000. Other suppliers pulled out. The results are shown in Figure 6.1.

Even the upline manufacturers have suffered. While the Japanese assault began in small cars, over a period of 25 years they began to penetrate further up-market. First, they developed mid-sized cars, then even larger vehicles. Each of the three largest suppliers then launched luxury divisions, with their own vehicles. Toyota introduced Lexus, Honda developed Acura, and Nissan brought in Infiniti. Mazda also planned a luxury division, Amati, but had to pull out when it overstretched itself.

These cars had an even more dramatic impact. Traditional luxury car suppliers in the US like Cadillac, Mercedes-Benz and BMW had spent years cultivating their market images. Their cars stood for tradition, for

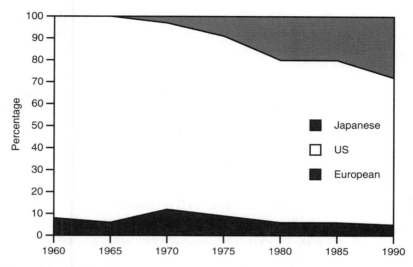

**Figure 6.1**   Market shares of European, US and Japanese producers in the US, 1960–90.

quality, for technical superiority. Their cars commanded a substantial premium. When the Lexus LS400 was launched in 1989 few believed that it was a significant threat to these long-established marques. Yet image only suspends disbelief for so long. One drive in the Lexus was enough for most people. Beautifully engineered, comfortable, technologically innovative, supremely silent and half the price of many of its competitors, it captured US hearts and wallets instantly. Mercedes-Benz had a reputation that had taken 100 years to establish. Lexus were outselling them in just 24 months. In 1993, Lexus' US sales were 50% more than its older rival and growing nearly twice as fast.

So the Europeans, after a few decades of success in the USA, began to fall back, retreating to safer ground. Although some of them have made forays into unexplored territories, such as South America, Eastern Europe and China, these are of marginal consequence. They are back where they started, back on home territory. The problem now, however, is that their competitors, having chased them out of North America, are pursuing them there also.

The impact of the battle for market share in North America over the last 30 years is that the world's motor industry is now increasingly dominated by five main vehicle manufacturers. They already dominate two of the three largest car markets, Japan and North America. GM, Ford, Toyota, Nissan and Honda account for 81% of car sales in the USA and Canada. They also account for two in three cars sold in Japan, although this is mainly Toyota, Nissan and Honda. In the developing countries they (again particularly the Japanese manufacturers) already dominate the markets in Indonesia, the Philippines, Taiwan and Thailand. Through joint ventures other Japanese suppliers control the majority of sales in Malaysia and India and are increasing their presence in China and the former Soviet Union. Yet, in Europe, the share of the top five is only 30%. So why have they failed to penetrate Europe to the same extent? The reason is simple, the battle for Europe has not yet been fought.

# Japan – the inviolate homeland

The Japanese market has managed to avoid any serious penetration by importers by maintaining very high trade barriers, although they are not called that. Potential competitors in the market have also been distracted by fighting a rearguard action at home. As a result, the market share of imports is around 4% in Japan, or 180,000 cars a year. These few sales that are made are fought over by more than a dozen, mainly sub-scale, competitors.

# The attack on Europe

The largest European manufacturers, Volkswagen, Peugeot, Renault and Fiat, having tried to expand overseas are once again concentrating on winning market share at home. For Renault, Peugeot and Fiat, that has meant a retreat not just to Europe but even further, back to their traditional markets of France and Italy. Yet, the four suppliers are still very powerful in the region. Between them, they control 53% of the market.

Outside Europe, their business is marginal – particularly in the next largest markets, the US and Japan. While Volkswagen has been successful in China, Brazil and Mexico and Fiat has had some success penetrating Eastern Europe, their volumes in these markets are not significant in world terms. The sad fact is that the largest European competitors have been pushed back into a defensive position.

As a result of this concentration in Europe, smaller competitors such as Volvo, Rover, Lancia, Alfa Romeo, and Porsche are all likely to face difficulties in the future – even those with generous parents. One of the industry's prestigious veterans, Rolls-Royce, is in deep trouble, strategically. The weakness of smaller suppliers is not just an issue in Europe, however. Japan has weak suppliers too, – particularly Isuzu, Subaru, Suzuki and Daihatsu – small competitors without the scale necessary for long-term independence. The same is true in South Korea, where more recent entrants into the automotive arena like Kia, Ssangyong, Daewoo and Asia Motors will all face difficulties trying to find new sales outside their home market.

The biggest battle to come is in Europe. It is the largest vehicle region in the world in terms of annual sales, yet it is stagnant. Sales growth will therefore be hard for vehicle manufacturers to achieve. It is a high-cost region for manufacturing yet it is more fragmented competitively then either Japan or the USA. In addition, traditional European competitors are vulnerable simply because they have not achieved the global scale necessary for long-term success. All of the world's top five competitors are now present in the region. Worse, the top three Japanese suppliers are adding substantial capacity in the region, just as they did in the USA. This new capacity is more efficient than that present today, in some cases much more efficient, and adds to what is already too much.

The response of the Europeans to date has been confused. They initially tried to build defences, using trade barriers, to protect themselves. These were moderately successful for a few years, although their success varied. In France and Italy penetration of Japanese importers remains minimal. It is greater in Germany and the UK and greater still in the smaller markets like Sweden, Belgium and the Netherlands. The Japanese penetration is highest in some of the smallest markets, however, where trade barriers have been largely non-existent. In Ireland and Finland for example, their share of new car sales is nearly 50% a year.

The trade barriers were always intended as a stopgap. They were meant to be a means of allowing European competitors time to develop their plants, to reach world-class standards. Although this was not in the best interests of consumers in the short term, European governments felt that it was necessary to protect what they regarded as a strategic industry. They therefore imposed quotas, to restrict the number of Japanese imports into the region. Current EU legislation, however, states all trade barriers have to fall in 1999, and that after that date, the Japanese will be given free access to the region. The idea was that local suppliers would have until then to invest, to reach world-class standards.

The trouble is that one country in Europe let down the side, the UK. A reluctant European, the British government was less concerned about the European good and more worried about its own economy. Its only domestic vehicle supplier of any significance, Rover, was a marginal competitor in world terms and had limited prospects. The government, under Margaret Thatcher, also believed strongly in free-market competition. The UK had also benefited in the past from encouraging automotive transplant factories from Ford, Peugeot and GM.

The UK government's priorities were therefore to stimulate investment and so employment. It mattered little if that damaged its domestic
car industry; after all there was little left to damage. If by encouraging
more competition this displeased the EU, so be it.

As a result, the UK government allowed the Japanese to set up transplant operations. Nissan was first when it set up a plant in Sunderland in
the 1980s. Next came Toyota and then Honda. By 1999 their combined
output is expected to be nearly a million cars a year – equal to nearly 8%
of European demand and adding to an already over supplied market.

The component suppliers, the foot-soldiers in the competitive battle,
are following. The effect of the battle in the US and the new transplant
operations in Europe is that the major European car and component
producers are now trapped. They are in a high-cost region, without the
economies of scale available to their competitors, they have little
business outside, and have nowhere to run.

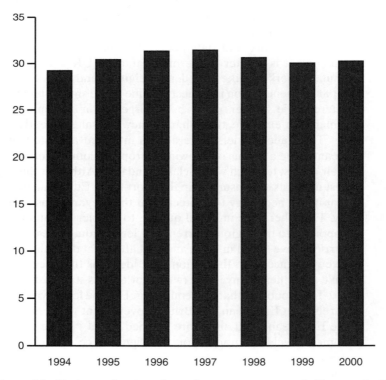

**Figure 6.2**   Forecast of registrations of new passenger cars in Europe, the US
and Japan, 1994–2000, in millions of units.

Worst of all, the markets in the US, Japan and Europe are forecast to be stagnant over the next five years (Figure 6.2). Growth for vehicle manufacturers must therefore come from new markets or by beating competitors in traditional ones.

# Japanese dominance is still incomplete

It is absolutely crucial to be able to distinguish real competitive stability from potential change that may disrupt the equilibrium. Apparent power based on historical, positional assets must not be overrated against market-driving capabilities. The Japanese at first played the old world-car game: a single product, with only minor adaptations for different export regions, shipped worldwide. Their competitors thought that an undervalued yen and an industrial culture peculiar to Japan were the sources of their competitive advantage. They thought that import barriers – quotas, voluntary agreements, and so on – would stop them advancing further. This was precisely because they believed in the competitive importance of assets and failed to recognize that of capabilities. The Japanese vehicle manufacturers then proceeded to demonstrate that they could transplant their factories and apply their superior capabilities in other locations and cultures.

The impact on the world automotive industry's supply side has been colossal. Western vehicle manufacturers have not been able to shelter from the capabilities-based assault behind asset-based barriers. They have had to try to pursue world-class performance standards. They have been forced to adapt their processes and supply structures to the Japanese model, even though there have been some local modifications. The world components industry is also being forced through enormous changes as a result, as we shall see in Chapter 7.

The Japanese started by emphasizing cost, and then design and quality. They then deployed their speed-of-development capability to drive their invasion of foreign markets. Others are catching up on quality – more the American vehicle manufacturers than the Europeans, so far. Once established onshore in Europe, the Japanese may shift gear again, slowing their innovation rate somewhat and re-emphasizing cost – which is the ultimate competitive differentiator, in any business. Their range of capabilities allows them the flexibility to change strategies and thereby to stay ahead of the game.

# The impact on global car manufacturing: the transplant phenomenon

As we have seen, the Japanese car industry has successfully accomplished the first part of its assault on world markets. This has been done, despite an envelope of relatively limited market growth during their initial foray, by means of direct assaults on their competitors' home markets. The imposition of trade restrictions has had no long-lasting effect. In fact, it probably stimulated the Japanese to cross the Rubicon and establish transplants, which they have now done on a substantial scale. In the US this high-performance, new capacity continues to displace existing less-competitive US capacity, triggering numerous plant closures. Having established production facilities, the Japanese have since followed by transplanting engineering and design capabilities to strengthen their hold further.

A similar movement has been underway in Europe for some time. Europe has historically been more protective of its automotive industry than has the United States. To circumvent the EC restrictions, Japanese manufacturers have made substantial investments in onshore facilities, notably in the UK. Much political tension continues to surround these moves. The more protectionist countries – and manufacturers – want onshore Japanese production to count as part of the import volumes. Currently, however, these facilities are excluded.

Again, these attempts by the EC may slow Japanese penetration but efficient capacity will, in the end, displace the less efficient. This competitive displacement phenomenon will, once again, be caused because of the large gaps in performance that exist.

The gaps in productivity, quality and flexibility between Japanese and Western-managed assembly plants have been thoroughly documented, notably through MIT's International Motor Vehicle Programme (IMVP). It is ironic that this initiative should have had to be taken by academics and sobering that there was initially quite a lot of resistance to accepting its findings and conclusions. A characteristic attack is made by two French academics, de Banville and Chanaron, in their book *Vers un Système Automobile Européen*[1], accusing the authors of *The Machine that Changed the World* of inadequate analysis, 'nippo-mania' and being cleverly 'inspired' by the Japanese automotive lobby.

These charges might be more convincing if the authors in any way analytically proved their hypothesis (or hope) that a separate, distinct and defensible European automotive industry can exist. The IMVP comparisons of assembly-plant performance and subsequent work on components suppliers do appear to have been diligently carried out, however unpalatable the resulting conclusions. Perhaps the most disturbing findings concern the ability of the Japanese to achieve equivalent results abroad as they can at home. Their superiority does not rest on features peculiar to the Japanese environment but on an uncompromising devotion to going back to the basics of the processes – again and again.

The impact of the transplant factories on the positions of the Japanese vehicle manufacturers in Europe will be considerable. From negligible onshore production in 1987, the Japanese manufacturers as a group are expected to be supplying a third of their European market volume from it by 1999. This will help them even up their penetration across European countries and to move their total European penetration from 9% in 1989 to an expected 15%–16% by the end of the century.

The manufacturing gap is matched by an equally serious product development gap, long-since demonstrated by research at MIT and Harvard. The Japanese have been shown to require 40% fewer engineering hours to develop a new car, to do it in 25%–30% less elapsed time, and to use 40% fewer staff in the development team. Moreover, this is not done by recycling more old designs: the Japanese were observed to use half the proportion of carry-over parts in their new designs, which were therefore individually 'newer' than those of their Western competitors.

# Note

1.   De Banville and Chanaron (1991). *Vers un système automobile Européen.* Paris: Economica

# 7

# From slaves to partners: the restructuring of the components industry

## The performance gap in components

Most importantly, the Japanese vehicle manufacturers have not achieved their remarkable results by themselves. With vertical integration levels significantly lower even than those common in the West, they could not have done so. Japanese automotive components suppliers also outperform their Western competitors by a wide margin.

A study performed for the European Commission by the Boston Consulting Group (BCG) and PRS in 1990 showed huge gaps: sales per employee 40% to 100% higher, and even greater discrepancies in stock-turns – a good measure of manufacturing efficiency. Yet Western firms had returns on net assets at least equal to those of their Japanese competitors. No wonder there were 20% to 30% differences in the prices of components.

Those gaps seem, if anything, to have widened since. In 1992, BCG reported that while Japanese vehicle manufacturers remained 30% more productive than Europeans, the components manufacturers were 150% ahead! The size of gap identified has, of course, been challenged by the European components industry. But it is hard to deny that a substantial one exists. Yet, the components industry is supposed to be one of the strongest elements of the European automotive industry!

The quality gap is also large. Japanese vehicle manufacturers in Europe have experienced build-quality levels in components of 25% to 35% below their domestic standards. Reject rates in Japan have moved from almost the 10% level in 1960 to 1% in 1970 to 0.1% in 1980 to the parts-per-million range in the 1990s – an improvement of a large order of magnitude every decade. Some UK suppliers, helped by the transplants, have achieved the Japanese level of the 1980s in the 1990s.

## The causes of the gaps

The causes of the gaps are illustrated by the example of components and sub-systems development. In the hands of the Japanese, in many instances this is accomplished with 30% to 40% less expenditure in terms of time and money. A root cause of this better performance is the much earlier involvement of suppliers in the product development process. The experience of specialized suppliers influences the design choices made by the vehicle manufacturer. Costly errors and dead ends are avoided (Figure 7.1).

In the West, events and activities are handled largely sequentially, resulting in delays and ineffective feedback loops. In Japan, there is much emphasis on team-working across specialized functions, both within the vehicle manufacturer's organisation and into those of its suppliers. The breadth of capabilities is harnessed. This is made possible

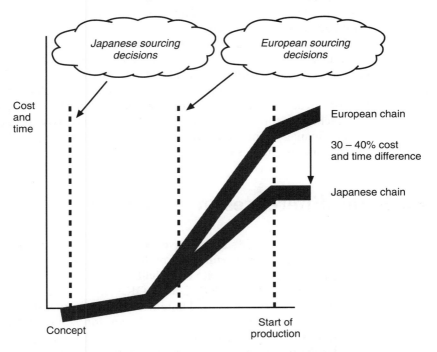

**Figure 7.1**   The product development gap in components. (*Source*: EIU Motor Quarterlies)

by a partnership-based relationship between vehicle manufacturers and their suppliers. The suppliers sell their capabilities, rather than just an end product. Their customers are intimately involved in their efforts to improve their own capabilities. Suppliers and sub-suppliers at different levels in the development and supply chain work closely together, on a long-term basis, to improve cost, quality and product performance. Suppliers are expected to take the initiative on technology choice, engineering, and continuous improvement in products and processes.

This is in stark contrast to the competitive/adversarial form of relationship which was traditional in the West until relatively recently. In this, design control rested primarily with the vehicle manufacturer, who contracted for supply on an arm's length, competitive basis. In many instances, the supplier received 'built-to-print', contracts that were negotiated on an annual basis. The emphasis was on price, and competition was encouraged by the vehicle manufacturer using multiple suppliers for the same product.

This adversarial approach has now changed and there is a much more co-operative approach between component suppliers and their customers. Even so, although the working relationships between vehicle manufacturers and component suppliers in the West have improved, they are still very different from those in Japan. While many talk of 'partnerships', the façade often breaks down when the going gets rough – then price becomes king, once again.

Professor Richard Lamming's assessment of customer/supplier relationships in the UK – *A Review of the Relationships between Vehicle Manufacturers and Suppliers* (DTI/SMMT, 1993) – is eloquent on this: lack of trust, undeveloped two-way communications, lack of movement towards true tiering, poor implementation of EDI, inconsistent approaches to supplier assessment, CAD systems, cost transparency, project management and even the delegation of responsibility for systems and assemblies itself.

# Regional differences in structures

Superficially, the world's automotive components industry appears to be well-structured and powerful. Each of the major regions – Europe, North America and Japan – is the home of half a dozen giant suppliers. Bosch, Valeo, Magnetti-Marelli, ZF, Lucas, GKN in Europe; Allied-Signal, TRW, ITT, UTC, Eaton in the United States; Nippondenso, Aisin Seiki, Hitachi, Yazaki, Sumitomo Electric in Japan, for example. All of these have automotive sector sales well in excess of $1 billion per year. This excludes the tyre companies, some of whom are also very large players.

Despite GM's high levels of vertical integration, there are still many large independent component suppliers in North America as well as a great many more small ones.

In Europe, the top 25 suppliers share about 40% of the market. As in the US, there is also a very long 'tail' of medium and small suppliers. European automotive components industry structures were archaic until fairly recently but are undergoing considerable change. The industry was very fragmented, with vehicle manufacturers sourcing mainly from their national supply bases. Although there has been an accelerated shift towards pan-European and global sourcing, this pattern is still comparatively common.

Germany dominates the European supply industry, with over 45% of production. This is proportionately higher than its share of vehicle production and results from the strong technology positions of many of its firms. Relationships between vehicle manufacturers and suppliers in the West were traditionally one-sided and authoritarian. This attitude is changing, although with some difficulty in some instances, as vehicle manufacturers are forced to delegate more responsibility to suppliers in order to survive competitively themselves.

The Japanese components industry is also concentrated at the top but has a different structure to those in the United States and Europe. Japanese components suppliers, unlike their independent Western counterparts, have mainly developed within 'families' (*keiretsu*) linked to individual vehicle manufacturers. There is, however, increasing cross-supply between families. The supplier associations (*kyoryukokai*) are also important mechanisms for mutual support and the sharing of best practices.

The most significant difference with the West has been, as stated earlier, in the form and practice of relationships. As a rough measure, the Japanese vehicle manufacturers outsource 75% of the components they need. The real figure is higher, if the outside purchases of their own in-house components operations are included. Of the 75%, most comes from a limited group of highly capable 'Tier-1' suppliers. There is also a smaller proportion that comes from the 'Tier-2' component producers. Below this, there are thousands of small sub contractors and materials suppliers in 'Tier-3'. Suppliers in one tier are expected to work harmoniously and effectively with those in other tiers.

This tiering is an essential complement to the process of delegation-with-involvement: the vehicle manufacturers could not practise it directly with thousands of supplier firms. There has to be delegation within delegation. This makes it possible to sustain relationships of sufficient density and quality – difficult under Western structures, in which vehicle manufacturers attempted to relate to too many firms directly and encouraged adversarial positions between them.

# The need for alignment and change

It is perfectly clear that, as in vehicle manufacturing, the production of components will have to align to the *de facto* Japanese world-class standards. To compete directly, this will include replicating the structures and relationships within the industry.

Again, the necessary changes have been precipitated by the Japanese and their transplantation. When the Japanese vehicle manufacturers established themselves in the United States they had no formal local content requirement imposed on them. They could have imported most of their components from Japan – particularly given their disappointment with the existing local components industry they found in the US. In fact, they encouraged Japanese suppliers to follow them and set up greenfield operations. As a result, a series of such manufacturing investments were made by Japanese firms, starting in the late 1970s. There has also been significant Japanese–US joint venture activity.

This solution was not so readily available to the Japanese in Europe. First, the local supply industry was viewed as being far stronger and better-qualified technologically. Second, high local content levels were required from early stages of transplant vehicle production. Third, it was made clear from the outset that a mass transplantation of Japanese suppliers would meet strong opposition.

Only a few joint ventures have been established in Europe and remarkably few direct investments. The UK has received the major share, in parallel with the creation of the transplant vehicle assembly plants. However, the Japanese approach has not involved simply purchasing from the strongest existing European suppliers. The transplant manufacturers have only made partial use of these and have put a major effort into developing a new local supply base, working with selected cadres of suppliers, some of whom have been quite small. This has given them more freedom to develop and train them to their standards of performance. It should also be an issue of concern to the largest and strongest, locally-based suppliers who were shunned.

As a result of this policy the new Japanese entrants in Europe do source most of their components from within the EC – although some of the statistics are rendered suspect by the definition of European content as relating to the 'last substantial manufacturing operation' taking place there. Perhaps an example will illustrate the 'looseness' of the term. A factory one of us visited recently in the UK was assembling subsystems for Nissan in Sunderland. While these were regarded as 'local content', 90% of the components actually came from Japan and the added value of the British supplier, which acted as an assembler, was less than 5%. It is clear, however, that this is the exception, rather than the rule.

Nissan, the first of the major transplant firms into Europe, has moved rapidly towards the 80% European-content level agreed with the UK government for its UK operations. By European standards, it has picked a small local supplier group: just under 200 of them, mainly UK-based, and with only a minority having technical or commercial links with Japanese suppliers. Around 70% of Nissan's components in Sunderland come from the UK, although there are moves to bring their hitherto largely distinct UK and Spanish supply bases closer together within a European structure.

By keeping its supply base limited, Nissan has been able to forge continuous, long-term links with its favoured suppliers – a group which has remained fairly stable. It sets them rigorous performance targets and supports them with a considerable supplier development programme. The quality target is zero defects. Nissan emphasizes variable production cost, just-in-time delivery, and an active role in process and product development. Most importantly, it selects suppliers with a management that is responsive to its style of conducting operations. Honda and Toyota, the more recent entrants to the UK, have followed a similar track, although Toyota has moved towards a more pan-European supply base more quickly.

Progress within the suppliers to the transplants has been encouraging in some cases, although significant performance gaps still remain. Professor Dan Jones and Andersen Consulting (The Lean Enterprise Benchmarking Project, London, 1992) have compared productivity and quality levels in comparative UK and Japanese suppliers. Despite the gaps, many UK firms are now significantly ahead of their other European competitors, creating a renewed interest in the UK as a supply base for European vehicle manufacturers.

# A process of global convergence

Given the changes of the last 15 years, all car manufacturers now want to achieve the same goal: to have suppliers design, deliver and install systems and components. They want to delegate design and expect to see a progressive shift from build-to-print to design-in, with black-box supplier engineering within the 'systems'. They would like to develop the whole engineering chain with suppliers. They want synchronous supply chains with them, in development as well as delivery. In short, they want suppliers to act as co-makers that are confident in their engineering, while the vehicle manufacturers retain control of the key design areas.

The end effect will be a convergence of standards and structures in the global components industry, as is happening in the vehicle industry.

Even though the transplant vehicle manufacturers have had to take somewhat different approaches to creating satisfactory supply bases in North America and Europe, they are forcing this process.

There were 300 to 400 direct suppliers to each vehicle manufacturer in Japan in the late 1980s, around 2000 in the United States, and 500 to 1500 in Europe. There is now a vigorous drive to get these latter numbers aligned to the Japanese pattern. Western vehicle manufacturers clearly understand that more effective suppliers structures are a major element of their own competitiveness. They are forced in the direction of greater delegation by the constraints on their own internal resources. They need capable, competent, financially-strong Tier-1 suppliers, with the critical mass to operate globally. Few suppliers meet the last criterion, including the Japanese.

## ...which is still far from complete

This transition in the component supplier business is still far from being complete or effective in the West. How far Europe still lags behind Japan is shown in Figure 7.2. In order to be able to innovate, and to make both step-change and continuous improvements, suppliers will need an array of capabilities that few of them yet have. Mastery of specific product and materials technologies, design for manufacturing and assembly and design for cost are examples. Suppliers also need world-class manufacturing engineering, as well as testing and process control and superior management of materials flows. They also need strong project management capabilities and far more direct involvement on the part of senior management.

Too few suppliers come forward with sound, well-developed ideas for improvement at present. Techniques such as design-to-cost and value analysis are not sufficiently widespread. Internal capabilities in design and manufacturing need to be rebuilt, or recaptured from the vehicle manufacturers – having a real black-box capability is still a major source of differentiation. Most suppliers want to go down this route but few understand how. Moreover, many aspire to being Tier-1 systems suppliers but few can hope to achieve it. Very careful thought needs to be given to positioning in the new tiered structures.

There are some interesting divergences of routes on the way to the common goal. The ultimate industry model involves substantial delegation of responsibility for both product and process improvement to suppliers. Europe and North America still have a good way to go before they achieve Japanese standards of co-development. The goal, clearly, is to match 'Japan-in-Japan' performance – which has largely been achieved by the transplant assemblers in their domain. These players appear to be pushing their selected supplier groups to perfect their

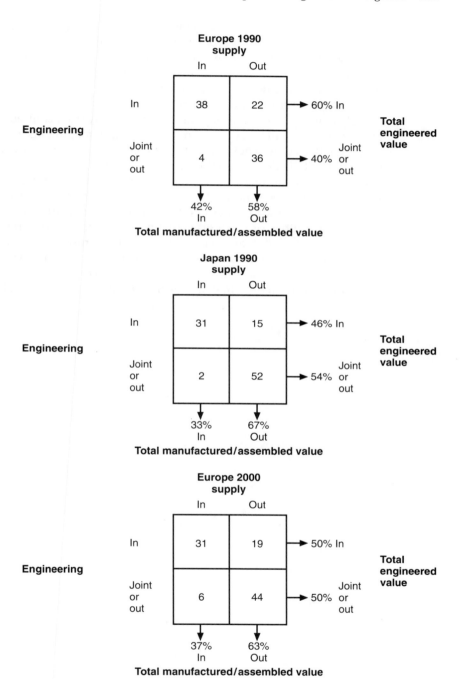

**Figure 7.2**   Division of responsibilities between vehicle manufacturers and suppliers. (*Source*: EIU Motor Quarterlies)

production processes first, working to existing Japanese components designs. Responsibility for product innovation will be delegated at a later stage. Western vehicle manufacturers appear to be applying the reverse sequence, possibly because of their pressing need to get more new products out in the face of Japanese competition.

Perhaps most difficult is the change in attitudes and relationships. Vehicle manufacturers say they want to move away from contracting for parts, with price the key, and limited mutual commitments based on arm's-length trading. They say that their goal is to contract for capability, with substantial mutual long-term commitments, where prices reflect costs, and there are relationships based on partnership sourcing or joint ventures. In practice the problem often remains as before, when the going gets tough, they relapse into the old domineering attitudes.

The difficulties are exacerbated by the continuing differences in philosophies, attitudes, approaches, information structures and systems between the vehicle manufacturers – particularly in Europe. These impose additional 'systemic' cost and performance penalties, over and above the structural ones that arise from the fragmentation of scale.

**8**

# The last frontier for competitive advantage? Distribution, the aftermarket and the customer interface

## Distribution: a neglected sector of the industry

Much of the attention paid to the automotive industry is concerned with the design, development and production of vehicles. The one to two billion dollars required to design a major new car and the scale of the industrial operations involved tend to impress and hold the imagination. A first visit to an assembly plant is an unforgettable experience, from the great coils of steel being received at the beginning to the moment at which a finished car is fuelled, started for the first time and driven away. But that, of course, is not where the industry ends – not by a long way.

The car has to have a buyer, an owner, an operator. Some buyers come to take delivery of their vehicle at the assembly plant – a method mainly popular with North Americans purchasing in Europe. Part of the market also consists of fleet operators buying in bulk. But the majority of cars are still sold to individuals, spread throughout the developed world through a dealer network.

Massive and complex distribution structures have been created to match the personal transportation needs and demands of individuals with the output of the huge industrial machine of the automotive industry. However, it receives much less public and media attention. The significance of this sector to the industry is quantitatively revealed by the estimate of its costs given in Figure 8.1. Yet these bald numbers do little justice to the efforts, the people and indeed the passions involved.

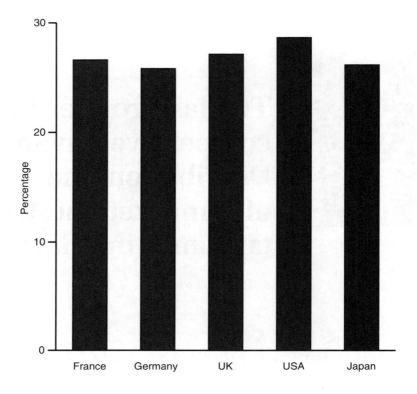

**Figure 8.1**   Cost of distribution to the motor industry as a percentage of sale price. (*Source*: Booz, Allen & Hamilton)

Distribution and the interface with the end customer are absolutely critical to vehicle manufacturers. This is also an area fraught with tensions, problems to be resolved and opportunities for the future. In many respects, this is the part of the industry that has evolved least in recent years, or, indeed, decades.

# A fragmented sector, remarkably similar throughout the world

Car distribution continues to be conducted principally through large networks of relatively small, independently-owned, franchised dealers. These are typically small or medium family or privately-owned businesses, usually with less than five outlets.

Although there are some variations between major world regions and countries, the underlying principles are fairly similar. Vehicle manufacturers argue that their products are difficult to present and sell to the customer. Most crucially, they claim that complexity and safety considerations make it essential to tie service and repair into a franchised distribution channel. The financially-independent dealers are therefore put into networks, based on the granting of a franchise to distribute the vehicles of a given brand.

Dealership agreements in the United States generally allow multi-franchising, i.e. a dealer representing more than one brand, which explains why this format is more common in America. Conversely, it is rare in Europe, where the manufacturers strongly defend the principle of exclusive or selective distribution. This is formally incompatible with article 85 of the Treaty of Rome. However, a special dispensation – the Block Exemption, or Regulation 85.123 – was negotiated in 1985, to last 10 years. This has allowed the single-franchise dealer to remain. In general the US exhibits the most advanced methods of dealership organisation. It is probably followed by Japan and then the UK. The structures in continental Europe remain the most traditional.

Despite these differences in approach, there are underlying global similarities in the practices dealers adopt. These are revealed by comparisons of dealership productivity – the number of new vehicles sold each year. Using average figures for the franchised networks in their home markets – where they should show their best – we see remarkably limited divergences. From Rover in the UK, through Nissan or Toyota in Japan, to Ford or GM in the US, the average number of vehicles sold per dealer ranges from 250 to 450 cars a year. The most significant exception is Mercedes-Benz, with its network of owned outlets in Germany. These are twice as productive as the world average. Other exceptions are Renault, Peugeot and Citroën, with their very extensive networks of small sub-dealers or agents in France.

## Continental European distribution remains very traditional

Dealerships in continental Western Europe typically are small, family-run businesses, with one or two outlets, franchised by a single manufacturer. Consolidation of these networks has been glacially slow. In France, there are over 50,000 main dealers and sub-agents, mostly with six or fewer employees. There are also a number of manufacturer-owned outlets, mainly in urban areas where the cost of property makes independent dealerships non-viable.

The major manufacturers recognize the high cost of these very dense distribution structures but also value them as a strong defensive barrier against competitive incursion – especially in France, with the removal of the national 3% ceiling on Japanese sales. The French manufacturers are adamantly opposed to multi-franchising and large dealer groups, because of the threat these could pose to them.

A similar though less extensive structure exists in Germany: some 15,000 main dealers, mainly family-owned, with a smaller second tier of sub-dealers and repair shops. There are also some manufacturer-owned branches, notably in the hands of Mercedes-Benz. Again, there are no large dealer groups and very little true multi-franchising. VAG dealers generally handle both the VW and Audi brands, a historical combination that their franchisors appear to regret but find difficult to undo. The attitude of the manufacturers is similar to that in France and little real rationalization of networks has taken place, for similar reasons. The one exception is BMW, which has had a consistent strategy of thinning out its network and raising the quality of its dealer outlets.

Italy is similar: the multi-franchising that does occur is mostly across the different brands within the Fiat group, that is, Fiat, Lancia, Alfa-Romeo, etc. Italian franchised dealers tend to rely on new cars as the core of their business, with little attention paid to used cars and with relatively low service and repairs income.

A somewhat different situation prevails in continental Europe for imported marques. Vehicle manufacturers selling into a country in which they do not manufacture generally have much smaller and tighter distribution networks than the domestic majors. They suffer from scale and image disadvantages because of their limited individual market shares. Importing and distribution companies have acquired a considerable degree of power in some instances – and not only in purely importing countries, with no national manufacturers. Where a dealer network has been built from scratch, they have often enjoyed considerable delegated authority to design and create it. In several instances, the manufacturers have sought to buy out their importers, in whole or in part, in order to strengthen their own hold on the market.

## The UK is significantly different

The UK's distribution pattern, though significantly different, does not yet represent a breakthrough in distribution practice. The leading vehicle manufacturers have far fewer dealer outlets in proportion to their national sales volumes than their continental European counterparts. This makes the average annual dealer throughput much higher than the European average. In addition, the set of dealer networks in the UK has been contracting steadily for years.

The market is also notable for a number of specific features not replicated elsewhere. One of these is the disproportionate importance of the fleet market, which represented up to 70% of new vehicle sales at its height. This is made up of large, 'genuine', fleets and an extensive company car sector. The 'genuine' fleets exist where a large number of vehicles, typically of the same model, are sold to government agencies, public enterprises, and sales or service companies, for example. The company and executive car sector is much more fragmented and exists where employers provide cars specifically for their employees. These developed mainly because the company car offered tax advantages to both parties. Latterly, however, they have become a 'perk', part of the overall employment package.

Although the tax concessions offered on company cars have been largely eroded, except for genuine high-mileage business users, the habit of giving them to employees remains. Middle and senior ranking employees of large companies expect a new car every two or three years and they expect it to be maintained for them at minimal effort. For many the cost of the fuel is also included in the package.

Fleet and company car sales have considerably distorted the UK's distribution sector. Car producers are, in effect, making substantial direct sales – in all but name – to bulk purchasers and professional intermediaries, such as leasing and contract hire companies. The latter sector has itself been consolidating into very powerful groups.

In addition, the dealership network itself is highly concentrated. UK public companies are extensive owners of car dealerships. Although the top 100 dealer groups own only 20% of the dealerships, the top 10 control 40% of the market. The biggest dealer groups own, overwhelmingly, the most productive outlets. Despite this, the groups are less powerful than their size might suggest: they are not allowed by the car manufacturers to control more than a limited number of dealerships of a given marque. They therefore operate largely as holding companies. Moreover, their added value is not always evident, beyond the exercise of more disciplined financial reporting.

## The distribution system in Europe looks inherently unstable

The whole set of relationships between manufacturers and dealers in Europe is shot through with tensions. The selective distribution system itself has come under attack. Despite the Block Exemption, there has been increasing national and EU pressure on the more restrictive elements in dealer contracts, such as obligations to buy parts only from the franchisor. The whole system has been attacked by consumer groups and has come under scrutiny by national governments as well as the European Commission. This is mainly because of the pricing inequalities between member states and the industry's attempts to restrict the right of EC citizens to buy cars wherever they wish within the Community. Despite this pressure, the Block Exemption will probably be renewed,

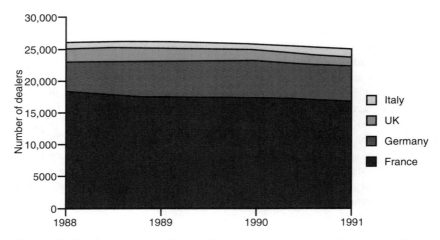

**Figure 8.2** Dealer networks of major European marques in their home markets. (*Source*: Sewells)

thanks to intense lobbying by the industry. It may not be left unmodified, however.

In reality, no one is making excessive profits through some sort of collusion in distribution. The regulators simply keep getting dragged in to try and fix the industry's distribution conflicts. The problem is the cost-inefficiency of the current system, which actually adds more to the cost of a vehicle than does the assembly plant. Most market research shows end consumers to be sceptical about whether it adds corresponding values, by making shopping for cars a satisfying experience. Unsurprisingly, perhaps, the profitability of dealerships is low and declining, often to below the survival level – particularly if the replacement cost of the site is included in the calculation. Consolidation of dealer networks is taking place at an extremely slow rate (Figure 8.2).

The performance of dealers also varies wildly. The best know their products thoroughly, systematically prospect their territories and build lasting relationships with their customers. They do not require endless support and policing from the manufacturer. Indeed they may even extend a loyal customer base into the used car business – even though they often receive half-hearted support from the vehicle manufacturers in this. On the other hand, the worst dealers are episodic traders, moving from one franchise to another, with fast-rotating, poorly qualified and trained staff.

Manufacturers spend a treasure of effort and money in trying to develop and control their networks. Yet few get anywhere near the level of consistency achieved by, say, McDonald's. Automotive dealers are neither true independents nor members of a true 'strong-form' franchising system. Instead, they are an uncomfortable compromise, somewhere in between.

The whole system remains fundamentally adversarial and based on push-selling. Ironically, the vehicle manufacturers are largely cut off from end users and the market, despite the large investments made in customer care programmes. They still tend to build to forecast and to thrust vehicles upon their dealers with the help of sales quotas and incentives. Dealers in their turn push-sell what they have in stock or can readily access. This forces them into excessive discounting and other price-related promotions, often undermining the brand in the process. Even the most recent attempt to control the phenomenon, whereby vehicle manufacturers have reduced dealer margins to hamper their ability to discount, does not address the underlying structural issue.

## The US situation is fundamentally similar

Although it differs in some of the details and formats of franchising arrangements, US car retailing is structurally similar. A few very large single and multi-franchise dealer groups generate extraordinary sales volumes. Yet the average dealer productivity is not startlingly different from that in Europe although this may in part be related to the greater size and lower population density of the country. Dual franchising is common but has not proved to be a magic solution to the structural problems of the sector.

The US dealership population has been shrinking for the past 30 years. It is likely to go on doing so (Figure 8.3), as the increasing pressure of competition continues to shrink margins. The minimum viable size for a dealership will therefore go up. There is also a growth in the number of automalls, despite the resistance put up by car manufacturers. These, which offer several brands together, have therefore emerged as the logical extension of dual franchising. Within these, dedicated staff normally serve each franchise, to avoid excessive dilution of brand image. This also maintains service quality and consistency across the brands. One-third of all automalls are in California – the state most penetrated by imports. As imports and transplants have increased their share of the market, brands have proliferated.

Market research shows that US buyers consider half a dozen brands and actively shop across three or four, before finally buying one. This logical consumer approach is based on a preselection through public as well as word-of-mouth information and reflects the maturity of consumer experience in the country. The fact that separate brands are represented at separate locations is simply a nuisance.

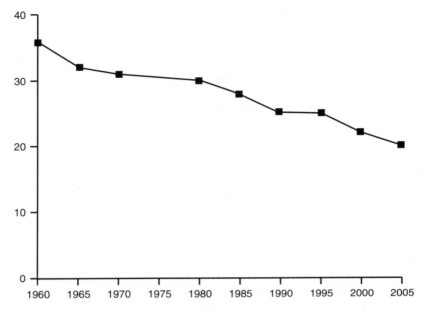

**Figure 8.3**    Total new car dealer outlets in the US.

However, this approach is in flat contradiction to the concept of building lifelong loyalty to a brand. It also works in contrast to the ideas of vehicle manufacturers, which would like to see car buyers working their way up the model range as they become older and wealthier. Worse, cluster sites, such as automalls, allow less-known brands to be viewed by consumers. This is why established manufacturers have hesitations about them.

As in the UK, furious battles have raged over the issue of direct sales to large customers, such as rental car companies. The resulting problem of large numbers of 'nearly new' vehicles coming on to the market – often bought back at a guaranteed price – distorts the used car business and its price levels, to the detriment of dealers. This in turn affects trade-in values and thus ultimately price realization on new car sales.

The only major attempt by a vehicle manufacturer to reform the traditional US franchised system is Saturn's, which uses much larger dealer territories, created from scratch. One could, however, argue that the creation of the Lexus and Infiniti franchises followed a similar pattern.

## Distribution in Japan

In Japan, the rather esoteric traditional distribution arrangements are being reviewed and aligned on more common practices.

Distribution in Japan started on a different basis. Each manufacturer sought to control its end market very closely. Direct selling to customers was used, often door-to-door. The salesperson would come to your house and offer the chance to drive the car he was selling. As recently as 1985, 80% of all sales were door-to-door. Separate channels were established for each carline within each marque. Toyota developed Toyota, Toyopet, Corolla, Auto and Vista as channels. Nissan has Nissan, Motor, Sunny, Cherry and Princ, while Honda has Clio, Primo and Verno.

While this approach had its virtues when the national market was growing it is a very expensive one. Manufacturers are also finding it increasingly difficult to attract new personnel and have even started to recruit saleswomen. The technique is being eroded as the market becomes more aggressive. This has accelerated in the last few years with sales in the market suffering from the first serious cyclical downturn.

Considerable rationalization and simplification is going on throughout the sales process. In some cases, a marque's dealer will be forced to carry all car lines, as has always been the case in the West. Car manufacturers are also increasing the numbers of cars sold in department stores and opening huge new 'mega-showrooms'. These are vast dedicated buildings on many levels that offer a Disneyland type of environment of challenges and entertainment. Their purpose is to market the producer's cars, new model ideas and technology. Often their purpose is not to sell cars at all, but simply to build brand loyalty and awareness. They work well. The most significant potential development, however, is the attempt to integrate the end-customer into the whole demand-driven, JIT-based delivery chain. This relies on interactive communications technology. Such a development could lead to the ultimate concepts of lean distribution and the 'virtual' dealership, with limited premises and very little in the way of display stock.

# A common set of problems and challenges, despite some regional differences

Despite the differences between major regions in the developed world, the underlying dealer and distribution structures are really much the same everywhere. So are the problems, which are really structural in nature. Western vehicle manufacturers are having to transform their supplier structures and relationships under the pressure of Japanese competition. They are moving to delegate more responsibility for product development and delivery to much stronger and more capable upstream partners. Yet no one – with the exception of GM with its Saturn brand in the US – has attempted anything as radical in the downstream distribution sector. Nevertheless, serious changes are needed, if distribution is to become as cost-effective as the rest of the industry. Although most manufacturers are exploring changes there is understandable hesitation because of the defensive role of the distribution networks.

Dealer networks are often imperfectly structured, because of the overlap of dealer territories. This is the major source of internal competition and discounting. Dealers are allotted exclusive territories and other dealers of the same brand are not allowed to solicit customers within them. The customers, however, are mobile and simply shop around. The territories – especially in urban areas – are often so small that they belong more to the age of the horse and cart than to that of the motor car. As a result, urban areas are often over-served and suburban ones under-served. Vehicle manufacturers, however, are reluctant to relinquish any point of sale to a competitor.

The emphasis at the interface between dealers and customers is also often misplaced. The current thrust of many dealers is predominantly to push cars, rather than pull customers. The tone tends to be based on price-orientation and mass advertising – at least in the volume car segments. Dealers concentrate on meeting the sales quotas imposed on them by the manufacturers. This encourages the selling of cars in available inventory, whether they really match the customer's needs or not. It also encourages high-pressure sales tactics and excessive discounting.

Staff compensation policies reinforce the importance of acquiring customers for single transactions, rather than retaining loyal customers who will repeat-purchase. This is consistent with a short-term profit orientation and encourages high staff turnover This in itself detracts from building relationships with customers. Only the most persistent and best managed dealers systematically develop their local markets and potential customer bases.

The priorities clearly ought to be reversed. Dealers should identify and prospect target customers. They should choose the mix of products and services as well as the marketing and selling environment through an analysis of local customer behaviour. They should also take into account the priorities of the vehicle manufacturer. The goal should be to expand value-added services, with the objective of keeping customers for life and 'pulling' the market through them. Staff recruitment, training and compensation should be consistent with this goal. Advertising and promotion should be consistent with the overall positioning and marketing strategy of the marque and product, as well as with local conditions. Relationships with customers need to be built up painstakingly, through the ownership cycle of each vehicle, and across successive cycles.

Doing this successfully requires a distinct set of relationship management skills. Ironically, these were common in the days of less reliable products and trusting local customers. In fact, the automotive dealer probably invented relationship marketing. Relationships are harder to create in an age of huge, mobile and fickle sets of potential customers, and in the face of an abundance of generally acceptable and functionally-indistinguishable products.

Similar changes are required at the interface between dealers and manufacturers. The emphasis should be on partnership and delegation, as it is beginning to be in relationships between suppliers and manufacturers. Today, the manufacturer often pushes his product on the dealer, with the help of the dealership agreement. This includes sales volume objectives and volume-based bonuses, and perpetuates the traditional approach of the dealership to its customers.

Again, this is a very crude and imperfect system. There should be more of a triangular relationship between the three parties: customer, dealer and manufacturer. Some dealers manage to create one, but this is the exception rather than the rule. For it to become more widespread, dealers would need to be much stronger in their capabilities, while vehicle manufacturers concentrated their sales and marketing efforts on analysing and steering, rather than pushing and policing. But it is hard to achieve this while manufacturers' distribution policies remain rooted in the concept of arm's-length trading with generally small independent franchisees.

# Dealers wage a war on several fronts, disadvantaged on most of them

Making individual dealers responsible for running six or so businesses at once in one location may also be structurally unrealistic. Dealers typically have different competitors for each of the businesses they run (Figure 8.4). Because these competitors are focused they often have much greater scale.

Dealers in effect have to compete with vehicle manufacturers in the sale of new cars to large buyers, which are sold direct in all but name. They face competition in the used car sector from a growing band of powerful second-hand vehicle specialists. Fast-fit operators, such as Midas, erode their share of the service and repairs business, while independent distributors impact their sales of parts and accessories in the aftermarket. Specialist body shops control much of the crash repair work, and powerful independent financial service providers compete in the lending and insurance sectors.

There are clear opportunities to unbundle and reconstitute the service offerings around more appropriate networks of outlets. For

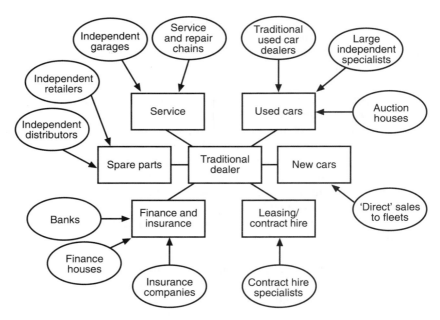

**Figure 8.4**   The multiple businesses of the dealerships, and their focused competitors.

example, vehicle purchase is an infrequent event and shopping is best concentrated in large units, where comparisons can easily be made and skilled salespersons housed. Conversely, routine service and repair needs the convenience of proximity and can use less skilled personnel – as the fast-fit and menu service networks have demonstrated. Again, however, removing the imperfections would require bringing in strong partners, with uncomfortable implications for the manufacturers.

In reality, franchised dealers only have a partial hold on the revenues arising from a vehicle once it has been initially sold. A simple measure of this is service retention – the share of the service market captured by all the franchised dealers in a country. Those shares vary widely: from 65% plus in Germany to 30–35% in the UK and 25–30% in the US. They appear to be linked to the period in history at which mass motorization began to take place.

The significant fact is that – Germany apart – a high proportion, if not most, of service, maintenance and repair activities are not carried out by franchised dealers. As a general rule, they keep a good hold on aftersales revenues arising from first-hand cars. They are strongly supported in doing so by their vehicle manufacturer franchisors, as it is well-known that the quality of aftersales service is a prime determinant of intention to repurchase the same brand (or not).

Dealers, with some individual exceptions, have not established the same virtuous circle for used vehicle ownership. Indeed, many consider used cars to be a nuisance to be suffered through trade-ins rather than a business opportunity in its own right. Most manufacturers are also ambiguous about this sector because their own urge to sell new cars from their factories outweighs their concern for the financial health of their dealers.

Once cars get into their third or subsequent ownership cycles, the franchised dealerships pretty much lose sight of them. The owners of older cars generally have neither the money nor the inclination to pay for servicing and repairs at franchised dealership prices. If they go anywhere at all, they go elsewhere – to the traditional all-makes independent repair garage, or to the fast-fit and menu service chains. Alternatively, they resort to Do It Yourself.

# The neglected opportunities of the aftermarket

The franchised dealer is supported by the vehicle manufacturer in service matters with training programmes and strongly structured distribution networks for proprietary spare parts. The independent sector is supplied by a very dense network of local, independent, parts wholesalers – called jobbers in the US, factors in the UK, *grossistes* in France, *Grosshändler* in Germany, *ricambisti* in Italy, and so on. It has to be dense, as independent garages cannot conceivably stock all the parts they might need to work on any possible make and model of car. They have to be able to obtain the parts quickly and locally, as they need them. The macroscopic structure of aftermarket parts distribution channels in Europe is displayed in Figure 8.5.

Apart from the fast-fit and menu service operators, which are highly-disciplined in both their own operations and their parts re-supply structures, the independent aftermarket remains something of a cottage industry. There are tens of thousands of garages and wholesalers involved, operating independently with no means of co-ordinating inventories. The structures are highly fragmented, duplicative and inefficient. The only exceptions to this rule are in the United States, where organizations such as NAPA have created structured and co-ordinated national distribution chains – the 'strong-form' warehouse distributors, with complete and integrated regional and local distribution networks. The so-called national factors in the UK are also slightly better off than the mass of independent factors, although not quite as strongly structured as the US majors; their downside is bureaucracy, in contrast with the local knowledge and motivation of the individual independent players.

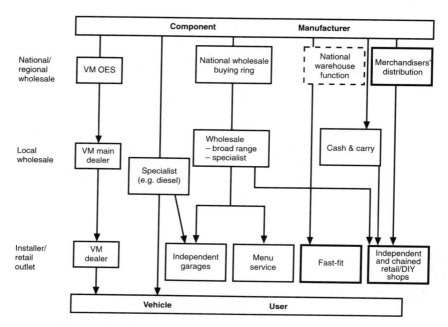

**Figure 8.5**    Macroscopic European parts distribution structure.

Aftermarket distribution in continental Western Europe remains traditional, despite the existence of quite large buying groups (which generally provide no additional logistical or management added-value). The Japanese independent aftermarket is weak – to a large extent because cars are scrapped at a young age or exported out of the country, thanks to the draconian safety inspections.

Independent aftermarket distribution remains almost wholly nationally-based. In Europe, only Bosch can claim any semblance of a pan-European presence, although others are trying. Few components suppliers have successfully penetrated this downstream sector – usually because their own product ranges are too narrow. Even though all economic analyses show that huge savings could be obtained by centralizing stocks of spare parts in a very few European or regional warehouses, the industry seems unable to change. To quote one major supplier-cum-distributor: 'Of course the theory is right. But no one is prepared to take the losses involved in clearing out all the little local players, who will fight to the end'. This subsector of the industry is a microcosm of the resistance to change which pervades it. But it must also be said that it is one of the most delightful, for the individuality and character of the players in it. The microscopic structure of one natural aftermarket – Germany – is shown in Figure 8.6.

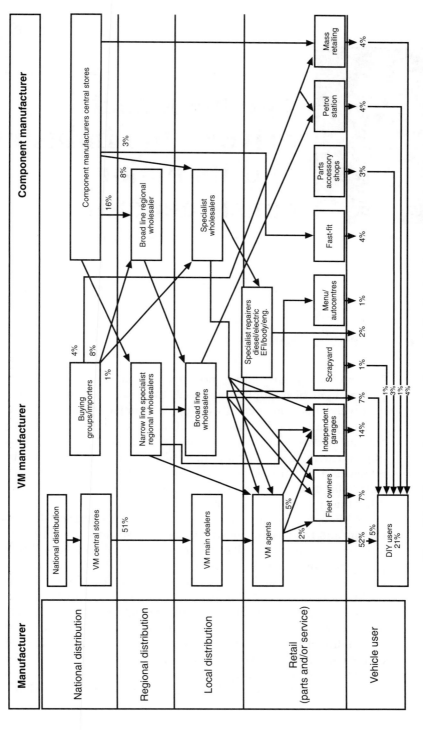

**Figure 8.6**   Microscopic structure of car parts distribution channels – Germany.

# 9

# The back seat drivers: the industry and its major constituencies

## The interested parties

The motor industry does not operate in a classical *laissez-faire* environment of multiple firms, each too small to influence the future decisively. It is fundamentally oligopolistic in nature and structures. It is also very large and important to national economies. It is of interest to external parties not simply because it is so large but also because so many others depend upon it or are affected by it, and some can significantly influence it. It is therefore worth looking at the role of what we have called the back seat drivers, the major constituencies of the industry other than its suppliers and customers.

Although there are many sectors that can influence the future of the car and the motor industry, there are two main constituencies that interact most strongly with it: governments and oil suppliers. While other parties are important, it is these two that exert the greatest influence on cars and how we use them. Demands for cleaner and safer cars may be made by their drivers, for example, but it is governments that will develop any legislative response. Governments also control conditions of use through taxation and their spending on the road infrastructure. The availability of suitable fuels to power them has a considerable influence on the choice of technologies and designs for road vehicles.

All three parties are interdependent. Should a government want to encourage the use of alternative fuels or engines it will have to implement its recommendations with the support of the car and fuel manufacturers. Should both sides resist any such legislation completely, there is really little governments can do, certainly in the short term. Many national governments are actually smaller and less powerful than the motor and oil industries themselves.

# The automotive industry as a generator of wealth

The automotive industry is a massive generator of economic wealth and employment. In the developed countries it accounts for roughly 13% of GNP. In 1900, 2000 people were employed in the automotive industry in the US. By 1910, that had grown to 76,000. Today, in Western Europe, Japan and the United States, one in seven people is employed in the industry, either directly or indirectly in materials, components or insurance, for example. Many of today's largest companies grew on the back of the car industry in the early 1900s.

Consider, for a moment, the industries and businesses that support the 50 million cars made every year worldwide. There are obvious industrial sectors such as oil, rubber, steel and glass that are heavily dependent on car production. The most important supplier sector is probably the oil industry. Most of the oil companies were already established at the turn of the century, supplying oil for lighting. However, electric lighting destroyed this business and they had to find new markets. The emerging car industry was the most obvious. On average, road transportation accounts for around a quarter of a developed country's total energy consumption and more than 40% of its oil use. Other forms of transport only use 5% or 6% of the total.The influence and importance of the oil industry will be covered in much more detail later.

The automotive industry is overwhelmingly the rubber industry's largest customer, while rubber manufacturers are themselves large users of oil-based intermediate chemicals. A good 25% of steel and glass production goes into road vehicles. There are also less obvious materials manufacturers in sectors such as ceramics, platinum and some plastics that are also very dependent on vehicle production. The largest buyer of these materials, in terms of volume, is often the vehicle industry.

Then there is a vast range of other businesses that get vehicles onto the roads and support them in operation. There are the franchised dealers and independent garages, other specialized repairers, filling stations and so on. There is the insurance industry, that covers the risk on the 470 million cars and billion or more drivers as well as the plant and machinery used to build the vehicles and infrastructure. There are the banks that lend to the vehicle and component manufacturers, to their distributors and dealers and to car buyers.

Cars and other vehicles are therefore directly and indirectly important to the economy in a massive way – and thus to governments. Most obviously, road vehicles and fuels can be taxed. They are a major source of revenue for the public purse. In the UK, road and motoring taxes are estimated by the Society of Motor Manufacturers and Traders (SMMT) to account for 12% of the government's total income. Once the costs of road maintenance and policing have been accounted for, the motor industry remains a net financial contributor to the national budget.

# The industry as a powerful stimulant of unfulfilled expectations

But cars are not just utilitarian tools or cash cows for governments: they are also emotive. People want cars. They want the personal mobility, the status and the fun that cars provide. For governments in stable, developed countries this is not an issue. If their citizens work hard they can afford the car of their choice. It is very different in the less developed countries (LDCs) however, and much more of a problem for the governments there. Many homes in the LDCs now have television sets that, because of the Western programmes transmitted, help to stimulate the desire of individuals for car ownership. In these countries few can afford such luxuries – average incomes are simply too low. Moreover, even if the economies were to develop rapidly, it may be ten years, or more, before car penetration can rise significantly.

In Brazil the average income per head is under $3000 a year. As a very rough measure, at 1990 exchange rates, GDP per head has to be more than $5000, on average, before vehicle penetration increases rapidly (Figure 9.1). The Greek car market doubled within a few years at the start of the 1990s after the $5000 average income threshold was broken. Even if Brazil were to achieve a consistently high level of economic growth, say 5% a year, it would take it a decade to reach the $5000 average income level in notional terms – and it would take it 21 years to meet it in real terms. So, the average Brazilian wanting to own a car will have to wait until 2015 before he is able to afford it. That's a long time to wait, if you want it tomorrow.

Even so, Brazil's average GDP is much higher than many other nations with large populations of car-starved consumers. Russia, China, India, Turkey and Indonesia have huge and growing numbers of car-

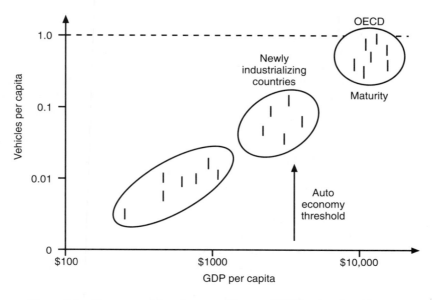

**Figure 9.1**   Car ownership v. income. (*Source*: EIU International Motor
Business, 3rd Quarter, 1993)

hungry people – yet few will ever be able to afford one. While this may
seem almost trivial to us in the developed nations, it presents a very real
problem to governments in the poorer ones. Increasing awareness of the
lifestyles and wealth of developed countries is raising expectations in
these countries. Expectations for a wide range of goods – refrigerators,
motor cycles, radio-cassette players and, of course, cars.

Even with the most ambitious economic plans these expectations are
difficult for governments to meet – and they know that such a mismatch
of reality and expectation can be problematic. This is particularly so if the
country's citizens are expected to wait more than 20 years to fulfil their
dreams. Such discontent can be exploited by extremist factions. Many of
the fundamentalist movements in the Levant region, for example, draw
support largely from deepening popular frustrations. Similarly, one of
the principal reasons for the dissolution of the Soviet Union was the
frustration felt by unsatisfied consumers.

The governments of these countries have a number of options – none
of them easy or comfortable. They can invest in vehicle production and
attempt to manufacture at a sufficiently low cost to meet the market's
needs. Alternatively, they can attempt to suppress the desires of their
citizens by controlling the media. China and Malaysia recently banned
the use of satellite dishes in an attempt to halt the flow of Western images
into the country. They can try to offer alternative dreams for their citizens
to aspire to – although demand for cars may prove difficult to redirect.

Or, finally, they can try to respond to whatever manifestation the unfulfilled expectations of their citizens produces.

Governments also intervene in the car industry directly. They impose requirements and constraints on car manufacturers and drivers. Initially, it was by imposing speed limits and by forcing owners to register their vehicles and fit license plates. Later is was through taxation, of the vehicles themselves and of the fuels they used. They set construction and use and homologation requirements, and impose checks on the safety and environmental conformity of vehicles on the road. In Europe, they are becoming increasingly embroiled in holding the balance of equity between end customers, franchised dealers and vehicle manufacturers, as we have seen in Chapter 8.

Vehicle safety has become a major issue for governments in recent decades. The automotive industry, like any other business, obeys the laws of industrial economics. A vehicle manufacturer will add a feature to his car, if it makes financial sense – that is if the revenue generated exceeds the cost of adding the feature. In the 1960s, Ford tried to sell a car on the basis of its safety features, with little success. GM and Chrysler also investigated safety, coming to the same conclusions. GM even offered air bags as a low-cost option, but found very little consumer interest. In the past, therefore, car producers did not place much emphasis on safety. The same problems arose if the vehicles wasted fuel, were dangerous or polluting. The market-place fails to address these issues unaided and governments, even the most *laissez-faire*, have had to intervene.

A number of key events prompted this change of attitude. In 1965, at the Rubicoff hearings, the US Attorney General forced the then president of GM, James Roche, to admit that the company spent almost nothing on vehicle safety. In his book *Unsafe at Any Speed* (1966), Ralph Nader created an outcry when he highlighted the dangers of the Chevrolet Corvair. Nader also highlighted the problem of air pollution, when he claimed that the car industry knew about the causes of the Southern California smog as far back as the 1920s.

# The industry's resistance to change

The industry has often fought hard against legislation. During the 1960s, in the US, it was discovered that brakes often failed because the hydraulic fluid boiled, vapourized and was then unable to activate the system. The car giants and the Department of Commerce argued that the government was *ultra vires*. It had no right to legislate on the matter. Formally, they were right. The car companies fought legislation on seat-belt anchor points, padded dashboards and safety latches on doors on the grounds that it would 'create stagnation among automotive engineers and designers' which would damage the economy. Some even tried to block the fitment of air bags, on the grounds that 'safety did not sell cars'.

Ironically, and despite this resistance, it has been the US, with the most free market-economy in the world, that has led the way in terms of vehicle and safety legislation. The Clean Air Act of 1963 set exhaust emissions standards; subsequent laws required the use of seat-belts, catalytic converters and safety glass. Ultimately, governments had to intervene much more extensively in the standards for the design of vehicles. More recent examples include corporate average fuel economy (CAFE) objectives, the fitment of air bags and anti-lock brakes, while California, in particular, is forcing the development of zero emission vehicles (ZEVs), as part of its very ambitious environmental goals.

Still the car makers resist. The big three in the United States, Ford, GM and Chrysler, claimed for many years that catalysts would not work. They also resisted legislation that would increase the padding inside vehicles to protect against head injuries on the grounds that it would reduce visibility. The added cost of up to $80 a car was not cited as the principal reason. They now claim that the development of cost effective ZEVs to meet Californian legislation in 1998 is impossible.

# Fuels and environmental policy

The shift to unleaded gasoline/petrol provides another example. The laws of thermodynamics mean that all heat engines operate more efficiently as the difference between the temperatures of heat source and heat sink increases. The further development of the internal combustion engine inevitably led to the use of higher operating temperatures in the combustion cycle. This leads to two problems: an increase in toxic nitrogen oxides as a by-product and damage to exhaust valves. Increased compression ratios also allow a better weight-to-power ratio in the engine but lead to problems of uncontrolled pre-detonation of the fuel-air mix in spark ignition engines. The cost-effective solution to both the last two problems, almost universally adopted between the wars, is to add an organometallic compound, tetraethyl lead, to petrol.

The compound itself is toxic but its production and incorporation into fuels are carefully controlled, while the law generally prohibits the use of leaded fuel for purposes other than fuelling engines – hence the cautionary notices commonly found on gasoline/petrol pumps. The decomposition product emitted from exhausts, metallic lead in the form of small particles, was not thought to present toxicity problems for the population. Saturnism, or the effects of lead poisoning – particularly on the development of children – has been known to the medical profession for generations. While workers in the lead-smelting and processing industries were obviously exposed, the most widespread source was the dissolution of lead from pipes in areas with acidic water supplies.

When some epidemiologists expressed serious concerns about lead pollution from motor fuels, they were roundly attacked by the combined automotive and oil industries and even accused of falsifying their research data. Ultimately, lead began to be driven out of motor fuel, not because it might be poisoning people but because it poisoned the catalysts used to oxidize unburnt hydrocarbons and nitrogen oxides in car exhausts. In the process, the vehicle industry presented a sorry spectacle of resistance to change and, in the case of Europe, internal disagreement about the extent to which exhaust catalysts should be made mandatory. Safety and environmental features are now an essential part of new vehicle marketing – and largely because of government intervention.

## Fuel economy and taxation

Governments in Europe and Japan have taken a different approach to legislation than the US government, particularly with respect to fuel economy. On average, 70% of the pump price of a gallon of fuel in Europe is tax. By taxing fuels, the Europeans have achieved better fuel efficiency than through the CAFE regulations in the US. These try to modify the behaviour of car producers through legal penalties, but keep the cost of fuel low. As a result, gasoline costs a quarter of the price charged in Europe. Acting on the supply side of the industry, rather than the demand side of consumer behaviour, introduces a major distortion of free-market principles.

# Providing the road infrastructure

Governments are also overwhelmingly the dominant providers of the road infrastructure, without which most vehicles are useless. The road infrastructure is regarded in most countries as an essential national asset. Its development has taken many years and cost a substantial proportion of the annual GDP of developed nations. There are also considerable costs associated with maintaining this asset. The most obvious costs are for repair and policing. There are many more costs, however. These include administration by local and national authorities, cleaning and lighting, parking wardens and courts to administer motoring offences.

The impact of this investment and upkeep is similar to that in the fuel and oil industries. There is a monolithic interest in maintaining the *status quo* in terms of jobs, incomes and wealth. As a result, both the road and fuel lobbies are particularly strong. Attempting to change either the use of conventional fuels or roads will therefore be a very difficult task. And, given the sums invested, this resistance to change is supported by a clear economic logic, at least in the short term.

It is certain that governments will continue to intervene in the industry in the future. Indeed, their influence is likely to increase. Future issues for governments include road pricing, restrictions of vehicle use within cities and tougher laws on safety and emissions. Many in the industry will doubtless continue to resist, certainly in the US and Europe. This raises the question, why? Why does the industry continue to swim against the tide? It would seem far more sensible to change direction, to take the initiative, to assist in the development of legislation. As we will see later on, this is typically the approach taken by the Japanese and it certainly seems to have paid them dividends.

The industry is frequently defensive about itself – often unnecessarily so. Information is sometimes manipulated to generate a more favourable image of the industry and of motor vehicles themselves. The vehicle manufacturers have a great deal of difficulty on occasion in presenting a united front, and in working with governments early enough to help them explore the most productive legislative and regulatory options. This parallels the historically fraught relations they have had with their component suppliers upstream and distributors and dealers downstream.

One important difference between governments and the industry is that while governments are typically forced to act nationally, the industry behaves internationally or globally. This mismatch offers risks and opportunities to both parties. Strong governments, such as that in California, can force vehicle manufacturers to invest heavily. If other governments do not follow a strong legislative lead, such as that on ZEVs, that investment can far outweigh the revenues. Similarly, the scale of the industry means that it can have considerable influence over policy formulation, particularly in countries that are heavily dependent on it for employment.

# The oil and fuel suppliers

Leaving electric-powered vehicles aside, there are many potential fuels and prime movers for propelling cars. The family tree of potential heat engines is shown in Figure 9.2.

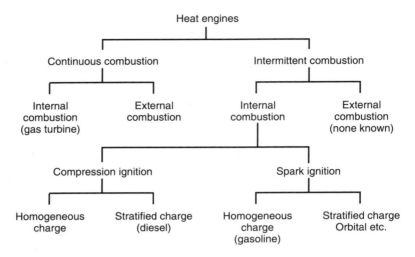

**Figure 9.2**    Heat engines useable in automobiles.

Both the historic and the ongoing development of the passenger car industry are heavily shaped by the choices made between these alternatives. In 1805, when the first 'car' was demonstrated in Philadelphia, the battle between alternative fuels began. Initially, the favoured means of propulsion was steam, although internal combustion engines burning liquid hydrocarbons and electric power were also strong contenders. At one early stage, three-quarters of vehicles in the US were electric-powered. As the car developed so did the different means to propel it.

If you were considering buying a car in the United States in 1905, your decision would have had less to do with the reputation of the manufacturer, the price or the performance of the vehicle than it would today. It would almost certainly be determined by the choice of propulsion system. Electric, steam or internal combustion? If you chose the third option, should it be 2-stroke or 4-stroke, one cylinder, two or four? Should the fuel be gasoline, kerosene, alcohol or naphtha? You might also have to select the valve types and the method of ignition.

Steam cars were favoured initially – mainly because of their lower price and the familiarity of consumers with that source of energy. Until 1920, there were more than 100 suppliers of steam cars in the United States. Steam cars had problems, however. They took time to start, water froze in cold weather, they were complex and had a comparatively short range.

Electric cars were also popular during the early years. At one stage, there were at least 36 electric vehicle manufacturers in the United States, although by 1928, only three were left. Electric cars were seen as silent and clean, certainly compared to their gasoline competitors. The major drawback for electric cars was their range and, when people started to travel outside cities, that drawback became overwhelming. This perception persists today.

As a result, the long-term winner in the fuelling race was the internal combustion engine, despite the noise and fumes. Today its principal fuel is gasoline/petrol – although diesel is also a major fuel for cars in Europe and for trucks and buses almost everywhere. The first vehicle patented to run with liquid fuel was in 1826, when Samuel Morey demonstrated a form of internal combustion engine for motorized transport. However, it was George Brayton who took the big step forward in the 1870s and patented the first real 2-stroke engine of a design that would be familiar to us today. Indeed, even Gottlieb Daimler advertised his 4-stroke engine as being built under licence from Brayton.

In 1901, Olds Motor Works introduced the gasoline-powered Curved Dash, costing $650. At the time the Locomobile steam car cost 50% more. Although the price of the Dash was still twice the average annual wage of a production line worker, the car was within reach of many of the professional classes. At around the same time, a major oil discovery pushed the price of oil down to five cents a barrel. The fall in price of both the vehicle and its fuel assured gasoline's success over the alternatives – although the development of reliable ignition and starting systems were also important.

Today, the oil and motor industries are strongly interdependent. In 1990, 60% of the oil used in the United States was consumed by cars as fuel. Oil is not only essential for gasoline. It also provides plastics for the interior and increasingly the exterior of the vehicle, bitumen and tar for the roads and of course much of the energy used in the production of cars themselves. The motor industry represents one of the largest markets for the oil industry's products.

# The interdependence of the oil and automotive industries

Oil has considerable geo-political importance. The availability of oil and increased mobility were critical in gaining strategic advantage during the two world wars. Oil has brought enormous wealth and influence to historically weak nations. It has also brought them a great deal of trouble as the industrialized countries attempted to establish control over their reserves. Wars have been fought over access to oil. Even the price of oil has also brought us to the brink of war, such is its influence on developed economies.

The supply of oil and over-dependence on foreign sources of it was also responsible for the decline of the American car industry during the 1970s. When oil was in short supply in 1973, consumers turned to smaller, more fuel-efficient vehicles. As Detroit initially ignored the trend, most of the smaller cars sold tended to be Japanese. The foothold that they managed to achieve then allowed them to develop their presence throughout the next 20 years. The Japanese control nearly a third of the US market today.

The oil crisis was also responsible for a fundamental change in the materials used in vehicles. To save weight, suppliers turned away from steel and cast iron towards plastics and lighter metals such as aluminium. The decline of the older materials industries was caused substantially by dependency on oil.

Ironically, given many of the political events of the last 30 years, the prospect of oil running out is not a major consideration today. Despite the increased use of oil, reserves grew by more than 50% in the 1980s as new discoveries were made. There is enough oil to last another 50 years at current rates of consumption. In addition, the prospect of one of the oil producing countries holding the developed nations to ransom is also less likely, as oil is now produced in so many parts of the world.

Yet oil is still close to the top of world agendas. In the last 20 years, America's dependence on foreign oil has doubled. Nationalism, fundamentalism and the influence of non-OPEC nations are major concerns in the countries where the most oil is used. In the future, as in the past, the governments of the oil-using nations can adopt one of two broad policy options. They can attempt to secure an uninterruptable supply, or they can try to decrease their dependence on oil. The key issue that will determine the long-term future of the oil industry is government policy – more than supply and demand, more than OPEC and more than the 'Seven Sisters' that control the supply of oil. Change will be difficult and slow, however.

It is also the less-developed nations that would suffer most from any decline in oil demand. Many of the economies of the Middle East, South America, Asia and Africa are heavily dependent on the sale of oil. In Nigeria, for example, 95% of hard currency earnings are derived from the export of oil. Any drop in demand could have a disastrous effect on these economies.

# The potential for long-term change in fuelling structures

Despite these barriers to change, there is a threat to the oil industry that may be difficult to fight. If, by 1998, the Californian legislation on non-polluting vehicles is implemented, demand for petrol and gasoline will begin to fall in the developed world. Although its impact will be small for many years and demand could rise in less-developed countries, it is a seed from which major change could grow. Its scale appears in Figure 9.3.

Although it is pollution that has caused the Californian authorities to act, they were not driven primarily by a concern for the wider environment. Pollution and smog caused by motor vehicles have resulted in health problems around Los Angeles. The effects of this pollution have been enhanced by the geographic and climatic conditions in large metropolitan areas. While public authorities are keen to promote a better atmosphere, their interest is primarily in their area of jurisdiction. It has long been argued that electric vehicles do not solve the pollution problems, they simply move them from the tailpipe to the power station. This is not a concern for the Los Angeles authorities, however. Electric vehicles will solve their problems, even though it will mean more pollution in the desert, where the power plants are located.

It would be unfair to suggest that the Californian legislators do not care for the wider environment. They clearly do. They have simply faced up to the realities of today's technology. If they want pollution-free vehicles in 1998, they will almost certainly have to be electric, and that will mean that the pollution will be transferred elsewhere.

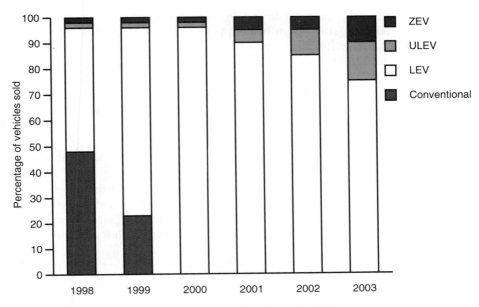

**Figure 9.3**   Effects of California legislation.

# The role of legislation and limitations on substitute fuels

The final decision on alternative fuels will be determined by legislation. None of the alternative fuels proposed today can compete with gasoline and diesel on economic terms. For any alternative fuel to become established, some sort of government intervention will be required. That may be directly, as in California, or indirectly, through taxation. The options are fairly restricted in the short term. Even Jerry Martin of the California Air Resources Board has said that 'new blends of gasoline will be the mainstay long into the next century'.

'Synthetic' fuels have to be synthesized from something combustible – at great cost, compared to fuels refined from oil. Apart from some pilot projects in the US following the first oil shock in 1973, the only serious attempts to make oil from coal took place in two beleaguered countries – Germany in the 1930s and 1940s and South Africa more recently. Substantial though these efforts were, they are puny compared with the scale of demand. Cars in the OECD countries today gulp more fuel in a weekend than Germany's panzer divisions consumed in a year.

The non-competitiveness of bio-fuels has been amply demonstrated by the large-scale alcohol experiment in Brazil, which seems to have benefited the sugar cane growers more than anyone else. A draft EU directive suggests taxing bio-fuels at one-tenth the rate for four-star leaded petrol – hardly an appealing prospect for finance ministers! The land requirements and associated environmental problems make them a doubtful proposition, at best, for large-scale use.

While some further improvements to the thermodynamic efficiency of the internal combustion engine are possible, they will be relatively marginal. There is no magical technological fix for consumption and emissions problems within the existing patterns of vehicle design and use. Nitrogen oxide and hydrocarbon emissions per vehicle-mile have been significantly reduced already; no catalyst will solve the problem of carbon dioxide emissions and the possible greenhouse effect. Hydrogen as an alternative fuel offers clean combustion and the absence of carbon dioxide emissions but poses enormous problems at both the generation level – requiring a vast increase in nuclear-generated electric power for electrolysis – and in storage and distribution, not to mention on board vehicles.

The enormous scale of the investment in today's fuelling infrastructure is a huge barrier to change. The network of fuel stations is designed primarily for gasoline/petrol and diesel. Although they could be changed to methanol or other liquefied bio-fuels, they would be useless for electric or hydrogen-powered vehicles. Similarly, the lead times in the oil industry are enormous. When the oil companies make an investment in exploration or refining they frequently anticipate a payback decades later. Simply based on the amount of investment being made today, they are likely to resist strongly any attempt to reduce our dependence on oil, particularly in the transportation sector. There is, in fact, a strong argument for reserving fossil hydrocarbons for this sector and as feedstock for the chemical industry, where they are difficult and costly to replace. Coal and nuclear energy are most easily applied to major industrial heating and power generation, while natural gas is preferred for smaller domestic and commercial heating. If massive changes in drivetrain and/or vehicle design, and use patterns are required to solve the problems, it is difficult to see how they will be implemented by the vehicle and fuel industries acting on their own.

# 10

# The Triad club: outsiders need not apply

## The dominance of the Triad countries

The countries of the industrialized Triad – North America, Western Europe and Japan – dominate the automotive industry. This dominance is reinforced by all that has happened in the sector in the last few years. The world industry is thus structured into three mega-regions – East Asia, North America and Europe – which fits the lean development and supply model for passenger cars and light trucks. Tightly-coupled innovation and supply chains in the upstream part of the industry will increasingly link vehicle manufacturers into tiered supply hierarchies.

Although the underlying technologies and designs are increasingly common throughout the world, complete vehicles still differ significantly between the regions, because of differences in highway infrastructures, driving habits and government regulations. There is unlikely to be a true 'world car' for a long time – and still less a 'world heavy truck'.

The economics of just-in-time clearly dictate that vehicles be assembled close to end markets and that components be sourced primarily within the mega-regions. Within a mega-region, there will be specialization as a function of competitive advantage. High-technology, scale-intensive components will come from the more advanced countries within it. Low-technology, less scale-intensive and more labour-intensive items will be sourced from lower factor cost areas. This is limited by the proximity of customers, whether these are vehicle manufacturers or suppliers. If lean distribution takes hold, this will further tighten the interdependencies within the overall delivery system.

The effective 'reach' of sourcing depends on the nature of what is supplied. Sequence In-Line Parts, those that must fit the vehicle final assembly sequence exactly, will be manufactured virtually on site, or at least within a 20 to 30 km radius of the final assembly plant. Seat assemblies are a typical example. At the other extreme, some high-value, low-bulk/weight, low-variability components, such as integrated circuits, can come from the most competitive sources anywhere in the world. Most items in between can in practice be sourced on a mega-region-wide basis.

The preoccupations and priorities of the major automotive companies are known. The major challenges to competitors in this industry are in product development, the technology with which to differentiate products, and in building their innovation and delivery chains. These require companies to work on an extended enterprise basis within a mega-region and sometimes globally.

Japanese penetration will continue to increase. It will continue to provide the impetus for rationalization and globalization in the industry, notably at the supplier level. Technology will also be shared worldwide, so that leading components suppliers will have to be global too.

The Japanese-inspired revolution in the Triad regions is rapidly widening the performance gap between them and the rest of the world in cars and light trucks. For those outside the mega-region, inadequate domestic scale will be a fundamental barrier to the development of high-technology components.

The automotive environment is therefore likely to become increasingly unfavourable to countries that lie outside the Triad 'mainstream'. This exclusion will not primarily be the result of tariffs or quotas to protect it, for it is the result of practical economics, not arbitrary discrimination. An integrated economic zone such as the NAFTA is simply likely to become the home of powerful players, in terms of scale and competitiveness, which outsiders have little chance of challenging on their home ground.

Thus the future structure of the world automotive industry can already be glimpsed. The end-game in passenger cars as well as light trucks and vans will be played in the three mega-regions: Japan, Eastern Asia and the Pacific Rim; the NAFTA combination of the US, Mexico and Canada; and Western and Central Europe. There will also be some countries on the fringes of these regions that will face the opportunities and challenges involved in integrating themselves into them – South Korea and Turkey, for example.

There may be some future wild cards for the longer term, such as Russia or India in heavy trucks and China in cars, light trucks and components. In each case, however, the local market must be carefully segmented for demand potential and the supply base closely examined for the possibilities of integration into the mega-regions. The idea that developing countries can, by force of will, government intervention and subsidy build up autarchic, integrated industries is inconsistent with the technological, economic and competitive realities of the industry.

# Countries that have played a strategy of integration into a mega-region

The policies of governments and companies must be evaluated against this global industry framework. Some countries have stepped up to the challenge and managed to enter the mainstream industry.

### Spain

Spain provides the earliest example of a country that reversed its earlier autarchic strategy and achieved integration into a mega-region. Spain's automotive industry remained isolated and largely self-sufficient until the late 1970s. A minimum 90% local content was imposed on nationally-made cars and imports were discouraged by extremely high customs duties. National producers received special tax and investment incentives, on condition that they achieved certain export quotas. Cars sold in the national market were expensive and often outdated. Exports were limited, despite the subsidies.

The 'Ford Law' ushered a new era of integration into Europe, in anticipation of the death of Franco and of Spain's ultimate integration into the European Community. Basically, Ford made Spain an offer it could not refuse. Ford was about to enter a new market segment in Europe, the supermini class, for the first time, with the original Fiesta. It could therefore take market share from its competitors in Europe and therefore required additional production capacity, preferably in a low-cost country. As the car would sell throughout Europe, it could easily promise to export two-thirds of the volumes from wherever it was produced. As a result, national local content could be reduced to 50%, while still earning an export surplus. By avoiding the need to rely on Spain's autarchic and uncompetitive components sector for technology- and scale-intensive components, the production cost would be highly competitive, even with the necessary transhipments.

Since then, GM has followed Ford, investing in a major assembly plant in Spain to build its smallest volume car, the Corsa. VW likewise, has the Polo produced in Spain by its affiliate, SEAT. Nissan builds 4 × 4s in Spain. Coupled with rapid internal economic development, this has enabled the country to become Europe's fifth largest car builder, producing almost two million units in 1992. A large number of vehicle manufacturers now sell in the Spanish market, as imports from the EC have been liberalized, although the three leading domestic producers still control over half the national market.

Thus Spain has become an integral part of the European automotive mega-region. The country has clearly profited from its shift from a policy of autarchy to one of integration. This has been facilitated by the interest that vehicle and components manufacturers have had in Spain, both as a market and as a potential low-cost supply base. Other European governments were also willing to grant Spain access to their automotive markets while it remained partly protected during a transition period, as part of the price of reintegrating Spain into the European family of nations.

## Belgium

Belgium is an often-forgotten earlier example. It assembles over a million vehicles per year – a huge output, compared to its national market – and hosts major plants belonging to Ford, VW, Renault, GM and Volvo. Its historical advantage was central location within Europe and the availability of good-quality labour, particularly with the run-down of the traditional base of heavy industry. The plants are simply viewed and operated by each manufacturer as an integral part of their production network – thus Renault's Haren plant is planned into its French assembly plant structure.

## Mexico

Mexico provides another successful example of this change in strategy and continues to consolidate its position as a player of growing significance in the global industry. Government influence has always been a significant factor in the development of the Mexican automotive industry. Its growth and that of the local market have been directly tied to a series of government decrees. The Mexican government pursued a policy of automotive autarchy for many years, consistent with general economic and political philosophies dating back to the 1910 revolution. The financial crisis of the late 1970s made their inadequacy obvious and Mexico made a fundamental change of tack in the direction of liberalization.

This has produced dramatic success in the automotive sector. The industry continues to restructure and is poised for rapid growth and increased exports of vehicles. Vehicle exports have already risen from only 3% of output in 1980 to over one-third; components exports are substantial and still rising. Imports are also growing since they were liberalized in 1991 but remain limited so far. Car production is expected to reach 1.25 million by 1996, from 835,000 in 1993 – itself a trebling of the 1987 level. Mexico is already the world's 12th largest commercial vehicle producer, after Brazil and the CIS.

The NAFTA agreement positions Mexico to become a major component of an enlarged North American mega-region. Local content requirements will be reduced from 36% to 29% and ultimately to zero. The US will reduce its light truck import duties from the NAFTA countries to zero in stages and will remove tariffs on cars.

In five years Mexico will eliminate its car import duties. It will do the same for trucks in 10 years; duties on parts will also be phased out. Mexico will allow foreign ownership of parts producers. Once again, the successful automotive play is part of – and also a justification for – a much wider-ranging politico-economic realignment for Mexico.

### Canada

Canada is a relatively large market and producer but its future role may be more modest. The Canadian market has declined steadily, by 25% from 1987 to 798,000 cars in 1992. There may be some recovery, in line with the economy as a whole. But this is a completely mature market, which will therefore cycle around a low growth trend, possibly reaching the one million mark by the year 2000. Many competitors sell in it. As a producer, Canada has long been integrated into the US system, through the Big Three.

Local production was close to one million in 1992. This was expected to increase to 1.5 million, in response to US demand. Both levels are clearly higher than would be expected in a self-sufficient country. Canada has clearly gained from its early integration into the US-based North American mega-region. Now, however, there is a real threat of transfer of production to Mexico, with its much lower factor costs, within the NAFTA framework and this could hit the industry hard. Canada's prospects may be better in components.

### Turkey

Turkey provides the counter-example to Spain – a country that could be part of the European automotive mega-region but is having difficulty in doing so. Domestic sales of passenger cars have grown steadily, at 7% per year, for the last 10 years. Demand for pick-ups is strong. But the market remains constrained by low incomes, while economic growth is offset by a fast-increasing population and national prices are high. Imports surged when tariffs were reduced in 1990 and then fell again when they were raised once more. Vehicle taxes are among the highest in the OECD, at 45%–50%.

The government has made a serious attempt to develop an automotive industry and puts transport and infrastructure high on its list of spending priorities. Until recently, the country had a long tradition of autarchy, which extended to the automotive industry, with local content requirements of up to 100% and never less than 50%.

The market is expected to continue to be supplied mainly by national production for the time being, with no government encouragement of imports in the short term, even though local vehicles are often outdated. Total vehicle output was 302,000 in 1992, of which 285,000 were cars. Some exports have been achieved, particularly to Egypt but the volume is very small at 7800 units. An increase in exports to developing country markets is hoped for, as new manufacturers invest in Turkey – notably Toyota, with 200,000 units of capacity. Limited deals have been struck with European vehicle manufacturers for importing vehicles against exports of Turkish components.

Rationalization of production by specialization and integration into Europe, on the Spanish model, would make good economic sense for Turkey. The proposition, however, comes 20 years later, when growth and competitive prospects within Europe are a good deal more sombre. Moreover, European governments are a good deal less keen about including Turkey in the EU than they were about Spain.

# Some countries have accepted that they cannot play a major role in the world automotive industry

### Australia

Australia struggled for a long time to sustain its domestic industry. It is now on the way to abandoning it. With a market of some 400,000 cars and 550,000 total vehicles per year, adequate scale is hard to achieve. The government has tried for years to reform the industry, in order to create a sector that could deliver quality cars for domestic consumption at competitive costs. The Car Plan, in operation for nearly a decade, has reduced the manufacturing groups from five to three and the number of locally-produced models from thirteen to six. Nissan, which had 10% of the domestic market, pulled out in 1992.

Productivity remains stubbornly below world standards, vehicle prices are rising faster than inflation and the local industry is making heavy losses. Imports were 20% of the market in 1987, are now 35% and are expected to rise further. Production has fallen from 384,000 in 1984 to 262,000 in 1992. As import tariffs are expected to fall further, it seems unlikely that domestic production can survive much longer. Component exports have risen and may rise a little more, because of the export credits they earn, which can be offset against duties on imported vehicles. However, local component suppliers are not likely to achieve the critical mass needed to survive in global markets unaided.

### Chile

Chile has also virtually given up on national production and relies on imports. At one stage, the domestic market was heavily protected and 30 assemblers produced locally under licence. During the 1980s, free-market economics and reduced protectionism, with import tariffs falling to 15% in 1991, curtailed this activity. There is now only one local producer, Franco-Chileña, building 3000–4000 units per year. Local content requirements are now also very low, at 13%. Heavy commercial vehicles were assembled in the 1970s but are now imported, with only a local coach assembly operation remaining. Protection for local vehicle producers is expected to end in 1995. More than 200 models are on sale from 30 manufacturers, with the Japanese leading in cars and light commercials. The market is fairly small – 54,000 cars in 1991, with only four cars on the road per 1000 inhabitants. Sales are expected to reach 89,000 in the year 2000, with a shift from pick-ups as the road network – currently in a poor state – improves.

# Other countries are scaling back their ambitions and liberalizing their markets more gradually

### Columbia

Colombia continues local production but has given up any attempt to do more than satisfy its domestic market. The local industry is based on kits and has grown only slightly over the last decade. Until recently, the government controlled the number of investors in it, setting quotas for the types and numbers of vehicles. These controls are now being eased, allowing manufacturers to make their own investment decisions more freely. The import restrictions set in 1983 are being removed, in order to encourage competition. Closer relations with the Venezuelan industry are also expected. Price controls on vehicles are being abolished but national price levels are very high by world standards. A total of 32,000 cars were produced and sold in 1990 together with 15,000 commercial vehicles. Low incomes restrain demand and vehicle penetration is minimal, at two cars per 1000 population. With liberalization, sales are forecast to reach 52,000 in the year 2000, with a rising demand for pick-ups also. Bus demand will rise sharply because of the age of the existing parc. Production, however, will rise to only 34,000 cars in 1996. The growth in demand will be satisfied by imports.

## Taiwan

Taiwan is another example of controlled liberalization. National economic growth has accelerated again and is expected to continue at about 7% per year to 1996, with good longer-term prospects. Unlike most of its South-East Asian neighbours, Taiwan has a vehicle market in which cars predominate, at about 70% of total units. The market grew very fast from 1986 to 1989 – at over 25% per year. Growth temporarily ceased with the 1990 property and stock crash but volume reached 541,000 vehicles in 1992, of which 412,000 were cars.

Vehicle penetration in Taiwan remains low, at 11 cars per 1000 people. The market is expected to grow further, with the help of the six-year infrastructural development plan. Despite high tariffs (42.5% on cars and 48% on trucks) imports grew from 15,000 in 1982 to 185,000 in 1989, reaching 43% of the market before falling back to 24%. Tariffs are expected to fall to 25% for cars and 35% for other vehicles by 1996, which should relaunch import growth. Although direct imports from Japan are banned, most vehicles are Japanese designs, built in Taiwan or the US. This ban may be lifted soon, in return for greater access to Japan for Taiwanese components.

Sales of locally-built vehicles trebled over the last decade, to reach 400,000 per year. The 50% local content rule is likely to be relaxed. Production capacity is expected to increase and production to rise to 550,000 units over the next four years. Vehicle exports, however, have never become significant and are not expected to, although components have done far better. Thus Taiwan is aiming at a modest expansion of its automotive role through controlled liberalization but has no aim to become a major world player.

# A few countries are still pursuing the chimera of autarchic development

Many countries have – or have had – ambitions to develop their own fully-fledged automotive industries. The challenge is considerable and most countries outside the Triad core members have, as described above, either moved to become part of the mega-regions or started to withdraw from the race. There are still some significant efforts to 'go it alone' and build an industry capable of satisfying the domestic market and of successfully exporting to the rest of the world. Critical factors for the success of this strategy are a sufficient internal market to provide the base-load volume and a stable and predictable economic environment. These are not easy criteria to satisfy.

## Brazil

Brazil has long sought to build a strong automotive industry. But the country lacks the direction and stability to sustain it. The domestic market remains stagnant, with Brazilians buying fewer cars than in 1980. The government's past automotive policy was strongly autarchic, with imports virtually banned and export surpluses strongly subsidised, as part of the Befiex programme. This policy proved a costly failure, after some initial successes.

In a partial reversal of policy, the domestic market has been slightly opened to imports, which have captured about 3.5% of sales. But this is enough to reveal the old-fashionedness of many local products. Import tariffs have been considerably reduced but are still high. Vehicle production in 1992 was at half its 1980 level. Argentina remains the largest export market, and a further integration of the Brazilian and Argentinean markets and industries is expected.

This will not be enough to lift the isolation of the Brazilian industry from the world. Very rapid adaptation and heavy investment would be needed to bring it up to world-class standards. The domestic market is expected to reach 610,000 cars per year by 2000. This is simply not enough to justify isolated development in a period when the world industry is becoming global in nature and more scale intensive. The economic and political difficulties of the country are major disincentives to outside investors. The constitution of the NAFTA threatens to put Brazil truly out of the world automotive game. No South American common market can compete as a base, even if one could realistically be constructed.

## South Korea

South Korea has been aggressively developing its automotive industry for many years. This policy has been strongly driven forward by the national government, which sees the automotive industry as a national development priority. The country as a whole has achieved high rates of economic growth, which are now falling somewhat. Automotive production, domestic sales and exports have continued to grow at double-digit rates, spurred by government support. Production increased 360% from 1985 to 1992, reaching 1.7 million units.

South Korea is a player of consequence. Both production and sales are dominated by Hyundai, although four other manufacturers are also present. The domestic market and the industry have been heavily protected, through both fairly high duties (17–40%) and cumbersome administrative procedures. The structure of the industry is changing rapidly, through further investment by and collaboration with foreign manufacturers, such as that between Mercedes-Benz and Ssangyong. Hyundai itself obtained much of its technology under licence from Mitsubishi.

The government plans to increase capacity to four million vehicles per year by the year 2000. It is expected to go on playing a very active role, forcing the industry to focus on improving its level of technology. It wants to reduce the current dependence on foreign suppliers and partners, and to rationalize the components sector. The domestic market is expected to reach 1.65 million units by 2000, from 0.9 million in 1992, an 8% annual growth rate. The major outlet for the increased production volumes is therefore intended to be exports, notably to Europe and Asia. This may prove to be a heroic strategy in the face of a maturing global market and industry, with the rapid consolidation of the mega-regions.

## Malaysia

Malaysia is another case of a country deliberately targeting the automotive industry as a national development priority. In contrast to Brazil, Malaysia, as one of the 'Tiger' countries, is an economic success story. It is expected to go on growing at 8% per year through 1996, with good longer-term prospects. However, the domestic market is quite limited, having reached 181,000 in 1991 and then fallen back in 1992. Internal demand is constrained by low incomes and high prices. Domestic sales, however, are expected to increase to 275,000 by 2000. Differential tariffs and taxes favour commercial vehicles over passenger cars, and local kit assembly over vehicles imported in built-up form. The latter attract charges of 140% to 300%. Duties on components imported for local assembly operations are far lower, at 13%.

The government has strongly encouraged local assembly and production, with eight assemblers and one manufacturer active. The total number of vehicles produced and assembled reached 232,000 in 1991. Proton accounts for two-thirds of car production and 40% of all vehicles. It is heavily dependent on Mitsubishi technology and expertise and has cost at least $200 million in so far unrecovered investment. A new 'second national car project' has been agreed with Daihatsu, in order to produce lower-cost vehicles and stimulate the market further. Other projects are planned for light commercials.

Conversely, the government will encourage the expected rationalization of assemblers and raise required local content to 60% in 1996. Production – as opposed to assembly – is expected to double to 200,000 units by this date. However, hopes for a strong export-led components industry have failed to materialize. Again, the objective is to develop this sector further and to upgrade its technological content. Great hopes are pinned on exports to the ASEAN quasi-free-trade area, for both vehicles and components. As a result, Malaysia is the latest and smallest starter in a race for autarchy which it has probably lost in advance. Some argue that 'Malaysia has wasted its time in the automotive industry', to quote an opposition economist. Others suggest that its industry may become a satellite component of a Japanese-dominated East Asian automotive mega-region.

# 11

# Bleak House?
# The state of the
# automotive industry
# today

## A maturing industry

The material presented so far shows that the world automotive industry is in its mature phase. Those markets which have the level of GDP per capita to pay for extensive motorization have mainly been exploited. Volumetric demand for personal transportation has probably reached its peak. While it will not rapidly decline, developed societies will not be able to support a significant further extension of it either. Few countries are candidates for entering the First World. Most will not be able to afford mass motorization. A great extension of it would, in any case, hopelessly overload the environment and the world's energy resources.

Product and market segments have converged throughout the world and multiplied – a typical phenomenon of maturity. Industry growth is being sustained in part by government-mandated enrichment of vehicle designs but mainly through a frantic marketing-driven race for more products and more features, more frequently. Everyone wants to 'create more value' – which in fact means to sell higher-priced products.

The market is filled with irrationalities: cars that can be driven at speeds far in excess of legal limits; acceleration and handling properties far beyond the competence of most drivers; an increasing dependence on image, rather than objective value to the end user; more and more extravagant appeals to individualism and differentiation, when the car is fundamentally a tool of everyday life. There is a real risk that consumers may rebel, or simply transfer their interest, attention and premium spending money to other products and services.

The private car is heavily promoted as an instrument of personal freedom. Yet the freedom achieved becomes rapidly less as more individuals manage to acquire it. Society is expected to pick up the multiple consequential costs of mass motorization: investment in the road infrastructure, deaths and injuries, the degradation of urban and rural environments. There are already signs of rebellion against these impositions. Politicians, governments and voters are likely to become better informed, more mature and more discriminating about these matters with time. There may well be a generational change of attitudes on the way.

# A competitive restructuring on a planetary scale

The vehicle industry is fundamentally oligopolistic in nature, because of the scale effects and critical mass requirements. It is in the throes of the restructuring of its supply side. The Japanese have driven this change at the level of the vehicle manufacturers. Contrary to some received opinion, they did not flatten industry scale curves when they discovered lean production and engineering. They simply got their extended enterprises to perform to levels much closer to the theoretical curves. But the improvement in performance that resulted was such that they were able to upset the competitive equilibrium of the whole world industry.

Had they not been inhibited by a series of import restrictions and restraint agreements, they might have achieved dominance earlier on, through massive direct exports. Sooner or later, as a result not only of the strengthening of the yen but also of the requirements of lean production and supply, they would have been forced to transplant their factories. Ironically, the restraints to trade may have worked to help the Japanese vehicle manufacturers overcome their reluctance to transplant their operations into foreign cultures. Their global dominance is not yet achieved. Yet the emerging pattern is clear: by leap-frogging their competitors, the Japanese vehicle manufacturers have triggered the shift from national and regional oligopoly to global oligopoly.

The supply side of the industry is manifestly in an unstable intermediate condition. There are far too many players and a gross oversupply of product. Go to any motor show and see the number of manufacturers offering product ranges that are similarly structured and the plethora of products that are functionally identical. What is striking at most shows is not the degree of real innovation but the lack of it. There are very few really new products.

The old US industry offered a reasonable model of a self-regulating oligopoly, with the pecking order of GM roughly twice as large as Ford, itself twice as large as Chrysler, and American Motors the marginal price regulator. Because of its different fuel taxation policies, the US remained a largely separate island, in terms of product characteristics. With world market segments to a large extent homogenised, it is hard to escape the conclusion that the future world oligopoly of car manufacturers is not likely to exceed half a dozen in number.

The industry already suffers from chronic over-capacity. New, highly-competitive production capacity is driving out the old. But the adjustments are not being made fast enough. There is permanent over-optimism in volume forecasts, whether at the overall market and industry level, or in predicting the success and market penetration of new products. Everyone appears to assume that cyclical rebounds will be permanent and that their new model will win.

Underlying technologies and major design and development programmes will require world volumes to amortize their costs. Local product adaptation, applications engineering, production and sourcing will be organized into mega-regions, incorporating both First and Second World countries into tightly-managed innovation and delivery chain structures. Interestingly, the least well-structured mega-region is the Asian one. This should logically be Japanese led and structured. In fact, most of the other players in the region with any serious ambitions seem to be aiming for some degree of autarchy while borrowing Japanese technology and expertise. Witness South Korea, Malaysia and – to a degree – Taiwan. China has shown no great inclination to let Japan create its automotive industry for it. It is tempting to attribute this reluctance to become part of an automotive mega-region to continued resentment over Japan's aggression in the 1930s and 1940s. A more plausible explanation is the determination of these countries individually to pursue maximum economic growth, with co-operation and integration very much secondary considerations. But not everyone can make the automotive industry a strategic development priority and win. It may simply be too late for new entrants.

The world automotive components industry is being driven into radical restructuring as the vehicle manufacturers tighten their supply chains. Tier-1 players will have to have considerable technology and engineering resources – and a global reach. The existing regional oligopolies are moving towards a global oligopoly. Tier-2 and Tier-3 players may be able to survive on a regional or even a local service basis.

Again, there will be a homogenization of the business segment structures and a partial worldwide coalescence. The alignment to world standards of performance – Japanese-determined – will cause an enormous shake-out of resources. The Boston Consulting Group estimated that almost 50% of the employment in the European components industry would have to go for it to match Japanese levels of productivity. While the figure has been contested in the industry, whose gains in performance may have been underestimated, there is no doubt about the direction of change.

The Japanese components manufacturers have not been encouraged to transplant themselves into Europe. Yet they are penetrating it indirectly: the transplant vehicle manufacturers have initially pursued a strategy of having local suppliers improve their processes for making Japanese-designed components. They have not automatically sourced from the established large European firms. Local content needs to be closely looked at, too: the goods may be purchased in Europe (the basis for the measurement of local content) but the intellectual property remains in Japan. This is particularly true for the most critical components, such as electronics hardware and software.

## The obstacles to change

If God is so clearly on the side of the big – and better-organized – battalions, why is the result so long in emerging? The reason is that the automotive market and industry are imperfect, in the terminology of economists – as are most other markets and industries, in reality.

We are not talking about the classical economic theory of competition, based on a multitude of small players, none large enough to be able to try to influence the rules. The automotive industry is highly political. However much it may seek to portray itself as operating on free enterprise principles, it continuously seeks to influence political decisions. This is inevitable: an industry which encompasses up to 13% of GNP cannot be wholly a matter of *laissez-faire* for national governments. Old, outclassed industrial capacity does not simply disappear overnight, in recognition of the superiority of the new. There is generally a protracted and costly struggle first. This is equally true in non-industrial parts of the sector: the multitude of small, independent, aftermarket, parts distributors ought to be displaced by new, efficient, continental-scale players. But they will not give in that fast. The industry – like most others – is full of vested interests.

In some cases, barriers are quite deliberately maintained. The clearest case of this is the franchised distribution and retailing system for cars. Most vehicle manufacturers have an immense vested interest – a life-or-death one in some cases – in maintaining their hold over a set of small, separate, franchised dealers. Dealer bodies and associations may complain about the manufacturers' behaviour but have very little power to counteract it. The idea of powerful national distributors who might pick and choose between marques and models on the basis of their experience of what appeals and sells is terrifying to the manufacturers. The automotive industry refuses to contemplate the transfer of power from producer to distributor that has already taken place in so many other consumer products, whether durable or consumable.

## Future prospects

Whatever the temporary impediments, economic rationality usually wins out in the end. Ultimately, there will be a world oligopoly of vehicle manufacturers. They will still be the architects of the industry. They will read markets and anticipate their needs. They will determine the product concepts and make the choices of technology to incorporate. They will own the product brands. But, they will delegate much more, to stronger and much more capable partners, both upstream and downstream.

The upstream partners will be a limited set of global Tier-1 systems suppliers. These will be the major developers and maintainers of the technology that goes into vehicles. They will in their turn be supported by Tier-2 and Tier-3 partners.

The downstream partners could well be major national or even regional groups that take on the responsibility for distribution, retailing and after-sales support of vehicles. They would develop the strategies and capabilities for these activities. They will be the Tier-1 players in distribution. In their turn, they will be supported by Tier-2 and Tier-3 partners: local franchisees and sub-franchisees, whom they will be free to choose. In this vision, much of the traditional distinction between franchised and independent aftercare could disappear.

Geographically, Europe will be the primary battleground for the next few years. The reason is twofold: the failure to rationalize the European car industry, leaving six major volume players, each strong in a national market but thin elsewhere in Europe, and only two large upline specialists; and the fact that no European car manufacturer is global. If car manufacturers reduce their upstream and downstream integration but broaden their geographical spread, then the Europeans start with a fatal handicap, compared to the three Japanese and two American majors. They are large but weak and are all in defensive positions. All have failed to crack the largest single national market, the United States. None has decisively broken out of its national *laager* in Europe. They can sustain defensive barriers around these national home bases but they have been unable to create an effective common one around Europe.

For better or for worse, the UK has encouraged the three major Japanese suppliers to transplant onto its territory. The European restraint agreement is only temporary. It does buy time for the European manufacturers to improve their competitiveness. But it does not get them out of their defensive positions. The choice is a painful one: suffer the consequences of having missed the step-change to globalization, or attempt to close off Europe as a separate mega-region within the global automotive industry. The latter option may no longer even be open.

Having survived the Japanese onslaught on their home market, at tremendous cost, the two US majors – GM and Ford – are by no means out of the game. They have long been the most global players – since long before the Japanese started to transplant themselves. They know how to run multinational enterprises on a large scale. They have made enormous efforts to improve their capabilities and this is beginning to show through in their performance. The situation in the US has probably now stabilized to close to its future equilibrium: dominated by the two US and three Japanese global players. Others will gradually get squeezed out, as they fall behind in the race for global scale and resources.

Asia will be the other area of major change and consolidation. The Hyundais and Protons will not be major global players on their own. Pacts will have to be formed. With the Japanese majors, if that is politically and culturally acceptable. With the US majors, perhaps. Or with Europeans: the only semi-global European is Volkswagen, which has put down a strong stake in China.

Whether they will have the financial resources to co-develop an Asian pole is debatable, however. Major horizontal strategic alliances are not easy to set up and manage well: there is always a tendency for one partner to try to use the alliance to achieve dominance. The Volvo-Renault fiasco clearly shows the dangers of politics overshadowing industrial logic. Cultural barriers and historic loyalties are difficult to overcome. Another global player may be born of a future alliance but its integration process will start a generation behind that of the others.

Global automotive markets are well into the maturity phase. The industry itself still has some way to go to match them. There will be much structural change required. Some of it will be difficult and painful.

# Summary of Part Two

Enormous structural and competitive changes can and do take place – even in mature industries. Considerable effort may be required to understand, master and effectively exploit them, rather than having to suffer their consequences:

- Segmentation is rarely as obvious as it seems and is also constantly changing. A product-based segmentation may be appropriate in the growth phase but be replaced by a market-based one as the industry matures. Segmentation is not fixed but changes according to demand and the actions of competitors. It can certainly be changed by competitors alert enough to the opportunities.

- Scale curves can be shifted. What was once sufficient, in terms of scale, can be made sub-optimal by the investment of competitors. That may be investment in plant, in products, in distribution or in the encouragement of new legislation. Shifting the scale curve is a major strategic opportunity for any business, but is frequently overlooked.

- Radical changes on the supply side – often related to increasing scale of operations – can completely reshape an industry. Mass production involves the standardization of components and the division of operations into repetitive tasks, both elements becoming highly reproducible and thus requiring less direct control. Lean production reverses the day-to-day relationship between demand and supply, and also involves considerable delegation of authority. Such changes can lead to huge competitive upsets.

- Capabilities, that enable one to determine one's future, matter more than assets inherited from the past. Thus apparently secure market positions can be swept away by a competitor with a new approach to production. Well-established brands, frequently capitalized on balance sheets, are far from invincible. The market is ultimately rational. If a competitor develops a product that offers better value, without the image associated with established brands, it will win – as long as it is given the necessary support throughout the supply chain.

- Strengths can become weaknesses and vice versa. Massive variations in product offerings, intended to give consumers more choice, involve a different trade-off with manufacturing efficiency and therefore cost. Less choice can mean lower cost and so strategic advantage. Greater manufacturing flexibility and leanness can make it possible to reconcile greater variety with limited and acceptable increases in cost.

- Maturing markets need very different strategies from growth markets or those at other stages in their lifecycle. This may appear simple, yet few businesses seem to realize this or practise it. Few managers seem to want to accept that their markets are maturing and change their strategies accordingly. After all, it's not an easy message to convey to a shareholders' meeting. It also runs against the ego of the ambitious manager.

- Management of the 'extended enterprise' is crucial. Companies and products do not exist in isolation. They depend on suppliers and distributors, who are critical to the success of a product in the market-place. Managing a business or deciding a product strategy while ignoring the upstream and downstream parts of the supply chain is sub-optimal. It also offers major opportunities to competitors.

- Attempts to defy the laws of economics through import quotas and other restraints on trade, for example, will fail in the long term. Consumers may still have imperfect knowledge in many markets but information flows are improving, thanks to the growth of the media and communications industries. Barriers of any sort that try to protect a region or part of the supply chain are usually inefficient for the market, and in the long term for the suppliers within that market.

- Manufacturers need to manage the whole of their supply chain but they also need to look wider too and to manage the back-seat drivers – the other industries and bodies that depend on their particular sector. Companies need to ask themselves, 'Who else has a vested interest in my industry?' 'What influence could they have?' 'What can we do to keep them on our side?'

- In many established industries in the Triad the emergence of entirely new competitors from other parts of the world is unlikely. Locally-based, non-Triad suppliers face almost insurmountable barriers to gain the scale necessary for success. Growing local markets and low factor costs are not by themselves enough to break into a major global industry. On the other hand, neglecting such markets may be to hand a vital opportunity to another established competitor.

# Markets and
# the outlook
# for demand

# 12

# Global cooling: the overall prospects

## The political outlook

In general, political stability is expected to continue in the core regions of the Triad. Little political change is anticipated for most countries during the next few years, although a number of countries are expected to confront new challenges. Many parts of Western Europe, for example, are likely to experience problems due to the influx of economic refugees from Eastern Europe and Africa. Similarly, ethnic difficulties are anticipated in India and parts of Eastern Europe.

There are a number of potential flash points, however. We have considered the likelihood of military activity that would affect the future of the automotive industry in a number of regions. Of the possible conflicts considered, there were a number that were significant in that, were they to occur, then the demand for passenger cars in that country or region would be severely impacted. The most prominent of these are in the Pacific/South China Sea, where conflicts could arise over land and mineral rights, in the Middle East and North Africa, where a number of issues could spark military activity, and in the former Eastern bloc nations, where civil war or cross-border incursions are possible or likely. There is also the possibility of civil war in China.

Unrest is most likely in Eastern Europe. Although the likelihood of some automotive markets being effectively destroyed by war, at least temporarily, is small, the possibility of armed conflict affecting car demand in some countries is real. The highest chance of military action was felt to be in the old Eastern bloc countries, with a probability of civil unrest highlighted in the projections. Only the CIS, however, risks following the pattern seen in the former Yugoslavia.

Such unrest is only detailed to the extent to which it is likely to affect the rate of economic and social development. Other areas where civil disturbances may be anticipated include parts of South America and India. The chance of some sort of war in the Middle East is also high.

# Drivers of demand

There are several major drivers to change in the Triad. First, growth rates will generally be low and manufacturers will need to differentiate themselves by some means other than price in order to gain greater market share. These markets are likely to be characterized by:

- Automotive end customers who are increasingly knowledgeable about what they buy. This is expected to force vehicle manufacturers to change both their products and their delivery mechanisms.
- A market for passenger cars that is being increasingly fragmented by more varied and selective end customer needs.
- A rapid growth in environmental pressures particularly on emissions, fuel economy, component recycling and vehicle use.
- Increased competition as national and regional barriers continue to fall.

These pressures for more varied and environmentally acceptable cars, together with the growth in competition, are expected to create real issues for survival, forcing many vehicle manufacturers to enter alliances or consolidate further.

In less mature markets the issues are not as complex. The principal drivers of new passenger car demand in the less mature markets, such as many of those in South East Asia and some of the former Soviet bloc countries, are much simpler. Demand is typically determined by:

- The political environment and its stability;
- The rate of economic development;
- The ability of consumers to fulfil their desires for passenger car ownership and move away from rail and public transport. This is largely a function of the real income levels and the distribution of wealth in each country.

Even so, competition will be just as tough. The total volume of cars manufactured and sold in these markets is much lower than in the more mature countries. The growth rates are much higher, however, and the expectations of consumers and legislators easier to meet. Vehicle manufacturers in mature markets are therefore likely to be attracted to these countries to achieve their growth objectives. Many have already entered them, often quite aggressively, to plant seeds for sales beyond the year 2000. The degree of competition present is none the less expected to rise considerably, ensuring that potential new car sales in these markets become far more difficult to achieve for individual competitors.

# The automotive outlook

Sales of passenger cars are forecast to grow by 2.4% a year to the year 2000. The breakdown by country and region is given in Figure 12.1. The highest growth rates are expected in Asia and South America. In China, India and South East Asia the rate of growth is expected to be considerably higher then the average. China is forecast to grow at an annual rate of nearly 22%. Car demand in most of South America is also forecast to grow at well above the world average.

| | | | |
|---|---|---|---|
| China | 21.9% | Czech Republic | 4.1% |
| Norway | 11.1% | Greece | 3.8% |
| Mexico | 11.0% | UK | 3.3% |
| India | 10.8% | Canada | 2.7% |
| Peru | 10.0% | **World** | **2.4%** |
| Malaysia | 10.0% | US | 2.3% |
| Sweden | 9.8% | Spain | 2.3% |
| Finland | 9.8% | Denmark | 2.0% |
| Venezuela | 8.3% | Portugal | 1.5% |
| Taiwan | 8.3% | Luxembourg | 1.4% |
| South East Asia | 8.3% | France | 1.3% |
| South Korea | 8.2% | Eastern Europe | 1.3% |
| Philippines | 8.2% | Western Europe | 1.2% |
| Argentina | 8.1% | Switzerland | 1.2% |
| Thailand | 7.7% | Japan | 1.0% |
| Hungary | 6.8% | Netherlands | 0.9% |
| Colombia | 6.7% | Poland | 0.8% |
| South America & | 6.4% | Brazil | 0.6% |
| Mexico | | Italy | 0.5% |
| Uruguay | 6.3% | CIS | 0.3% |
| Bulgaria | 6.1% | Belgium | 0.2% |
| Chile | 5.3% | Germany | 0.2% |
| Ecuador | 5.2% | Romania | 0.0% |
| Indonesia | 4.8% | Austria | −0.4% |
| Republic of Ireland | 4.3% | Yugoslavia | n.a. |

**Figure 12.1**   Forecast of compound annual growth rates for new car sales by country and region from 1992 to 2000. (*Source*: EIU, Global Car Forecasts)

Little growth is expected in the largest markets. For Western Europe, the United States and Japan, the world's largest economic regions, passenger car registrations and production are expected to remain relatively flat during the forecast period to the year 2000. Growth will be particularly slow over the next few years in much of Western Europe and Japan.

A number of structural changes are taking place within the mature markets for passenger cars. Most notable of these is the level of market saturation that has now been achieved and which constrains further new growth in many countries. In the medium term, the anticipated growth in legislation, higher taxes and restrictions on use will make car ownership increasingly less attractive than today. This will affect the usage rates and so the frequency of replacement. There is also expected to be a much greater emphasis on alternative forms of transport such as rail travel, particularly within Western Europe.

The high growth rates anticipated in most of Scandinavia are misleading. The huge decline in demand for passenger cars in Norway, Sweden and Finland, due to the recession in these countries, has led to annual sales well below normal levels. As these markets recover, car demand is expected to return to previous levels. From such a low base, this generates very high annual growth rates. As the markets are simply returning to their historic levels, these growth rates are distorted.

Most of Eastern Europe is expected to experience below average growth. Most of the former Eastern bloc countries have suffered during the last few years. The transformation to free-market economics has led to considerable hardships. Savings have been eroded and, for many, incomes have fallen. While demand for cars has remained high, most of the consumers that can still afford them are buying used vehicles from Western Europe. As a result, demand for new cars has fallen and is forecast to continue to fall before a recovery is anticipated in 1995.

There are exceptions, however, such as Hungary and the Czech Republic, where free-market philosophies are already bringing benefits, and new car demand is forecast to grow above the world average.

# 13

# World War Three: the European battleground

## The main battleground

If Europe is to be the main battleground, what are the options for European vehicle manufacturers and governments in this, potentially the most bloody of battles? Sadly, there are few left. The position of the European motor industry's suppliers is not good, even if their sales figures within the region appear superficially attractive. In contrast, the position of their competitors is strong. Continuing the military analogy, the Europeans have little ammunition left. They cannot fight with superior technology or lower costs, because the economies of scale of their competitors are greater. They cannot fight using improved production processes, shorter replacement cycles or innovative designs. Their competitors already set the world standards for these. The options we have identified therefore are largely unattractive. At a broad level, there are seven:

(1)   Try to make friends with the Japanese
(2)   Legislate against non-European competitors
(3)   Adopt guerrilla tactics
(4)   Follow the UK's example
(5)   Take the path of controlled degradation
(6)   Forge some global mergers
(7)   Adopt Chrysler's example, become a virtual VM.

## (1) Make friends with the Japanese

An obvious military option is to call for a truce, negotiate a peace, and divide up the territory along mutually agreed lines. There are a number of practical problems with this, however.

First, the European car industry cannot negotiate a truce with its competitors on its own. It no longer has enough to offer. It cannot say, 'OK, we are happy to stick to a Japanese share of, say, 25% in Europe (it is about half that today) provided we can build our share in Japan and the USA'. Although this is an arbitrary figure, too much above this would lead to inevitable casualties among the four major Europeans.

The trouble is, why on earth should the Japanese accept the offer, when they can simply continue to penetrate the European markets as they are today? It is offering them a small slice of the cake, when they are perfectly capable of taking much more. Their share in some parts of Europe is already nearly 50%.

Second, even if they agreed to a truce, to a fixed share of the market, the European car industry would remain in a hopelessly weak position. The main manufacturers would remain dependent on a high-cost region. Given that, and their increasingly marginal share of the world cake, developing new sales in the other major markets would be even more difficult for them than it was in the past. Worse, the Europeans would have lost the competitive initiative in their domestic markets; they would not be defining the competitive arena at home. That position is not sustainable.

To achieve some sort of truce in Europe would therefore need massive government intervention on a broad scale. The EU would need to find some sort of bargaining counter, some incentive or threat, that would ensure the Japanese agreed to limit their attack on the automotive sector. For example, the EU might threaten legislation that would exclude the Japanese from competing in other economic sectors. It would be easiest to select areas where they are weak today, such as retail banking or insurance. Unless they offered an equitable and mutually agreeable arrangement to limit their assault on the motor industry, they would be excluded from these markets.

This, however, also has serious problems. First, it is unlikely to be in the interests of consumers to limit competition in this way, especially in the long term. Second, there is always the risk that one part of the EU must break the spirit of the agreement, as the UK did with the car industry. The third major problem is the capability of the EU to negotiate a binding agreement. Foreign policy problems over the Gulf War, the civil war in Bosnia and even the Uruguay round of GATT show it often encounters problems in showing a unified face to the outside world. As a result, although the idea of a negotiated peace may be attractive in theory, it is unlikely to work in practice.

## (2) Legislate against non-European competitors

If the EU had the will, it could re-erect trade barriers. It could maintain the quotas beyond 1999 and could extend them to cover the transplant factories as well. This would certainly be favoured by the French in particular.

Trade barriers mean interfering in the laws of economics. A little like medieval fortifications, trade barriers can offer protection from attack but they can also leave the inhabitants isolated. Trade barriers could also result in a damaging trade war that could extend to other products. They are also rarely in the interests of consumers and encourage uncompetitiveness.

Trade barriers therefore have to be applied selectively and for a limited time. The EU has already given the industry until 1999 to reach world-class standards. Is this going to help? There are two critical questions.

First, can the European vehicle manufacturers achieve world-class standards by 1999? The answer is probably no, unless there is a massive restructuring of the industry supply chain. (That is, they become virtual vehicle manufacturers, as discussed in option 7.) If the structure remains as today, then the investment required in plant and technology is probably beyond the purse of the four largest vehicle manufacturers in Europe. They all experienced heavy losses in the early 1990s, all have enormous investment in brown-field sites and limited resources. Some also suffer from inertia. All of them are already behind world-class levels and falling further behind each year. So, the likelihood of each of the top four manufacturers becoming world class by 1999 when the quotas fall is very low indeed.

Second, if they were given extra time, would that improve their chances? No, not really. Not unless they seek alliances or radically restructure the supply chain. They are behind now and are falling further behind each year. There is little chance that they can catch up. To make it worse, each of the top four manufacturers in Europe would remain overly dependent on sales in the region, already lacks the scale and breadth necessary to be global and could not afford the investment required, without massive government support. Indeed, they would become even less competitive, because of their dependence on a high-cost region.

Trade barriers hold competitors back, they do not fix the long-term problem. They will not make European vehicle manufacturers world-class because legislation creates a protectionist region and an industry that is not economically sustainable. As the industry accounts for such a large proportion of GNP, this creates an economic and social time bomb. One other major drawback: if you protect one industry with trade barriers, they'll all want it – and many other segments of the economy would face the prospect of only being competitive within one region.

The option of raising trade barriers is unlikely to be valuable in itself. If it is combined with other options it might be. If the EU and automotive suppliers sought global alliances, or the industry was heavily restructured, then trade barriers might play a part. They may also be useful if the EU were to offer massive investment to the industry, to help it become world-class. They may be applied selectively – for example, against the South Koreans, who have enjoyed tariff-free entry to Europe so far. On their own, quotas will not solve the problems.

## (3) Adopt guerrilla tactics

When the US was fighting in Vietnam, it had every strategic advantage. The problem was that saying 'you're beaten' had no effect on the enemy, who kept on fighting. They simply did not understand what 'you're beaten' means. The result, of course, was that the US had to engage in a costly and protracted guerrilla war that became politically and morally unacceptable.

There are lessons here that may prove useful to the Europeans in defending their motor industry. Never let the competitors win, never stop fighting. Like the Vietnamese, this means fighting at the micro rather than the macro level.

Fighting at the macro level means developing new cars that are better than those made by the Japanese and achieving better market share. As we have seen this is likely to be extremely difficult, given the position of European manufacturers today. Fighting at the micro level means encouraging sales of European vehicles in preference to those made by the Japanese, even though they may be less competent. This was one of the strategies adopted by Ford and GM in North America, and with some success.

Micro-level fighting is competing for the hearts, rather than the minds, of car buyers. It uses marketing and advertising at a regional and a local level to encourage nationalistic buying. It is, in effect, an attempt to turn the clock back, to the time when everyone bought locally-manufactured vehicles. The difference this time is that they buy local products because they want to, not because they have no other choice.

It is, of course, a dangerous policy in some respects, in that it encourages ethnocentricity, regionalism or nationalism. Focused correctly it can reflect national or regional pride, as happened when the strategy was adopted in North America. There, nationalistic buying was a statement of confidence in the economy and the country. It said 'I believe in what made America great'. Ironically, this micro-level competition is also that most used by the Japanese in Japan. The trade barriers are not to keep out competitors explicitly, but simply because they reflect national sentiment. Japanese buyers, in general, prefer to be loyal to their own economy and to their own industries.

If this strategy were to be consciously adopted it should, of course, be regional, pan-European. The national level is too small and, in fact, already superseded in industrial and market terms. Yet this is unlikely on the demand side. While the European Union now exists, it still has some way to go before the majority of its citizens feel 'European'. Most still regard themselves as German, Greek, Spanish or French first and European second. Even if they did feel 'European' there is no guarantee that this would change buying behaviour. Indeed, the country that promotes itself most as the home of the 'Young European', Ireland, has the highest penetration of Japanese vehicles in the region!

Micro-level competition is most likely to be successful in specific countries, where nationalist sentiment remains strongest. These are probably France, Italy, and perhaps Germany and the Iberian Peninsula. Ironically, the British, despite their lukewarm approach to Europe, are no longer particularly nationalistic in their consumption patterns. Neither are the other countries, although this may be partly because they no longer have – or never have had – large indigenous motor industries. Even Sweden, where Volvo is based, is not dominated by its local producer today. Even so, the markets of France, Italy, Germany, Spain and Portugal are substantial, accounting for nearly three-quarters of all new car sales in the region. If the citizens of these countries could be encouraged to buy with their hearts and not their minds, the braking effect on future Japanese sales in the region could be considerable.

Each of these markets is already reasonably nationalistic in its buying patterns, although they are becoming less so. In Spain and Portugal, nearly two-thirds of all new cars sold are made by the top four European manufacturers, Volkswagen, Peugeot, Renault and Fiat. In France, 60% of the new cars sold are made by the local manufacturers while another 16% are made by Volkswagen and Fiat. In Italy, Fiat accounts for nearly one in two cars sold, while Peugeot, Renault and Volkswagen take up another 29%. In Germany, Volkswagen accounts for a third of sales while the other large European producers are responsible for an additional 14%. If you add the sales of BMW and Mercedes-Benz, then European-owned vehicle manufacturers account for nearly half the market.

One of the problems with this strategy is that it means reversing a trend. As recently as 1987, Fiat accounted for 60% of sales in Italy, yet its share is falling sharply. It is a similar story in France for Renault and Peugeot. To make this strategy work, this trend would have to be stopped and reversed before the share of the indigenous manufacturers falls even further. If it gets much worse in some countries, like Germany, the trend may become irreversible.

There are several other major drawbacks to this strategy. If it did work, it would probably discourage any industrial restructuring. It would, in effect, partly push the industry back from a regional oligopoly to a national one. That is counter to the direction of current economic forces. The strategy would also encourage competitive inertia.

The distribution network is a critical part of this strategy – it is the front end of the battle, where the industry and the buyers meet. It is here that the consumer must decide that his nationalistic sentiment overrides his financial and economic logic. No wonder the European vehicle manufacturers are so sensitive about the issue of the renegotiation of the Block Exemption!

The final major problem with this option is that it serves the producers, not the consumers. Some would argue that that is in the national interest. That said, it is probably possible to maintain a strategy of micro-level competition for quite a long time, if everyone plays the game. After all, the Japanese have certainly managed to maintain it pretty well since the Edo period ended and the country supposedly opened up with the Meiji Restoration in 1867.

## (4) Take the UK government view

By the end of the 1970s the UK knew that its indigenous motor industry would never reach world-class standards, even if the government did not acknowledge it publicly. British Leyland was an industrial dinosaur. All the government could hope for was a sustainable niche, or to ensure that Leyland survived until it became saleable. The sale of Rover to BMW in 1994 was the final acknowledgment of the UK's position.

As a result, the British government decided that the best it could do was attract new suppliers. This would increase employment, stimulate exports and develop the manufacturing sector. If the vehicle manufacturers were Japanese, perhaps the components could be British.

In retrospect, their strategy has been reasonably successful, in terms of achieving its original objectives. Leyland became Austin Rover and then the Rover Group, used Honda to modernize its processes and was eventually sold. New entrants set up large manufacturing plants, generated export revenues and offered employment. Although the British share of the components business is not as great as hoped, the strategy generally worked well. Who cares if the UK has no national vehicle manufacturer? The economy has regained a strong industrial sector and, although some of the profits are repatriated to Japan, there is a good deal of local added-value.

Most of the objections within the UK to the loss of Rover were therefore largely emotional, it seemed. 'The country has a strong car industry and that's what matters,' said the government. Additionally, the UK share of components supply might grow, and further investment is likely from the Japanese component industry.

Of course, one of the major problems with the strategy was that it allowed the Japanese to circumvent EU import quotas and gain access to the rest of Europe. It played a major role in creating the problems that the region now faces.

So, what if this strategy was adopted throughout the region? The Europeans would have to accept that their vehicle manufacturers were unlikely to become world class again. They would have to welcome new Japanese investment with open arms. They would have to seek new parents or partners for their remaining indigenous manufacturers. They would have to accept that their greatest share of the added-value would be at the component level. On the positive side, if Europeans adopted this strategy, they might once again have the prospect of exporting large numbers of vehicles to the USA and Japan.

This is clearly an option, although not a very palatable one, particularly as few of the local manufacturers are ready to acknowledge their problems. If the Europeans did adopt this option, the Japanese and Americans would clean up. It would create a truly global industry – but without any major Europeans.

Yet this is precisely what is happening. All this strategy does is to accelerate the current trend. While we think we have watched the Japanese assault on the USA and have learned from it, it is the other way round. The Japanese have learned from past mistakes. Instead of taking 20 years to build their share to 30% or more, they are likely to dominate Europe far more quickly. The industry is so fragmented in Europe. It's so easy. They've already captured the small markets.

One attractive part of the strategy is that there is an opportunity in components, particularly electronics. Added-value and intelligence in vehicles is moving increasingly into electronic components and systems and away from mechanical actuation. If the European component suppliers could retain a substantial share of this business, they would remain on part of the high ground. After all, any employment is acceptable, from the point of view of governments, and if the objective is to retain some sort of control over the design, engineering and the 'feel' of future motor vehicles, then electronics may be the key.

The biggest losers would be Peugeot, Renault, Fiat and Volkswagen – the others in the 'Big Six', Opel and Ford, are already part of global operations. The major problem with this option is more emotional than rational. It is most unlikely that the European vehicle manufacturers would ever admit that they could not become world class again themselves. After all, Rover never did. This is therefore the single biggest reason why it will not be adopted, at least not explicitly.

## (5) Controlled degradation

As we have seen, it will be difficult for the European vehicle manufacturers to become world class without some radically new approach. That may mean rationalization, government support or the extension of trade barriers. One other option is through alliances.

Joint ventures and alliances are, by their very nature, unstable. They are therefore risky unless managed carefully. Many European companies look on them as marriages, as the joining together of two companies to achieve some mutual objective. They should be the open, supportive and long-lived relationships, they claim to be. Yet, this is naïve. Alliances are 'sleeping with the enemy', the joining together of two competitors, two companies that both need help to achieve their objectives.

The Japanese use alliances to gain market entry, to improve their share, to learn. In the US, Mitsubishi's Diamond Star plant is a means of avoiding foreign exchange exposure and increasing its market share. From there it supplies Chrysler with vehicles and engines that will be fitted into the US company's vehicles. It also assembles its own vehicles for sale locally. The relationship with Chrysler simply makes all this more acceptable, it is the Trojan horse. The same is true of Toyota's alliance with General Motors, Nummi, and of Suzuki's arrangement with Chevrolet. Honda's abortive relationship with Rover allowed it to learn about European vehicle buying and design. It also allowed the Japanese firm to sell more of its vehicles in Europe using the badge of a local supplier.

The difference is that while European and American companies are to a degree naïve about alliances, the Japanese approach them in a very structured and disciplined way. This was evident in a joint venture between a European and a Japanese component supplier. While both had similar objectives, their approach to the alliance was very different. The European supplier was happy to arrange for meetings that involved discussion of broader strategic objectives. Employees at all levels were encouraged to meet with the partner to help develop the relationship. However, they were never briefed, other than being told that the Japanese firm was a partner that would help it develop a new system.

The approach of the Japanese firm was much more systematic. It assigned staff at all levels particular objectives. It matched them to individuals in the partner company. Some were to concentrate on electronics knowledge, others on sensors and others on overall strategy. They were to collect data on the competitor, its markets and its *modus operandi*. They were also to give as much help as possible to the development of the new system – but they were not to discuss any other part of their own company's business.

The alliance achieved its objectives. It successfully developed a new system, which is being sold by both companies today. But it also resulted in a massive leeching of information from the European supplier, which is now more vulnerable to attack and more dependent on its Japanese partner for success. Conversely, the Japanese firm is now wiser and more capable. Critically, the system is now a vital product in the European company's future growth plans – and a marginal one for the Japanese.

The point and the opportunity are clear. Players in any business can gain strategic advantage from joint ventures and alliances. By putting a spy in your competitor's camp, you can learn from them.

This is therefore an option for European vehicle manufacturers. If they are technically behind, then they should try to learn from those that are in front. They should seek out the world's best practice, replicate it and improve on it. Competitive leeching is a means of leap-frogging competitors, a way of reducing them to a lower rank, a process of controlled degradation.

In theory this is a perfectly valid option. In practice there are several problems. First, it ideally needs to be organized on a pan-European level. Each of the top four manufacturers should have equal access to knowledge. It should also be applied at the component level, the research level and include distribution and marketing. The problem is: who's in charge? Alliances on many levels and covering many products and systems need centralized co-ordination. Otherwise it would be like trying to fight a war without any central command structure. But, where can this control come from? It is well outside the scope of the EU in Brussels and beyond the competence and scale of most national governments. There is no European equivalent of MITI (the Ministry for International Trade and Industry in Japan).

The second major problem is time. Competitive leeching takes years, sometimes decades. The position of the European industry is already weak. It is therefore unlikely to have the time to adopt such an approach.

The third barrier is cultural. In many alliances, one of the most important pressures for agreement arises from the egos of managers involved. Most European managers have little or no experience in serious commercial negotiation, particularly across cultures. They do, however, thrive in a culture where action is rewarded, where the ability to 'make things happen' is a sure sign of future advancement. Senior European managers are often obsessed with their status and are frequently driven by what is good for them, rather than what is good for the company. Indeed, the structure of companies often encourages individualism and selfishness, because it rewards these traits.

As a result, many managers 'cut deals' that are far from optimal and often not in the best long-term interest of their employers. While there may be short-term gains, and certainly short-term kudos, any longer-term difficulties are unlikely to arise until the managers responsible for the deal have moved on. Managers in European companies move between companies frequently.

Japanese managers, on the other hand, tend to remain with their companies throughout their working careers. They therefore have to live with the results of their decisions. Culturally, they also think more of the broader good, rather than simply of themselves.

There is therefore a serious cultural barrier in Europe (and North America) that creates latent problems in joint ventures and alliances from the outset. Roles and objectives are often badly defined in European companies. Managers tend to be more self-seeking. The benefits of the alliance are therefore less predictable. Overcoming these cultural problems to implement this strategy would be very difficult.

## (6) Forge some global merger

Another clear option for the European vehicle manufacturers is to forge some global mergers. This may be with partners outside Europe or within the region. The proposed partnership between Renault and Volvo was an example of the type of merger that is likely in the next decade. Unfortunately that merger did not come off.

The idea behind this strategic option is that these mergers are going to happen anyway. So why not encourage them? Why not make them happen? Having established that, the range of options is clearly very broad. Previous attempts at mergers provide examples. Ford could yet link with Fiat, and more probably with Mazda. After all, Fiat and Ford have already looked at the possibility of a broad link, while Ford owns 30% of Mazda. Both Mazda and Fiat are sub-scale and although Ford is large enough it is overly dependent on the US and Europe. This three-way link has an industrial logic, as it would allow the creation of a truly global capability.

Similarly, a merger of BMW/Rover with Honda would have advantages based on economic logic – whatever Honda's apparent pique at having Rover snatched away. The options for Volkswagen and the two French suppliers are less obvious. There are candidates outside Europe in a similar position that may offer possible link-ups. Chrysler is a regional player, with some skills that are relevant in Europe. Similarly, Hyundai, Kia and Ssangyong in Korea need partners to become global. Daihatsu, Suzuki and Subaru in Japan are also sub-scale regional competitors, needing broader support. There is also Volvo and Mercedes-Benz within Europe, although they are less attractive.

Within this *mélange,* there are some interesting possibilities. There may also be some vehicle manufacturers who are attractive to those competitors who are already global in their own right. But care must be exercised in this. It is easy, for example, to assume that BMW and Mercedes-Benz are particularly attractive because they are traditional and upline. This is not necessarily true. Although the value of BMW and

Mercedes-Benz may seem obvious, most of their competitors – and particularly the Japanese – will ultimately be capable of replicating their skills without much difficulty.

It is impossible to predict which mergers will occur, although they are one of the most obvious strategic alternatives. It is clear, however, that several manufacturers could benefit by merging – and that many will simply have to. It is equally clear that those who realize this first are most likely to find a partner that suits them.

## (7) Follow Chrysler's example, become a virtual vehicle manufacturer

Another option for Europe's car manufacturers would be to follow the strategy adopted by Chrysler in the US and move closer to what we have called the 'virtual vehicle manufacturer'. Doing this involves a radical change in approach and strategy, and the acceptance of a much lower share of the total added-value.

A virtual vehicle manufacturer is one that, at the extreme, does not make a car at all! It would be responsible for the design and integration of the car, particularly the electronics and the software, and define its feel, look and image – but it does not need to assemble it itself.

There is enormous emotional attachment to the assembly line today, yet the vehicle manufacturer's share of a car's added value is already only around a third of the total. A third of a car's value is accounted for by components, while roughly another third is absorbed in sales, marketing, distribution and dealer margins. The car manufacturer's share of the total value chain is therefore comparatively small. It is certainly much lower than that of major players in industries such as chemicals, financial services and oil, for example, which are much more vertically integrated.

The concept of the virtual VM is not, therefore, such a huge step. Assuming the car manufacturer retains control of the essential elements, it simply means divesting itself of assembly and other non-identity-specific products or systems. It may mean reducing the added value to less than 20% and it may mean concentrating on electronics and software, but it can allow much better exploitation of the comparative advantages of others. Imagine a car advertised as follows:

'The new BMW 9 series. Exterior design by Pininfarina, interior styling by Christian Dior, ride perfected by Lotus, communications and navigation by Southern Bell, entertainment by Sony, engine technology by Honda, assembled by the Renault-Fiat consortium... systems integration by BMW.'

The point is that a car can be developed and built by a number of different people each contributing to the finished product. The most important part of the process is putting all of the parts together – although not necessarily putting them together physically. It is defining the style of the car, the feel, the image, the quality and the overall ride and handling that are critical. The skill is in defining how the systems integrate.

The idea of a virtual vehicle manufacturer, although perhaps not as extreme as the example above, is therefore a valid strategic option for the European majors faced with a competitive hurdle. They could increase their use of the scale of others and thereby improve their competitiveness by out-sourcing more of the components and subsystems. It is, effectively, Adam Smith's (on Henry Ford's) notion of specialization taken a stage further – instead of each task being done separately, each subsystem is created separately. The assembler concentrates on the production line, the suspension expert on the chassis and the engine specialist on the fuel economy and performance, for example. The virtual vehicle manufacturer concentrates on how all these subsystems interact together.

Vehicle manufacturers in Europe could access world-class scale and technology by this route, because they would avoid the need for direct investment in these. Suppliers, who may already be global, or who may have a broader base of customers outside the automotive industry, could invest in the technology and capabilities. European vehicle manufacturers would be much better placed to compete with leaner competitors.

# Summary and conclusions

None of these options are particularly palatable for Europe's motor industry. Many also need government intervention if they are to work, which is not always easy. For governments, selecting the best option is dependent on maximising the long-term utility for the EU. That will make the decision largely political, and therefore fraught with problems and vested interests. Another and fundamental difficulty is that there really is no European government to take a decision. Besides, it may be that the British have already given too much away.

Are there any other options? Is there any other way that the Europeans can stop the relentless march of Japanese competitors? If there is, it would need to protect all of the major markets to be effective. If it only protected one region, the end game would be the same as today. If all the governments of Europe, the NAFTA, the ASEAN nations, the Southern Cone, China and India got together and said 'stop', they might be able to halt the Japanese advance. This is not a very plausible scenario.

# 14

# Peace in our time? The future for the NAFTA region

The future market for passenger cars in North America is relatively predictable. Long-term demand will be stable in the US and Canada, as it has been since the mid 1970s, as those markets are just about saturated. There will, of course, be the usual cyclical variations around it. The best opportunity in the region is in Mexico, with demand for passenger cars forecast to increase by more than 100% to over a million cars a year by the end of the century. This opportunity extends beyond sales into production, and there is expected to be a general southwards shift in capacity.

In terms of market positions, few dramatic changes are expected in the US and Canada, certainly in the short term. In the next few years, no significant new entrants are expected and most of the smaller manufacturers are likely to withdraw. The big fight will continue to be between the Japanese and the American vehicle manufacturers. Recently, this share battle has stabilized, with the Japanese holding just under 30% of the market.

The effect of these pressures is that some big names will face the prospect of withdrawal. These include the South Korean manufacturers, the remaining smaller Japanese suppliers and most of the Europeans. The biggest uncertainties exist for the specialist Europeans, BMW and Mercedes-Benz, the mid-sized Japanese such as Mitsubishi, but more especially Mazda, and Chrysler. Of these, the greatest hope probably exists for Mitsubishi and, ironically, its one-time partner Chrysler.

Mitsubishi has a remarkable history of success and seems unlikely to accept a sub-scale position, while Chrysler seems to keep 'pulling rabbits out of hats'. There is a real possibility that these two may also put aside past differences and join forces permanently.

In Mexico, Volkswagen is likely to lose its dominant position. Volkswagen's plant there has suffered many problems, particularly in the early 1990s. The poor quality of the vehicles and the delay in launching new models from that facility are major reasons why Volkswagen's share in the US and Canada has declined so sharply. While these problems are being addressed, VW's competitors, particularly GM, Chrysler, Nissan and Ford, are using the opportunity to develop their share in Mexico. They are almost certain to succeed in the short term, making VW's position in the region even more difficult.

Competitively, therefore, all the rough edges in the market will be trimmed fairly soon. The oligopolistic position of the top five global competitors (GM, Ford, Honda, Nissan and Toyota) plus one regional competitor (Chrysler, perhaps aligned with Mitsubishi) will strengthen. The NAFTA market foreshadows the future structure of the global industry. Ironically, it also marks a reversion to something approximating the strongly oligopolistic US and Canadian competitive structures in the era before the import and transplant invasions. In those now long-distant days, GM had twice the market share of Ford, which had twice that of Chrysler, which effectively acted as industry regulator. GM, with its superior scale and therefore cost position would regularly earn better returns. But it could not use its superiority to drive prices below the survival level for Chrysler, as this would violate anti-trust law. American Motors, the fourth domestic player, and the imports moved in and out of the fringes of the market. This was a stable, self-regulating, closed system – until it was upset by CAFE, downsizing and the Japanese incursion.

## The wild card

The long-term wild card in the North American market is the zero emissions vehicle. Legislation is in place that favours it and seems unlikely to be withdrawn. The potential impact is enormous, as it requires yet another fundamental redesign of cars. Such a step would throw the whole competitive system open again. It looks like another enormous imposition on the industry, forcing players to write off their colossal past investments in existing designs and technologies. Conversely, it can be viewed as a challenge that greatly favours those willing and able to develop and deploy the capabilities required to meet it. This could present the Japanese with just the opportunity they need to increase their penetration still further.

First, there will be a technological race to identify the preferred and most practical means of achieving low or zero emissions vehicles. That will carry on well beyond 1998, when the first ZEVs are due to appear. Battery technology is far from the only solution, although it is certainly the most obvious. GM's much heralded Impact is not necessarily indicative of the technologies that will ultimately be adopted.

Second, there will be the emergence of new component suppliers, who may attempt to change the structure of the value chain. Chemicals and materials companies with expertise in composites, fuels and different methods of propulsion could play a far more significant role than today. In addition, many of the common auxiliary subsystems, such as air-conditioning, engine control units and hydraulic steering systems will require fundamental changes to their design and applications.

Third, vehicle manufacturers may be forced to sell an essentially different product concept. The flexibility of today's cars may have to be sacrificed. ZEVs, certainly those using today's technologies, have a limited range and may only be appropriate for certain types of journey. They may also demand new skills from the driver/owner, require different financial arrangements for their purchase, and a new style of maintenance and storage. They are almost certainly likely to need a new fueling infrastructure.

Finally, for vehicle manufacturers, this first step towards ZEVs is almost certainly only the beginning of considerably tougher vehicle legislation. The US has in many respects led the world in terms of emissions regulations. US legislation has been adopted and amended in most of the other developed nations of the world. US controls are also becoming progressively tougher over time. Some countries are also looking at road pricing, banning vehicles from city centres and much higher vehicle taxes.

These changes are unlikely to have a major impact at the consumer level beyond the year 2000. They are, however, likely to influence the structure and direction of car manufacturers and their suppliers long before then. They are already a major preoccupation for the industry.

With the prospect of a new technology hurdle, the emergence of potentially new component suppliers, the complexities of selling a possibly different vehicle concept and even tougher legislation in prospect, the automotive industry in North America will come under considerable pressure to change.

What does this mean for individual competitors? Of the top five manufacturers in the US today, three are best placed to exploit the new challenges – Toyota, Nissan and Honda. The next best placed are the mid-sized Japanese competitors, Mazda and Mitsubishi. The traditional US competitors, the 'Big three', have resisted the changes and are not yet in a position to supply the market.

The potential impact of the wild card is very significant in the otherwise stagnant US market. For the last few years the Japanese success in the US has been tempered and they have even lost share. They have countered this by moving further upmarket, to increase their share of the total market's value, and by increasing their supply of components and unbadged vehicles to their competitors. At last, therefore, they may have the opportunity to increase their share directly once again. Were this to happen, the effect could be very significant. The two main indigenous suppliers, Ford and GM are large but vulnerable. Despite years of investment and many management changes, GM is still far from lean. Both have low margins and have suffered years of losses.

# 15

# The new empire: the globalization of the Japanese industry

The market for passenger cars in Japan grew by 50% in just a few years in the late 1980s. Since then, demand has stagnated. The number of cars per head in Japan is low, compared to other developed countries. There are only 300 cars per 1000 people, half the level one would predict in such a wealthy nation by applying the normal relationship between per capita GDP and car ownership. Although this may suggest that there is considerable room for growth, the market is in fact expected to stabilize in the future and little additional growth is anticipated.

Japan sets itself five-year plans. The latest plan puts much emphasis on the environment and the motor industry is a key area for attention. This, of course, makes sense. Average incomes are among the highest in the world and the country can afford to spend time investing in the 'quality of life' of its citizens. The motivation is wider, however. Japan sees a worldwide trend towards greater environmentalism, and proposes to take a leading role. For the motor industry in particular, the emphasis on environment-friendly vehicles will actually encourage the country's industry to maintain its competitive edge. If the drive for 'green' cars is strong at home, then Japanese vehicle manufacturers will be in a better position where the same views are taken abroad – notably in California.

In order to maintain demand for new cars and to encourage the country's citizens to replace their vehicles more frequently, the government has introduced a complex and very expensive annual vehicle test. Few older cars can pass the test. Most old cars are not put forward anyway because of the cost, which can approach $2000.

While this encourages the Japanese to replace their cars more frequently, future demand is being limited by increases in taxation. It is already constrained by the availability of parking spaces. Potential buyers have to prove that they have a parking space available before they can buy a car; these spaces are also becoming prohibitively expensive. Until recently, mini-vehicles – those under 660 cc – were exempt from many of the taxes and hurdles attached to car buying. These are now having their preferential status dismantled. The Japanese government is expected to raise the costs of vehicle ownership further. It is also likely that it will directly limit their use, even though congestion, particularly in the larger cities, is already a major disincentive for many potential car buyers.

The market for passenger cars in Japan is likely to remain stable. In fact, annual sales would fall were it not for the fact that cars will have to be replaced more frequently thanks to the new testing regime. The number of cars in use is in fact likely to fall slightly over the next few years. While this would be anathema to most other developed nations, there are two important reasons why it is unlikely to be a problem in Japan. First, the alternative forms of transport, notably the rail network, are excellent. Second, the social and cultural ratchet that affects car owners in the West, making it nearly impossible for them to give up their vehicles, does not apply to nearly the same extent in Japan. The Japanese are not nearly so tied to their cars as an inherent part of their lifestyle as are Europeans or North Americans.

Competitively, the market is dominated by local manufacturers. A few of these are expected to suffer, particularly those overly dependent on mini-vehicles, when government concessions are fully withdrawn. These include Suzuki, in particular, as well as Daihatsu. Other smaller manufacturers are also expected to come under pressure, including Subaru and Isuzu in commercial vehicles.

The market will therefore be increasingly dominated by the five largest local manufacturers: Toyota, Nissan, Honda, Mitsubishi and Mazda. They already account for four sales in five. Of these, the first three are likely to be the strongest, followed by Mitsubishi, despite its heavy dependence on the mini-vehicle segment.

The priority for these manufacturers over the next decade will be the drive for a global operating base. The first four of them are already well represented in Europe and the US as well as South East Asia and are likely to continue to expand their facilities. Mazda is also likely to expand more overseas, once its financial position has improved. This is, however, likely to be increasingly as part of Ford, rather than independently, as Mazda had originally hoped.

The drive for overseas expansion has a number of important justifications. The most obvious is probably to improve the cost effectiveness of Japanese vehicle manufacturers. Japan is not only an inherently expensive place to manufacture – the appreciation of the yen has made exporting from the country increasingly unattractive. Overseas expansion also overcomes trade barriers – whether or not these are legislated or simply an emotional 'anti-foreign car' block in the minds of consumers. By employing people in the countries where the Japanese vehicle manufacturer's sales efforts are focused, potential buyers seem happier to accept that they are buying a locally made car – even if many of the higher value components come from Japan and profits are repatriated there.

The most important reason, however, is the sense the Japanese vehicle manufacturers have that they need to be global physically as well as economically. This, of course, is absolutely right. A broad physical presence evens out the problems caused by fluctuations in foreign exchange rates and demand. It allows producers to shift their output and their efforts to where it is most advantageous.

The effect of these efforts to build facilities overseas is that vehicle production in Japan is beginning to fall. At one stage the country produced nearly 10 million cars, while local demand was less than half that. The country was heavily dependent on exports. Output is now falling and is expected to continue to fall as transplant volumes rise over the next ten years.

The outlook for importers is pretty much as before. Despite great efforts on the part of entrants and some concessions by the Japanese, demand for foreign cars is limited. They are therefore expected to continue to account for a very small segment of the market. Importers are also likely to find maintaining a presence in the market increasingly unattractive.

## The demographic time bomb

There is one other important factor driving the Japanese expansion, and not just in motor vehicles. It is the country's ageing population. One leading academic recently claimed that this would be the 'time bomb to end the Japanese fireworks display'.

The problem is significant, and it affects many other developed nations, particularly in Europe. The problem is most severe in Japan, however. Over the next 20 or 30 years much of Japan's population will reach the age of retirement. They will require pensions, health care and support for many years. Life expectancy is rising, which will further increase the cost of funding those dependents. Because of the falling birth rate in the 1970s and 1980s, there will be too few people in work to pay for this. That is, the taxes that can be raised from the working population are far short of the expenditure needed to support the dependants. This is a serious issue and is indeed a potential 'time-bomb'. Although Japan faces the worst shortfall, Germany, France and the UK will also face enormous difficulties. The effect of this will be significant.

There are two basic means of addressing the problem. First, increase revenues or taxes to cover the shortfall or second, reduce social expenditure. For each country facing the problem, it will be a combination of both measures. Simply raising taxes to a sufficient level to make up the shortfall would cripple each country economically. Similarly, social costs can also only be cut so far.

There will undoubtedly be a sharp increase in taxation in each of these markets which will adversely affect demand for cars. There will also be a much greater emphasis on the provision of pensions, health care and welfare from the private sector – to reduce the burden on governments. For each of the citizens of these countries today the future is a little bleak. Citizens face higher taxes and the prospect of having to provide their own pensions. They will also have to pay for a much higher proportion of their medical bills. For providers of pension funds, life assurance and savings plans the problem presents a huge opportunity. For manufacturers of consumer goods, including cars, it presents a big problem.

If real disposable incomes fall, because a greater proportion of them is required for future health and pension payments, demand for consumer goods will also fall. For the car, as the single biggest item of expenditure after housing, this drop in earnings could have a large impact on demand – particularly if drivers are increasingly put off by congestion. They may also be more attracted to other products. After all, the electronic fantasy world of virtual reality should have reached the mass market by the time this problem becomes serious.

Japan has clearly decided to tackle the problem far in advance. The country recognizes its future income shortfall and, realizing that taxing its own citizens would not solve the problem, is encouraging its businesses to expand overseas. By doing this, and by repatriating the profits, the country can raise its income without over-taxing its citizens. It is therefore essential that the largest Japanese firms invest overseas. They are key to the country's future prosperity.

It is a clever and far-sighted plan that will put Japan in a far stronger position than many of its major economic competitors in the future. It will also ensure that the 'time-bomb to end the Japanese fireworks display' will be defused long before it is due to go off. Sadly the same cannot be said for many of the other countries that face the same problem in Europe.

# 16

# Not all that it seems: the future for the Pacific Rim

## The region as a whole superficially looks attractive

The Pacific Rim is one of today's great bandwagons. Spectacular economic growth over many years and good prospects for the future are market characteristics that every industry dreams of. As a result, investment in the region, particularly in India and China, is phenomenal.

The motor industry is no exception, particularly as the number of cars in the region is so small. The South Korean government is placing massive emphasis on the development of the country's motor industry, aiming at the Pacific Rim, as well as Korea itself, as its key target markets. South Korea is the largest car market in the region today. The investment in other countries is just as great. Japanese vehicle manufacturers have numerous joint ventures in the next largest car market, Taiwan. They also have established relationships in Indonesia, Malaysia and Thailand. In China relationships with European vehicle manufacturers, particularly Volkswagen and Peugeot, dominate, although Japanese suppliers have begun to invest more recently. In India, a Suzuki joint venture dominates the market for cars, although again, many more new entrants have recently arrived.

But is the region as attractive as it appears? For the next decade in most of these countries, the answer is 'no'. While these countries will experience rapid growth and the penetration of cars today is low, increased wealth may not lead to major volumes of car sales for many years. The problem is that average incomes are still very low in many of these countries and well below the car buying threshold. Unsatisfied demand for cars is certainly high. But this is a little like planting a tree: no matter how much you tend it, the tree will still take 30 years to grow.

The common retort to this argument is that even the wealthiest 10% of the market in China is 100 million people and that is a big market already. The same applies to India. The argument is true and the wealthiest 10% represents a sizeable market today. Yet with little growth expected in the developed world's car industry, this new market will be hard-won. In short, there are too many vehicles chasing too few buyers in the region already.

As a result, the Pacific Rim will be a region with high growth, but small volumes and intense competition. While it has enormous long-term potential, the other important issue for entrants to consider is that it is already dominated by Japanese products. The South Koreans are also far more advanced in the region than the American or European producers.

# The outlook for the smaller countries in the region: Singapore, Malaysia, Thailand

In terms of specific market opportunities, the smaller countries in the region have little to offer. While there is an attractive market in Singapore, it is small and already well served. In Malaysia and Thailand demand for cars is growing rapidly. Their combined populations are equal to Germany and growing much more quickly. However, car sales are only 5% of the number sold in Germany today. Even if they grow at 10% a year, it will be decades before the market for cars in these countries is significant in world terms.

Options for potential entrants to these markets are also limited because they are already probably too far down the road with the Japanese vehicle manufacturers to change. This also makes it unlikely that they will develop their own motor industries. As a result, although superficially attractive, these markets offer little to those not already present. They are already competitively locked up and in any event too small to change the global balance of the industry.

# The larger markets: China, Indonesia and India

China, India and Indonesia account for 45% of the world's population, yet little of its wealth. They account for less than 1% of the cars in use today. The average income level in China is less than $400 a year; it is less than $300 a head in India and only $700 a year in Indonesia. These countries may appear to represent a huge potential market for cars in the long term. Yet all of this vast potential may never be realized. There are some real and important questions that may leave these embryonic markets just as they are.

In the short term, there will certainly be growth – and very rapid growth. For potential entrants, however, the options are limited. A great deal of capacity has already been laid down relative to local needs, particularly by the Japanese in Indonesia and India, and by Volkswagen and Peugeot in China. These markets have therefore already been infiltrated.

There is a tendency to extrapolate the short-term trends into the long term, to assume the growth will continue. There are several reasons why this may not be appropriate. First, and this may be an outside chance, there is a possibility of civil war in the two largest markets, China and India. Were this to happen then, clearly, the opportunity these countries present to Western and Japanese car manufacturers may never materialize.

China has a long history of internal revolutions after periods of instability. The critical point today will come when Deng Xiaoping, China's 'paramount' political leader, dies. The country could leap in one of several directions. It could follow the path of Singapore or South Korea and become an 'authoritarian democracy'. Alternatively, the country could become much more reformist. It could also return to orthodox values.

Each of these will have a huge impact on the growth and demand for automobiles. It is tempting to assume that the flood of Western investment has made the reform process unstoppable. Yet at some point the forces of individual enterprise and state control will come into conflict. The outcome of this conflict will depend entirely on the new political leadership and the relative influence of the military. While the drive to a market-like economy is the most likely option for the future, the possibilities of civil war or a return to a closed society should not be discounted by potential investors.

There is also a possibility of civil war in India if economic targets are not achieved. Political and social instability have characterized the country for many years. There is a very real risk of armed insurgency and the loss of central control today. The flash-points are in Kashmir, Jammu, Punjab and Assam. In Kashmir there is no obvious political solution, other than the region's independence. That is unlikely and India's military occupation of the region is expected to continue. Other states in the North and South are also keen to break away. Weak government could therefore result in many parts of the country pushing for independence. As this would be strongly resisted, some sort of breakdown of law and order is therefore a real possibility.

There is also the big question of whether or not China, in particular, is going to follow the pattern of economic development experienced in the West. It is by no means certain. Culturally, politically and socially, the country is very different from most developed nations today. An alternative approach, for example, would be for it to achieve growth by military force. Although not politically likely at present, it is an option. Even if China did choose the path of steady economic development, then a car industry may not be high priority. The development of the infrastructure and putting water and electricity in every home may rank higher. The car may remain a rich man's toy for many decades yet. That is, if they can control the expectations of their citizens.

There is another issue. China is rapidly becoming two countries. Huge areas are becoming rich – the special development regions, around Hong Kong and Shanghai. This also contrasts with India and Indonesia. It is possible therefore that the new wealthier parts of China could develop in a very different way to the rest of the country. This raises new possibilities, as well as new threats.

The overall conclusion, however, is that even with the most optimistic forecasts the markets in China, India and Indonesia will not generate the vast growth in demand that the world's largest vehicle manufacturers need. They are certainly attractive markets and may add another four million cars to the world's total over a period of 15 years. They will not represent another market the size of the US for a very long time indeed. Indeed, in terms of the world's total demand for cars, the addition of these countries represents a compound annual growth rate of only 0.5% – far below that which the major suppliers have become used to.

# Other constraints on growth

Assuming civil war is avoided in both India and China there are a number of other factors that may limit the growth in sales of motor vehicles. The availability of fuel, for example, is likely to be an important issue. Although there is plenty of oil for the 470 million cars on the world's roads today, the development of India, China and Indonesia could ultimately double that number. This increase in the number of cars would not only stretch the world's oil supplies, it would cause other problems too.

Congestion is already an issue in many parts of the Pacific Rim and such a rapid growth in traffic will make this considerably worse. The growth in pollution is also a concern. Most of the vehicles sold in these markets today do not have catalysts fitted. In addition, the governments in these countries are reluctant to legislate in favour of catalysts as this would increase the price of cars. Their priority is to satisfy their citizens, not to put financial barriers in their way. As a result, the growth in vehicles in use in the Pacific Rim will have a much larger impact on the world's total emissions than it would were it to occur in the developed world.

The growing emissions problem in Asia will have to be dealt with globally. There is, however, a dilemma here. Why should the wealthier nations, those that already have cars and that can afford catalysts, impose their wishes on the poorer less-developed nations that are only just beginning to discover the benefits of personal mobility? Conversely, how can the developed nations stand back and watch as the volume of pollutants in the world's atmosphere rises? After all, they are being good citizens, they have cleaned up their vehicles.

The most important reason for feeling nervous about extrapolative forecasts for the region is income levels. The average incomes in these countries are still very low. It will take decades for most of their citizens to be able to afford cars. The bigger problem still is that the citizens of these countries want cars now, not in two generations' time. This mismatch of reality and expectation is a potentially volatile combination and a significant issue for the governments of less developed nations.

Another important question for these markets is whether or not they will develop their own motor industries. The answer, at this stage, seems to be 'no'. First, there will not be sufficient local demand to justify a local producer setting up for many years. It is not like in Europe or the US in the early period of motorization – if you set up a new car manufacturer today, it must be done on a large scale or not at all. Second, each of these markets is already more than adequately provided for by foreign entrants. It is most unlikely therefore that an entirely new vehicle producer will emerge from these countries, other than as a partner of an existing competitor.

# The competitive implications

So, who will supply these markets? Which competitors will win? Volkswagen and Peugeot are in a strong position in China. Although the Japanese are investing, the Chinese remain uneasy about Japan and its ambitions. This mistrust of the Japanese may offer an opportunity for the South Koreans, as both nations are partners in having suffered under Japanese colonialism.

Volkswagen might consider allying with the Koreans and ensure the Japanese are kept out. The problem is whether VW will have the resources for such a manoeuvre, given its difficulties in Europe. Another scenario could see the Japanese supplying low-cost CKD kits to China as it does to Taiwan, or support the development of a local industry, as it did with Proton in Malaysia and Hyundai in South Korea. Their problem, in the case of Hyundai, is how to keep control of their partner. It is difficult to see anyone else in the frame.

Indonesia is already dominated by the Japanese and likely to remain that way, although a few specialist European suppliers such as BMW and Mercedes-Benz may be able to maintain their positions.

The real battle in the region is likely to happen in India, which is currently dominated by Maruti, a Suzuki partner. There have been several recent entrants, some of which are in partnership with Maruti's traditional competitors, Premier and Hindustan Motors. These include several European vehicle manufacturers, such as Mercedes, Opel and Peugeot. There are also two other important new threats to Maruti's position. First, Telco, the dominant commercial vehicle manufacturer, plans to enter the car market. On the one hand, its reputation is formidable; on the other hand, the history of truck manufacturers trying to get into the passenger car business is not replete with successes – the two are very different in terms of product and end-user markets. Second, competitors are working on a range of new mini-vehicles that will cost half the price of cars today. Based on India's ubiquitous scooter, these could revolutionize the industry and the market. Solutions such as this may be far more appropriate to the developing world's needs.

Overall, the Pacific Rim region is attractive, but it is no holy grail. The world's largest vehicle manufacturers need to grow. But they will not find major growth in their traditional markets and, although they will find high rates of growth in much of the Pacific Rim, the volume of vehicles sold there is very much lower. It will also remain that way for many years.

# 17

# No Eldorado: the future for South America

The future prospects for South America are very mixed. Some parts of the region seem to have overcome the problems of the 1980s – crushing external debt, economic and political instability, and the resulting tendency for military intervention. Others are still struggling to overcome these difficulties, while sadly a few seem to have learnt little in the last 20 years. Even the proposed economic free trade area, the Mercosur or Southern Cone, offers only limited hope for these countries.

The biggest success story of the region is certainly Chile, which holds a unique position. After a *coup d'état* in 1973, that stopped the country plunging into civil war, Chile became a dictatorship under General Pinochet. The military allowed the country to return to democracy in 1989. This is now firmly established and there seems little prospect of further military intervention.

An ambitious programme of constitutional reform has been proposed and although it will take time, this is likely to become law. Economic growth is now high, as high as many parts of South East Asia, and inflation is falling rapidly. External debt is not a problem for Chile, unlike it is for most of its neighbours. Indeed, foreign exchange reserves are high and there are strong capital inflows and exports. As a result, investment in the country is rising and its prospects are bright.

Although the population is small, car demand will rise – but the road network will need substantial investment first. Because of the poor state of the roads, sales are still dominated by pick-ups, most of which are supplied by the Japanese. Some European manufacturers have been successful in the car market. This position is unlikely to change dramatically in the short term.

The other country that seems to have begun to address its problems is Argentina. Although not as stable as Chile, the country has abandoned populist ideology in favour of an aggressive pro-business stance that has fostered an economic turnaround. The economy is growing, inflation is falling and the country is now a much more attractive prospect for investment. There are still problems, however, with a shortage of skilled labour and an inadequate infrastructure.

Sales of motor vehicles are forecast to grow rapidly here, particularly as average incomes rise. As the population is only just over 30 million people, the total market will never be huge – it is, however, attractive.

Until recently imports were banned and so local manufacturers, who are affiliates of European producers, dominate the market. The import ban is now being phased out and Japanese manufacturers are expected to gradually increase their share, particularly in pick-ups. Even so, this is one market where the Europeans have a strong position that will take many years to change.

The countries where questions remain are Ecuador, Paraguay, Uruguay and Colombia. These are countries that are attempting to reform their economic and political status yet are encountering problems. They could therefore become exciting new economies or fall back into financial chaos. Of these, the only country of economic significance is Colombia, the third largest country in the region in terms of population.

Colombia has considerable problems. The country and the economy are plagued by terrorism, tax increases and an energy crisis. Indirect taxation on luxury goods can be up to 45%, electricity is rationed and there are continual problems with guerrilla forces. In many of Colombia's neighbours these problems would have resulted in military intervention, yet this is unlikely in this case.

The country has had some success in diversifying away from its dependence on coffee and is addressing its electricity shortages through an agreement with Venezuela. Although inflation is a problem, it is less serious than in other countries such as Brazil. There is also a strong desire to improve the country's prospects – far more so than in other parts of the region.

The prospects for Colombia, Ecuador, Paraguay and Uruguay are uncertain. If there is sufficient impetus for the reform programmes to continue, then these countries could develop rapidly. If not, then they face a future similar to their recent past – with considerable political and economic instability.

The countries where problems are most likely to continue are Brazil, Venezuela, Peru and Bolivia. Of these, Brazil and Venezuela are probably the most important. Venezuela suffered two coup attempts in

1992 and there is little prospect of this social unrest ending. Surprisingly, though, the economy is growing and the prospects for the sale of motor vehicles are reasonable good. However, once again, with a small population, the long-term volume prospects are limited.

Brazil seems to be a constant source of despair – it is the promise that never comes true. Years of expectation have never materialized in this, the region's biggest country. Corruption seems to have become endemic, inflation is out of control and the country remains crippled by debt. The economic forecasts for the country give little reason for hope and the currency continues to devalue. In 1990 there were 68 cruzeiros to the dollar. By 1996 a dollar will be worth 8,000,000. Worse, the country suffers from weak leadership and there is little prospect of radical reform. There is also little of the desire for reform that seems to exist in Colombia.

To illustrate the problems of doing business in Brazil, in January 1994 General Motors announced that it would increase the prices of its vehicles by 1% a day. At the end of each month therefore, a car will cost nearly a third more than it cost at the beginning.

None the less Brazil is an important market for motor vehicles – although increasingly less so. In 1980, it produced nearly a million motor vehicles, making it the seventh largest source in the world. Since then, production and sales have slowly declined, while other countries' have grown. Although still large, it is increasingly less significant.

Despite incentives and government support the motor industry in Brazil seems stuck in a constant dream state. The major competitor, Autolatina – a joint venture between Ford and Volkswagen – is finding life harder since import duties were reduced. Still, it has introduced new models, as have its main competitors, GM and Fiat. However, the government which, in the past, offered protection to its motor industry seems to have adopted a much more free-market approach, perhaps realizing that it cannot achieve a world-class position. For local suppliers, many of which have invested heavily, the prospects are not inspiring.

Overall, the prospects for South America are mixed. Some countries will experience rapid growth in car demand, while others will continue to stagnate. For the world's largest vehicle manufacturers looking for new growth, the region offers some hope but not a lot. With the growth anticipated in each country, the total number of new cars sold in the region by early in the next century should be little more than 1.5 million, an increase of only a few hundred thousand.

# 18

# Marginal additions: the rest of the world

## The former Eastern bloc countries

The markets in the rest of the world offer some additional sales but few are of any great significance in the medium term. The area currently receiving the greatest attention is the former Eastern Bloc.

In some Eastern European countries such as Poland, the Czech Republic and Hungary prospects are improving. In the Czech Republic, in particular, economic conditions are looking much brighter – and certainly much healthier than in its previous federal partner, Slovakia, which was more 'sovietized' and dependent on armaments production.

The Czech Republic is growing and with the sale of its indigenous vehicle manufacturer, Skoda, to Volkswagen, the outlook for the car industry is positive. It is, however, a small country with only just over 10 million people. While demand for cars will rise progressively, the scale of the opportunity is strictly limited. The same is true in Hungary which has a similar population.

In Poland, with nearly 40 million people, the reform programme is likely to limit demand for a few years. GDP has fallen sharply over the period of the reforms and average incomes continue to fall. The GDP per head is well under $2000, which is far below the normal take-off level for passenger car sales. Again; the positive prospects are really in the long term.

There are also some similar long-term opportunities in parts of the former Soviet Union, notably in Khazakstan and the Ukraine. These new republics have large populations and considerable mineral wealth which should ensure economic development.

Other parts of the former Eastern Bloc seem to offer little, certainly for the time being. Bulgaria, Romania and Bosnia have small populations, are in various states of economic chaos and are comparatively poor. Most of the citizens of these countries have much more fundamental priorities than motorization.

The biggest questionmark hangs over Russia. Seemingly an attractive market, it has a large population and, before the collapse of the Soviet Union, had a not inconsiderable market for passenger cars. Both sales and production were well over a million units a year.

In the last few years, many companies and investors have looked on this historic performance superficially and assumed that demand will continue to grow. After all, Russia's sales and production were only 10% of those in the US, despite a population similar in numbers. Many Western manufacturers thought that this was just the opportunity they needed to satisfy the considerable pent up demand. Additionally, as the local manufacturers' cars were so badly made, it should have been relatively easy to displace them.

Before the collapse of the Soviet Union the chairman of Volkswagen at the time, Carl Hahn, once said that if he could produce a million Golfs and send them to Russia, he could sell them all instantly, such was the demand. So desperate were many to own a car, that they would put down considerable deposits many years before it was to be built. The only problem was, what to do with all those worthless roubles.

Yet, even in a best-case scenario, the problems that affect Russia and the Commonwealth of Independent States will take 10 to 15 years to resolve. If the present administration remains in power, then inflation should continue to fall and economic growth should return. Even then, the recession is expected to continue until 1994–95 at least. The economy was forecast to decline during 1993–94 and then grow at an average rate of 2.5% between 1995 and 1996. Inflation is expected to fall from a high of 2000% in 1992 to 40% in 1996. This follows the pattern of the Polish economy during its transformation to a free-market economy.

The main constraint to further growth is the reluctance of foreign companies to invest. Ironically, their concerns about political instability are only likely to make the situation worse. Many are justifiably discouraged by the remaining problems of foreign exchange availability. In addition, many companies are worried about conservative elements in the Russian government who want increased control over the activities of foreign investors. These politicians believe foreign companies are a threat, and are 'over-Westernizing' the country.

A major issue for the government is the arms industry. The problem is what to do with the millions of people whose jobs depended on cold war rivalry. The economy is still the most militarized in the world. Unemployment is already high and growing. According to Mikhail Malei, a presidential adviser in 1992, up to 25% of the population live off arms production. The government's programme for converting arms factories to the manufacture of non-military products was originally expected to last four years. It is now expected to take 15. At the end of 1992 most military factories continued to produce as before. According to *Izvestia*, only 12 out of 5000 arms plants had ceased production.

The government faces another major issue in the shape of the former 'colonies', the fringe republics that used to be controlled by the Soviet Union. Twenty-five million Russians live as minorities in these newly-independent states. In the past many lived as colonialists, often discriminating against non-Russians. The tables have now been turned and it is the Russians who are often abused, humiliated and treated as second-class citizens after many years of what the locals saw as exploitation. Many regions also face the rise of Islam. Azerbaijan and Tajikistan are already dominated by Islamic or nationalist regimes.

The feeling that ethnic Russians outside Russia are in danger is one of the few emotions that unites feuding politicians and their long suffering citizens. The Russian government is certainly unlikely to ignore the pleas of these 'colonials' as they offer it the opportunity to be seen as a defender of Russian values. Pavel Grachev, who was made defence minister in 1992, has said that he will not allow the honour and dignity of Russians to be insulted. To support the rhetoric, the withdrawal of troops from the Baltic states has been delayed until the local governments end 'discrimination' in the region. The rise of Islamic fundamentalism also creates opportunities for the hardliners. Many citizens reason that it would be preferable to return to authoritarian control than to submit to the will of Islam.

There are also difficulties for those opting to return to Russia from the outposts. Housing space is limited and jobs are scarce. In addition, returning Russians often have to face lower living standards and resentment caused by the large number of immigrants entering the cities. Many returning ethnic Russians cannot even speak Russian after several generations away from the country.

Although many Western states have woken up to the problems of Russia, the country desperately needs economic assistance if the free-market reforms are to continue. Even then a successful outcome is uncertain. Massive price rises, hyper-inflation and rising unemployment are a potent combination. Add to this the continued production of arms, difficulties in fringe republics and a growing sense of nationalism, and the mixture becomes highly volatile.

The continued existence of the CIS, of which Russia is the biggest part, is therefore questionable. A worst case scenario would see the country disintegrating under authoritarian or nationalist rule, with armed conflict or civil war virtually inevitable. Even a moderate scenario involves localized disturbances in the fringe republics.

Even if the country holds together, the near-term prospects for car demand are far from bright. The prices of new and used cars are still very high and inflation and difficulties with the currency have eroded savings. People currently have higher priorities than buying a car. Even those with enough money to afford a car will find ownership a problem. Fuel is still in short supply in many regions, limiting the value of cars to many owners. In 1991, Belarus received only 55% of the gasoline it needed. Turkmenistan received only 37%. To combat this, AZLK has developed a car that runs on vegetable oil. This is not due for production until 1998, however.

There were estimated to be just over 14 million cars in Russia in 1992. Penetration of passenger cars is therefore low, at 50 cars for every 1000 people. The highest numbers of cars in relation to the population are in Latvia, Estonia and Georgia. Many cars are old and poorly maintained because of the shortage of parts. The cars on offer are also outdated, despite the intention of local manufacturers to invest. Little wonder that many opt for a second-hand car imported from Central Europe – but this still requires hard currency.

Although latent demand remains high, the production and sales of new passenger cars in Russia are expected to decline sharply. The trend towards personal used-car imports, the shortage of fuel, high prices and the uncompetitiveness of local suppliers mean that annual sales are expected to fall from an estimated 880,000 in 1992 to a low of 500,000 in 1994. Many domestic vehicle manufacturers have found the transition to free-market economics hard and are facing falling profitability and even bankruptcy. Some analysts believe it will take up to 40 years for the automotive industry in the CIS to reach Western standards. Sales of new cars are expected to grow only slowly after 1994 to reach 900,000 cars a year by the year 2000, still below the levels achieved under communist rule.

This forecast for sales volumes may change significantly, however. Two alternative scenarios are offered. First, if economic and political stability were to be achieved rapidly, and funds and investments were to flow into the country, then the volume of cars sold could rise very rapidly to perhaps 1.5 million vehicles a year by the year 2000.

The alternative scenario is for the country to dissolve into civil war, similar to that seen in Yugoslavia. A virtual collapse of the car industry is then forecast, lasting for a number of years.

There is, however, one area of opportunity that seems more assured – trucks. Russia always had a large internal market for trucks and a number of very significant manufacturers. An economy in development also tends to need more, rather than less, trucks to support its growth. For truck manufacturers seeking growth Russia may be one major market worthy of detailed consideration.

# Other regions

Apart from those above, there are no other markets of significant medium-term potential. The market in Australia is stagnant and, through the attempts of the government to reform the sector, the number of car manufacturers is falling. Similarly, there are few markets of any great potential in Africa and indeed prospects for the continent are almost uniformly and depressingly poor. In the Middle East a few markets offer potential longer-term opportunities, including Turkey, Iran and Egypt. Turkey in particular offers an attractive production base for exports to both Europe and the East. The biggest issue in the region is political uncertainty. It is difficult to see how Iran will grow, for example, when fundamentalism is unlikely to promote the values that underpin economic development.

The overall conclusion is therefore unescapable: the Triad markets are likely to stagnate; there is no great source of new sales in other regions; and there is a growth gap, compared with what the industry might hope for. Vehicle manufacturers that have got used to high rates of growth have a problem. The only way to grow is to beat your competitors, to buy them out, to force them out of business. The competitive and structural outlook for the industry is clear – there will be massive consolidation in its ranks over the next few years.

# Summary of Part Three

- There is no such thing as a generic strategic option. Strategic options must be developed to meet particular needs. This adaptation requires knowledge, analysis, considerable understanding of the inter-dependence of the main issues and more than a touch of vision and creativity. That said, there is no 'right' option. Military strategies, often overlooked as models, often provide good ideas as they involve the same process of analysis.

- In order to develop good strategies, a number of things must be borne in mind. Two of the most important are the broader picture and the right time-horizons. If you are manufacturing hula hoops or some other short-term fashion item, a 20-year time-horizon is unlikely to be appropriate. If you are managing a country, or an investment in oil exploration, it may be. Time-horizons can be very long indeed. For example, the Chinese government recently defined a 100-year economic plan. If your competitors are willing and able to apply a very different time-horizon – whether longer or shorter – you may be heading for trouble.

• Remember cultural barriers when developing strategy! It is important to be consistent. Some US managers wrongly (or optimistically) assume that Europe is homogeneous, which is still far from true. Some British managers still seem to believe that the US, because of the common language, is similar to the UK in its market expectations and business practices. In some instances the result is merely hilarious. In others, it is disastrous. Strategic options for a business must not only be achievable, they must also be internally consistent, they must fit with the existing capabilities and *modus operandi* of the corporation. There is no point suggesting to a traditionalist organisation that it should become aggressive and acquisitive. Similarly, a second-rate management is unlikely to implement a first-rate strategy successfully.

• As the strategic options are being developed, put down some markers. What do you know, what is likely to be stable? It is as important to identify the areas that will not experience change as much as looking at those that will change.

• Look out for the wild cards. New legislation (environement or safety related, for example), new inventions, emerging competitors, changing market segmentation, shifts in the cost curve – events that have the potential to trigger radical and far-reaching structural change. Scenarios can be useful tools to identify the impact of such changes, and the correct response. Beware: scenarios are rarely understood by those outside corporate-planning functions. Many managers expect forecasts, not possible futures.

• Similarly, beware of overestimating the value of an apparent opportunity in a new market, while neglecting the home front. Becoming obsessed with apparently greener grass on the other side of the fence is a common failing of management – hence the vogue for diversifications in the 1980s, most of which did not have a happy ending. If apparently major opportunities are so clear, they become bandwagons. Strategies should be about 'going your own way', about finding a direction where you are not competing head-on with anyone. Fashion is a dangerous guide in business.

# PART FOUR

# *Options for products, vehicle manufacturers and the industry*

# 19

# Alternative technologies: options for the car itself

## Existing design structures are predicated on historical environmental conditions

The analysis in earlier chapters shows that there will be a sustained, if stagnant, demand for individual passenger transportation in the First World over the next decade, with insufficient growth in the Second and Third Worlds to allow a major change in the competitive equilibrium. It also shows that there will be latent instabilities and potential discontinuities associated with this:

- the problems with road space and the volume of emissions;
- the limitations of current technologies in dealing with these problems;
- the reliance on image-based factors to maintain prices and margins;
- the need for product proliferation and the frequent introduction of new products to sustain image;
- the waste of resources implicit in this;
- the current competitive stalemate, incomplete restructuring of the industry and the potentially massive shakeout.

There is a strong suggestion that the market is being force-fed – something that may not ultimately be the optimal solution to its needs.

The current industry philosophy is that product ranges will remain pretty much as they are today, based on four or five basic platforms.

These vary slightly in different parts of the world, notably North America, but for most markets consist of mini, supermini, small saloon, medium saloon and large saloon. There may also be some niche platforms, such as true cross-country 4 × 4s and highly market specific sports cars.

In general, each of the platforms has a range of engines and body shells that allow the vehicle manufacturer to meet a variety of market needs. These may include standard saloons, hatch or liftbacks, coupés and even multi-purpose vehicles (MPVs), or 'people carriers' as they are sometimes known. The principle variation is therefore size. All are typically capable of conveying four or more passengers at expressway speeds and with a range of 400 to 800 km between fuel stops. Moreover, the mainstream technologies are seen as basically fixed: monocoque body shells, petrol- or diesel-fuelled reciprocating engines, mechanical drivelines, and the increasing use of electronic controls.

The winners are generally those manufacturers who find the best equilibrium between product novelty – which brings conquest sales – and longevity – which improves returns on the development investments. However, these views rest on a number of historically-derived assumptions that may not always be valid. In terms of the choice of basic technology and design, it is worth remembering what happened in North America. From the 1940s to the late 1970s, it was assumed that the archetypal American car was – and would remain – a large, relatively crudely but robustly engineered vehicle using a large gasoline engine that drove the rear wheels through an automatic transmission. Car prices were kept relatively low by the long life of the underlying designs and a very slow rate of technological innovation. Differentiation in the marketplace was ensured through the annual model cycle, consisting of superficial changes in exterior sheet metal and trim.

The design was entirely predicated on low domestic fuel taxation and a lack of concern with levels of oil consumption. When fuel prices rose in the 1970s the basic assumption behind the design changed. The oil shocks and enforced downsizing completely changed the US car design philosophy, aligning it with the rest of the world. There is thus no absolute or eternal validity to the present pattern or approach to design. A number of quite radically different product line structures are conceivable, depending on external influences and criteria. It all depends on what demands the industry is going to have to satisfy. It is certainly not obvious that these will necessarily be set in the present pattern, to which the industry is geared and which it would naturally like to see continued.

# A wide range of design options exists for the future

There is a considerable range of alternative approaches to the technological basis of vehicles, to their basic designs, and to the management of product lines. A hierarchical tree of possible decisions about this is shown in Figure 19.1.

The first question to be answered exploring the possible product options has to do with the pattern of car use. Will this remain essentially the same, or will it be significantly modified? The left-hand branch of the diagram corresponds to usage patterns being broadly maintained, i.e. the existing dependence on cars and product choices remaining largely market-driven. It assumes that there is no strong imperative for governments to impose different usage patterns or designs, or to influence them indirectly through measures such as massively increasing fuel costs or stringent consumption or emissions targets.

Within this option, the technologies employed in vehicles typically change only in an evolutionary sense – continuing the historical trend. The designs and product range structures remain fundamentally the same from year to year. The decision over the design is largely made by the vehicle manufacturer, influenced by what the components industry can offer. The vehicle manufacturer makes its decision based on its best judgement on the future of the market and the activities of competitors.

The prime mover and the drivetrain evolve particularly slowly with this option. The typical solution is a reciprocating, internal-combustion engine, driving two (or sometimes four) wheels through a mechanical driveline. In this sense, moving from four-stroke to two-stroke Sarich-type engines, or extending the use of electronically-controlled multi-ratio automatic gearboxes is simply evolution within the branch.

What about body structures? Assuming that usage patterns remain as today, there are two main options for body structures: continue with the present materials and the design patterns they impose, or look for a known alternative.

In the first option, we stay with unitary (monocoque) sheet-steel bodies and the existing compromises between the number of platforms and the costs of developing them. This looks like business as usual. In reality, there are widely different ways of playing it, which relate to the frequency of renewal.

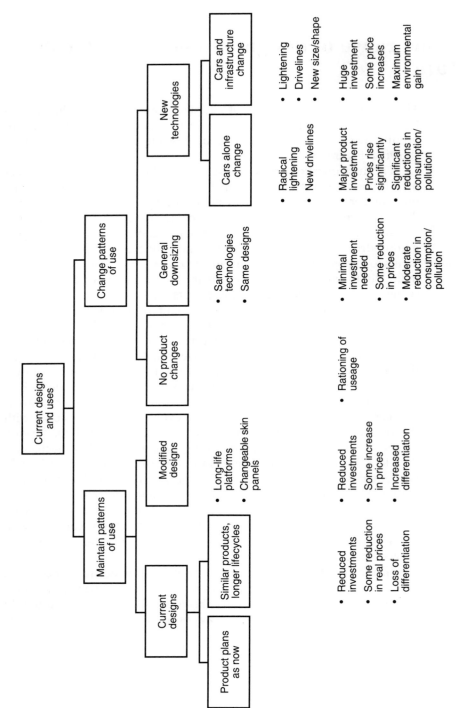

**Figure 19.1**  Long-term product options.

Despite accelerated product cycles, the economic ideal remains what it always was: to find the platform or product with a seemingly endless life, compared to the rapid rise and fall of most products in the marketplace. There have been such cases: the semi-utilitarian Beetle, Citroën's 2CV, the Renault 4; the Peugeot 504 and some upline vehicles. These are the real money-spinners in the motor industry, as can be seen when total cash generated by a model over its lifecycle is compared to total cash invested. Such an analysis showed the Renault 4, with its lifetime of over two decades, to have been one of Renault's most profitable products, despite the downward price pressures caused by age and the impression conveyed by a conventional approach to product costing.

# The semi-utilitarian option prolongs existing designs and technologies

Given the potential fragility of the image-hype-based marketing approach of many vehicle manufacturers today, it is possible that First World markets and the industry could switch back to the semi-utilitarian philosophy. This, after all, represents a financially very attractive strategy. No new technology is needed and there are no supplementary investments: vehicle manufacturers simply slow down the product replacement cycle.

It is difficult to claim that anyone would materially suffer from such a move, other than competitors who might get upstaged by those of their brethren who continue to tread heavily on the new product accelerator. A mature, long-running product almost invariably achieves better reliability than a new one, however much effort is put into 'right first time'. The striking quality and reliability improvements of the last decade have been largely achieved at the components level – which is where failures and breakdowns mainly originate. Much of the improvement has been in industrial processes. There is nothing fundamentally different between the designs of Japanese and other cars at the fundamental level – the Japanese advantage lies in the details.

Contrary to some opinion, lean production has not destroyed industry scale curves. It still takes a great deal of money to design a new car, to develop a new engine or gearbox family, or to introduce a new technology into a particular area of componentry. An increasing amount, in fact, because of the ever increasing performance requirements. A large bodypart press die is still a very costly item. The genius of the Japanese has been to bring their costs down close to the theoretical scale curves by the ruthless elimination of duplication, waste and general slack in the engineering and manufacturing chains. This has given them superior capabilities, in terms of the speed of new product development, and the quality and cost of outputs. Having started from a 'cheap but cheerful' positioning, they quickly shifted to emphasizing novelty, with a corresponding premium price-positioning. This was certainly a rational move for them, faced with volumetric constraints on inter-regional exports and initially limited presences and production capacities in the other two main regions of the Triad.

However, the differentiating capability of today becomes the mere qualifier-to-play of tomorrow. Once everyone is up to speed on design cycles and quality, the ultimate differentiator in a mature industry is cost. It is not inconceivable that, once they are firmly established in all regions, the strong competitors will revert to the cost-driven, long lifecycle approach.

It is also far from inconceivable that the market might favour this, particularly in Europe. Simply put, Europeans can no longer afford to pay themselves the way they have, especially in terms of social security and healthcare provisions. Over the next ten or 20 years, more of the burden will be shifted onto the shoulders of the individual citizen. This is likely to have a significant effect on personal disposable income. While the proportion of income devoted to travel and leisure in the UK, for example, has increased in recent years (Figure 19.2) the trend could well reverse as the squeeze takes hold on consumers. They could start significantly deferring their replacement purchases of vehicles. They might revert to being far more attracted to mature, proven, economical products. In short, the whole purchasing-behaviour pattern could change. The industry is certainly not altogether unconscious of the possibility.

Something along these lines happened in Sweden, Finland and Norway at the beginning of the 1990s, with the effect that car and commercial vehicle sales fell by up to 80% in just a few years. The citizens of these countries, faced with economic difficulties, put off the replacement of vehicles or gave them up entirely. This not only resulted in huge changes in demand patterns, it also changed the entire economics of car production and distribution in these markets.

The whole strategy of product-cycle acceleration and proliferation, heavy advertising, promotion and branding, and premium-price positioning is a wonderful device for avoiding having to deal with an underlying, serious, cost problem. Ultimately, it is a zero-sum – if not a negative-sum – game. If every vehicle manufacturer tries to reposition itself as another BMW, targeting the car-lover segments, then the only gainers are the advertising agencies.

In Europe, in particular, the industry is far from being fully rational in its structures. A shift in underlying market attitudes, coupled with one or more of the major manufacturers making a resolute push for cost-based dominance, could topple the whole existing edifice of the industry. Its ultimate structure could look much like that which prevailed in the US before the import incursion and downsizing. It is certainly clear

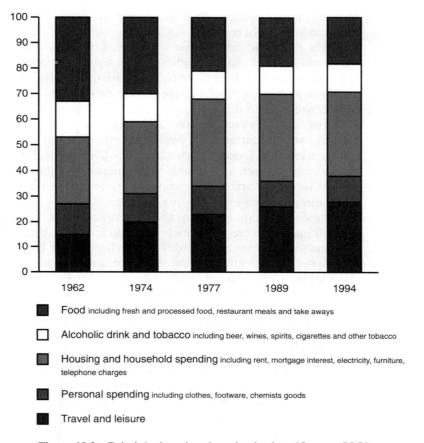

Figure 19.2    Britain's changing shopping basket. (*Source*: CSO)

that there is room for a major adjustment to the cost base in Europe, the
question is not if it will occur but when, and how.

# Alternative materials may allow other compromises between variety and cost

The other option, while maintaining existing body structures and
patterns of usage, is to look for some alternative structure without the
constraints inherent in today's model. This involves trying to find a means

of reconciling product proliferation and volatility, while maintaining reasonable levels of cost.

This approach was historically achieved in North America through the annual model change, with the underlying platforms and designs remaining stable for long periods. To ensure the vehicles appeared fresh and fashionable, superficial changes were made to the sheet metal and to the exterior and interior trim every year. The visual distinction was effective enough: a favourite teenager-trick was to identify make, model and year at night through the pattern of tail-lights. The technique relied on the relatively 'loose' design of the old US cars, with their separate chassis, non-stressed sheet metal and generous weights and sizes. The trouble is that the era of Dixie cup dispensers is over. We cannot simply adopt this approach using existing models.

A more modern version of this strategy has been explored using a space-frame structure and panels hung on it. It has been applied – in different forms – to vehicles as different as the Pontiac Fiero (steel frame and plastic panels) and the new Audi Advanced Space-Frame Vehicle (aluminium section frame and aluminium panels). It is also being explored by GE Plastics and DuPont, in particular, as a means of developing the truly plastic car.

The conventional European approach to product lifecycles has been to keep a basic platform for 12 to 14 years, with at least one face-lift halfway. There has been some tendency to shorten the cycle, in order to match the Japanese, with their faster rate of introduction of new products. Even face-lifts are very expensive though, if all the body panels have to be changed. This is why the industry tries to keep the cycles as long as possible. This severely restricts its ability to react to or anticipate market changes and the emergence of niche demands, however.

Using engineering thermoplastics instead of sheet steel, if you make 200,000 cars a year then you have the option of three different shaped models at any one time. You can also change the models not every seven years, but after two years or three years or four years. So if you have three models, you change one after two years, one after three years and the third after four years. Over a total period of 12 or 14 years you have a continuum, dynamic change all the time. This allows a vehicle manufacturer, not to change something just for the sake of it, but to adjust to trends. The consumers in Europe are going to change more rapidly; this trend is already visible in the United States and specifically so in Japan. Plastics allow vehicle manufacturers to respond

Plastics have other benefits. It is possible to print onto panels, through a process called ink diffusion. The ink can be diffused in special materials, where the ink does not leak through the molecules. This produces remarkable decorative effects – for example, a niche vehicle where the inside and outside is printed so that it looks like jeans. A next generation 2CV, for example, although the Ethos from Pininfarina had that potential already. A car that is washable outside and inside, with four openings in the floor, like scuppers. A bit of an alternative between a car and a motorcycle. With the potential that plastic offers, such as printing, a car can be decorated in a really innovative way. Given the interchangeability of the panels, there may also come a day when you buy your grandmother's car with plastic panels, you junk those panels and you buy a set that makes sense for you.

It is also possible to mould extremely thin films, that can be printed, coloured and then coated onto the panels – this is called in-mould decoration. The film sometimes has to be pre-formed and the panel is over-moulded behind it. The result is remarkable: the whole piece is fixed and finished, with no need for a paint line or anything else.

Plastic and interchangeable body panels therefore offer more freedom and flexibility. The concept of plastic body panels has existed for some time, of course, and there are already a number of vehicles that have plastic wings (fenders) and bonnets (hoods). One of the most notable of these is within the Saturn range, the new GM division in the US. To illustrate the use and value of plastic in fenders, Saturn dealers initially used a plastic fender as a doormat. When a potential customer entered a dealer's showroom they would stand on the fender, crumpling it out of shape. As the customer stepped off it, it would spring back, returning to its original form, unmarked.

Plastics certainly offer some advantages, particularly in terms of resistance to impact and repairability. Most sheet metal fenders need to be repaired following impact at speeds of around four kilometres an hour. Plastics need paint repair at around 12 kph. With steel, after an impact at between 4 and 12 kph, the fender is so damaged that you have to reshape and/or fill the sheet metal with polyester. Just a little above 12 kph and the sheet metal fender is irreparably damaged and needs to be thrown away. The plastic fender survives to around 30 kph and then becomes irreparable.

In the short term, the space-frame and body-panel – whatever the material used – is probably only suitable for a few specific and typically low-volume applications. The problems associated with the expansion of plastic materials at different temperatures have still to be overcome satisfactorily. In the longer term, it may well be applicable for niche markets, through a 'long, thin' approach, in which the underlying design lasts a long time and the annual volumes are small. Depending on the approach and the material used, styling refreshment, variants and personalization can be achieved at low investment cost. Whether it can ever challenge the economics of conventional designs at high volumes in the long term is questionable – especially if the emphasis in these shifts from novelty to cost.

# More radical options could be invoked under severe environmental pressures

The other branch of the design hierarchy diagram will only come into operation under circumstances which go beyond the interplay of current market forces. In practice, this means when radical new technologies are mandated by some sort of government action. Given its enormous investments in existing technology, there is no reason on earth for the industry voluntarily to offer vehicles involving inherently different performance/cost compromises. Such vehicles could be forced on the industry by governments if there was a greatly increased concern about energy consumption, environmental protection, or simply road congestion. There are several different possibilities.

One involves government intervention to reduce the energy consumption of vehicles, as happened after the Suez and 1973 oil crises. There is little incentive for vehicle manufacturers to carry this out themselves – few buyers select their car primarily on the basis of the amount of fuel it uses. No major product adaptation is possible or reasonable in this respect, against transient events. Anyway, designing vehicles with a built-in option for lower consumption is normally very unattractive in cost terms during normal circumstances.

The key issue here is the time over which a government wishes to limit energy consumption. Restricting the demand for fuel or the average mileage a driver is willing to travel can be done for short periods, when the need arises. A government can increase fuel costs through taxation, introduce road pricing or directly ration vehicle use for whatever period it wishes. Short-term measures, typically driven by a reaction to a specific event, such as the Gulf War, may not necessarily lead to long-term changes in vehicle design.

In the long term a more severe and prolonged squeeze on consumption and emission levels could lead to huge and radical changes in vehicle design. The first stage of this would be a general downsizing of vehicles, still using the existing technologies and designs. It is also fairly easy to reduce power within a given size of vehicle by fitting smaller engines. Downsizing moves could be prompted by drastic action on fuel prices, through taxation, severe horsepower taxes on vehicles, or CAFE-type measures. In these, the government put the onus on the manufacturers to build a mix of vehicles that meet progressively tighter average fuel consumption standards.

The US downsizing remains a classic example of such a move, although the means chosen – imposing the CAFE standards on the supply side, while balking at the political cost of increasing fuel taxes to the motorist – created all kinds of undesirable distortions.

For governments wanting to limit energy consumption, encouraging downsizing by whatever means could be a fairly low-cost option, although investments would be needed to re-balance capacity from larger to smaller vehicles and drivetrains. Such a move would almost certainly kill off much of the emotional appeal of cars and the branding hype. It might also actually reduce the cost of motoring. Moreover, it could certainly be compatible with possible long-term changes in attitudes towards cars in developed countries.

# Radically-different materials and drivetrain options could be used in extreme cases

More radical options are technically possible, involving substantial changes in products. If the problem is a severe squeeze on energy consumption and emissions levels, coupled with resistance to major reductions in mileage and/or product downsizing, then consumption and emissions could be radically reduced by changing weight and perhaps also reducing the performance for a given size of vehicle.

The feasibility of building cars with all-aluminium or plastic bodies has been demonstrated, although the economics are not yet proven in large-volume production. Weight savings of up to 30% are possible. Inertial mass is a major determinant of power requirements and therefore of consumption and emission levels. Reducing design top speed and acceleration will also have a significant effect on fuel use, while still keeping the same drivetrain technology.

Beyond this, there is a range of options for the drivetrain, from changing the fuel to changing the entire process of energy generation. At the broadest levels today, these probably range from reformulating gasoline to developing some sort of nuclear- or hydrogen-powered drivetrain, probably converting the fuel into electricity. The effect on energy consumption of these measures can be considerable. The problem is the equally great impact on first cost. Shifting the whole market and industry in this direction would require massive investments and substantial increases in vehicle costs and prices. These could only be mandated by governments, which would require enormous political clout to impose them or an exterior problem of grave and enduring proportions.

We can go further still, if we are prepared to change the whole utilization, technology and design basis of the market and the industry.

Electric vehicles are perfectly feasible, for instance, but they impose range penalties which greatly reduce the flexibility of the vehicle – certainly using existing technology. They are also smaller and generally less attractive. The emissions problem is to some extent merely shifted from the point of use – the car – to the point of energy transformation – the power station.

# The most radical options involve challenging the functional nature of the car itself

If we are prepared to be really radical and question the whole format of the conventional car and roadway, then other possibilities open up. We could have very small one- or two-seat vehicles, with very limited performance and range, taking up much less road and parking space, principally for getting to work. Lanes could be narrower and load-bearing requirements on bridges and other structures much reduced. This would probably involve compromises on passive crash safety – but these might be partly alleviated by lower speeds. Much more could be done to control vehicle flows. The technology largely exists already. The problem is obtaining fitment to the enormous vehicle fleet. Again, none of these changes are likely to occur without government influence and incentives.

# There are real practical obstacles to major change

The biggest problem and hurdle with very radical changes is the parc. When there are already 470 million cars needing lanes the width they are today, it is simply not feasible to change to small and narrow vehicles quickly. There is an old joke concerning a country that decides to change from driving on the right to driving on the left. To simplify the process it recommends staggering the implementation. From Sunday, 'all cars will begin driving on the left', they say. 'From the following Sunday, this will be applied to trucks as well'. Really radical changes to vehicle design and technology face the same hurdle – they cannot be brought in gradually.

The vehicle industry, like many others, is not a natural proponent of major change. The *status quo* may not be challenging, but it is profitable. Anyway, radical change typically brings about major competitive upheavals in an industry. The motor industry tends to be more resistant to major changes than many others.

For all the vast range of improvements made to the product, cars remain functionally what they were 100 years ago. You cannot miniaturize the transport of people, as you can the storage of knowledge or the process of long-distance communications. In the car industry, the basic transactional unit is an 80-kg adult, or a set of four of them, and that tends to limit the options.

You cannot have the vast technology leaps that have characterized the electronics industry, where the ultimate unit is the single electron. The whole trend there has been miniaturization, from the vacuum tube through the transistor to VLSI (very large scale integration) circuits. While electronic controls and communications have invaded the car and its environment in no uncertain way, they cannot solve the problems of achieving better actuation in what remains at heart a mechanical engineering proposition.

The automotive industry is fundamentally a user rather than a generator of technology. Its products are nevertheless enormously complex in their functionality and must – above all – be very tightly integrated in their design. There is none of the separation and interchangeability of hardware and software that is so characteristic of computers. Vast technology leaps have not characterized the industry in the past and, given its skills, are unlikely to characterize it in the future. This may be a weakness.

Because of these factors, the automotive industry has been the great innovator in the organization of production. This is perhaps why most books on the industry focus on this aspect alone. The automotive industry has been the great industrial innovator of the modern world primarily because it invented mass production and the large-scale application of Taylorian doctrines about the division of tasks and the specialization of labour. It then added to its own pioneering work through the discovery of lean production and the reversion to multi-skilling and the delegation of responsibility. The social and behavioural change that this represents within the work organization is nothing short of revolutionary. The contrast between an old-style and a new-style automotive components plant, for example, is truly striking. The industry's whole supply side continues to go through a gargantuan upheaval and reorganization on a planetary scale.

But it is less open to change in other respects, and particularly in terms of radical shifts to product design or function. The automotive industry has been isolated and resistant to calls for change in the past in other respects. In the future, it may find it beneficial to encourage change in these areas also, rather than attempt to resist it.

# 20

# A global oligopoly: options for the car manufacturers

## Car manufacturers are moving towards a global oligopoly

Vehicle manufacturers have had numerous ups and downs over the last 100 years. There is one general trend, however, that of consolidation. Consolidation on a national basis, then at a regional level and increasingly, today, on a global scale.

It was mass production and the birth of the corporation that caused the initial wave of consolidation in the automotive industry in the 1920s because, for the first time, there were economies of scale. Costs became critical and those unable to compete faced the prospect of bankruptcy or takeover.

Even those responsible for mass production and vertical integration encountered difficulties. Ford found it difficult to keep his company afloat during the depression after he borrowed heavily, while GM faced bankruptcy twice between 1910 and 1922 (Figure 20.1).

This process of consolidation is continuing. Like most businesses, the motor industry seems to reach equilibrium when it establishes an oligopoly, a steady state where there are, at most, half a dozen major competitors. This was true in the US before downsizing. It can also be illustrated by looking at the history of vehicle producers in Western Europe.

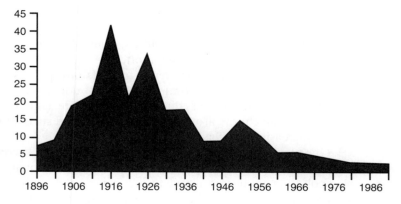

**Figure 20.1**  Number of manufacturers in the US from 1896 to 1993. (*Source*: Automotive News)

When car production began to expand in Europe after the Second World War each country was served by a large number of car and truck manufacturers. There were more than 25 car manufacturers in the UK. The next 20 to 30 years were a period of competitive rationalization, as the costs of model development and production increased.

By the 1960s each country was typically dominated by up to six major vehicle manufacturers. These produced and sold vehicles almost exclusively for their domestic markets. Then they started to export, becoming less dependent on domestic markets, competing on a regional or pan-national level. The extent of this export drive varies from country to country. German vehicle manufacturers were particularly good at developing sales in other countries. The French and Italian manufacturers were much less successful.

As before, a period of rationalization followed, during the 1970s. This time the consolidation was at a regional, rather than a national, level. The result, once again, was the dominance of six large manufacturers – but covering Europe rather than each country. From being a national oligopoly it became a regional oligopoly. Today, these dominant suppliers are known as 'Europe's Big Six'. They are Volkswagen, Opel (GM), Ford, Renault, Peugeot and Fiat, and they account for 75% of sales and 85% of production in the region.

This oligopolistic structure exists in each of the other major vehicle markets. Japan has five leading manufacturers – Toyota, Nissan, Honda, Mitsubishi and Mazda – which account for four in five cars sold. Similarly the US has six main suppliers, three Americans, GM, Ford and Chrysler and three Japanese, Toyota, Nissan and Honda. Together they account for nearly 90% of all new cars sold each year. The emergence of these dominant manufacturers has involved mergers, takeovers and bankruptcies.

Many famous marques have been lost. Still familiar names like Saab, Rover, Jaguar and Aston Martin are now owned by larger, regional parents while older marques like Morris, Triumph, Studebaker, Packard, Nash and Hudson are becoming forgotten.

Moreover, this natural tendency towards oligopoly is expected to continue. Now the trend is towards the global dominance of five or six manufacturers. This means that while there are still many smaller, national manufacturers around today they will find survival in the next decade increasingly difficult.

One other important point. While there is an overall economic logic that is driving the industry from a national, to a regional, to a global oligopoly, it is not just economic forces that are stimulating change. For much of the last 20 years, the process has been accelerated by one group of competitors, the Japanese. Their influence and control over the future consolidation of the industry is also likely to be immense.

## Winners and losers

Many national and regional competitors will face problems in the next decade as the industry rationalizes. Many will be forced to merge, cut back or seek alliances to survive. The key question for investors, car buyers, component suppliers and governments is: who will be the winners and who will be the losers? Where will the battle be fought? What are the factors that will determine success? The conclusions will be unpalatable for many, particularly the largest European competitors:

- There will be five main global car manufacturers, two American and three Japanese. No European supplier will become global unless it can merge with or take over a non-European competitor.
- The main battleground will be Europe.
- The key long-term competitive factor for success is scale, although there are a number of shorter-term issues that will influence competitive position.

Predictions about the prospects for this or that car manufacturer are made every day, particularly in the media. They are often superficial, even facile, and frequently rest on observations of the moment. As a consequence, they change with frustrating regularity. In reality, the prospects of the different vehicle manufacturers will be determined by two factors: the industry environment and their strategic positioning.

## The market and competitive environment will be harsh

The environment will determine the level of demand, both quantitatively (demand for individual transportation and unit volumes) and qualitatively (market segmentation, consumer preferences, price sensitivity).

The strategic positioning of each vehicle manufacturer will determine their ability to succeed. This is measured in terms of the company's positional assets and capabilities. The assets are the result of their historical performance. They are fairly visibly reflected in product lines, brand images, market shares, sourcing, manufacturing and distribution footprints, as well as cost and profitability structures. The capabilities are less visible but can be subsumed in their ability to manage the innovation, delivery and marketing streams cost-effectively.

We need to look out to beyond the year 2000, in order for there to be enough time for major changes to take place in an industry which has been fairly reluctant to accept change and especially rationalization. It is impossible to make a definitive forecast of what will happen to whom, and especially at what precise point in time. Despite that, it is important to reflect on the forces at work and on their possible effects in a harsh market and competitive environment.

Europe is the largest 'single' market in the global car industry. It is also the least well structured, the most fragmented – and the highest priced. This makes it the major future battleground of the industry. We therefore reserve the European market environment for particular examination and deal with the other regions first. Not surprisingly, the prospects in them are mixed, with some growth, some movement and some stagnation.

The US is currently experiencing a strong economic upturn, with an economy developing far more robustly than those of its Triad partners. This is naturally buoying up the car market and the financial fortunes of its manufacturers. This is a cyclical phenomenon, to be viewed against the background of very high levels of car penetration. The US market is clearly saturated, on a long-term view. Furthermore, the federal and trade deficit problems are by no means solved, any more than is the problem of the healthcare burden. Consequently, structural growth is not to be expected there. It is also subject to some non-negligible interventionist risks, such as tightened CAFE-type standards and the Californian emissions controls initiatives. The market is crowded with brands, many with marginal penetration and doubtful prospects of viability. The great changes of market share have already taken place, with the arrival of the Japanese transplants. This is not likely to be the arena for further such changes of position.

The internal Japanese market is rapidly approaching maturity and saturation, as indicated by its first experience of a serious cyclical decline. Government concessions to minicars are being withdrawn. The Japanese motor industry will become decreasingly dependent on its home market, as it continues to globalize and as the yen appreciates.

High growth rates in other markets, such as South Korea, China and other newly-industrializing countries of South East Asia, apply to markets too small to outweigh stagnation in the large Triad region. Third

World countries are simply too far from the threshold of the per capita income needed to start mass motorization, so that their impact on the global industry is small.

Demand-side prospects in Europe are not buoyant. Economic growth is not likely to be very vigorous, even once the continental countries come out of recession. Europe faces real long-term problems of competitiveness with the rest of the world. Automotive markets have clearly started to demonstrate the cyclical characteristics associated with maturity. In most of Western Europe, saturation levels have virtually been achieved in the vehicle parc. Reserves of potential growth in countries such as Portugal, Greece, the Czech Republic, and so on will only partly alleviate the problem.

There is a serious likelihood that real personal disposable incomes will be trimmed, as governments are forced to dismantle extensive welfare provisions and Europeans come to shoulder more of the burdens individually. This will have a direct effect on car buying intentions.

While this may not dramatically depress unit volumes in the short and medium term, because of the ratchet effect of cars being so built-in to everyday lives, it could well cause buyers to start behaving in a much more utilitarian and price-oriented manner. This would be particularly serious in Europe, where the market has been characterized by price levels significantly above those of the other Triad countries. The trend of recent years towards ever-stronger branding, supported by escalating advertising and promotional expenditures, in an attempt to avoid price-based competition, could be brutally reversed. The consequences for profits would be severe. In the longer term, there could be progressive disenchantment with the social and environmental costs of giving a high priority to road transport. The European market environment will therefore be characterized by low growth, financial difficulties and consolidation.

# A limited set of global players is already emerging

The strategic positions of individual manufacturers must be seen in the context of globalization. This is an underlying, long-term trend in the car industry, triggered by the downsizing of American cars driven by the CAFE regulations. It was first manifest in registrations, as markets became increasingly penetrated by imports but has been followed in production, through the increasing interconnection of the GM and Ford engineering and production systems, and the Japanese transplant phenomenon.

The emerging 'global' players are so labelled because of their relative omnipresence. Using 1996 forecasts, the geographical spread of the five most global manufacturers is plain to see. GM is still in the group by virtue of size and depth in North America, although it has lost much ground to the Japanese there, as well as its foothold in Japan. Ford – presumed in this analysis to have taken over full control of Mazda by then – will have begun to add the third leg to its Triad stool. The two largest Japanese, Toyota and Nissan, although still heavily dependent on Japanese production, will be on the path to having truly global market and production structures. Honda – the earliest to transplant abroad from Japan – is on the way, possibly less encumbered in the future by the removal of Rover.

The capabilities that enable these players to prosecute this strategy are vital. The Japanese redrew the engineering, manufacturing and sourcing approaches of the industry, as though on a clean sheet of paper. Critically, they have proven beyond doubt their ability to apply the precepts in distant locations and cultures, even creating complete local supply bases almost from scratch. Ford pioneered this approach within Europe and continues to try to globalize it. GM has made considerable headway in Europe, without yet transferring the recipe to North America.

# At the other end of the scale, a few players are in serious potential trouble

In Europe, Volvo has lost its link with Renault – apart from continuing the pre-alliance sourcing of engines. It has numerous problems: product positioning and eroding differentiation; over-dependence on the Swedish, US and UK markets, with falling shares and sales; inadequate scale for product line renewal; access to technology; and a poor cost position.

Fiat suffers from its 'fortress Italy' positioning, which affects both market footprint and product design and positioning. Its products are perceived as unreliable and its brand image is poor outside Italy. While its domestic market is increasingly penetrated by competitors, it has failed to break out of it. The ultimate value of the Fiat production and management model is not clear.

Daimler-Benz also contains the seeds of potential serious trouble – particularly in a scenario of increasing cost-consciousness in Europe. Its US position and quality image have been seriously eroded by Lexus. It remains over-dependent on its domestic market, Germany, which has not yet felt the impact of the Japanese moving upline. Its manufacturing integration and cost position are a liability. It is by no means obvious that ventures into minicars and Swatchmobiles can do much for it. The possibility exists that the group might seek to reduce the role of cars in its portfolio.

The smaller Japanese manufacturers – Daihatsu, Subaru and Suzuki – are very vulnerable to the maturing of the Japanese market, discriminatory measures such as the abolition of privileges for minicars, and the increasing difficulty of exporting against the yen rate. Suzuki's venture in Spain has collapsed, showing how hard it is for a small player – even Japanese – to go global. They are likely victims of the coming shake-out in Japan.

Similarly, it is difficult to predict a healthy future for the smaller Koreans, besides Hyundai, or manufacturers such as Proton. They are all too dependent – on parents for technology, on inadequate home markets, and on attempting to export into distant markets where penetration is increasingly hard to achieve for a newcomer.

## Those in the middle ground face difficult decisions to ensure their long-term survival

Mitsubishi could be a global player, with persistence. It has the backing of a major Japanese industrial group, good products and a history of commercial aggressiveness and success. It could go-it-alone but its more likely option is to find partners to accelerate its globalization – as it has begun to do in the Netherlands and once did with Chrysler.

By acquiring Rover, BMW has gained a valuable line-filler in the form of Land Rover, and potentially made some minor potential gains in range extension, vehicle design and UK sourcing. It remains more flexible than Daimler-Benz but will ultimately face the same structural problems: lack of world footprint and scale, over-dependence on Germany and a disadvantaged cost position. The worst aggregate threat is the progressive disappearance of the traditional segmentation boundary between volume and upline cars, as the Japanese move up the range and Europeanize their products.

Chrysler has survived for decades by outsourcing and nimbleness. It has perhaps gone further down the route to the 'virtual vehicle manufacturer' than most. The problem is how long it can conserve this lead and use it to parlay its disadvantages of scale. It may have to choose an alliance or merger soon.

Mazda's attempt to go global while Ford had other intentions for it has failed. It will probably have to reconcile itself to being the Japanese arm of Ford and thereby making some very valuable contributions to Ford, in terms of Japanese know-how, especially in new product development. MITI's attitude in the matter remains a question mark.

Hyundai has been the instrument of a classic government-inspired dash for growth. In this, it appears to have got the best of its alliance partner, Mitsubishi, which provided much of the original technology. Hyundai's ability to penetrate foreign markets much further seems questionable, particularly in an age of transplants.

Of the remaining Europeans, Renault has made the most valiant efforts to solve its cost problems, with PSA following and VW hardly started. None of these, alone or in combination, can solve the problem of being stuck in Europe, although VW alone has positions outside Europe. The most significant of these are in Brazil, Mexico and China. But Brazil is struggling, Mexico is in decline and China remains a long-term hope.

# The likely future of the players involves continuing consolidation of their positions

The critical issue for the two major US players, GM and Ford, will be to institute world-class best practice throughout their operations. GM will be striving to apply the medicine, developed at such cost in Europe, to its still considerable US operations. Ford is now in effective control of Mazda and may have a chance to benefit from Mazda know-how in a European assembly plant. It was the pioneer in creating Ford of Europe, in order to treat Europe as an integrated region rather than as a set of disconnected national markets. It is now striving to give itself truly global structures and processes, and is arguably the furthest down this route of globalization of any of the major players. It is probably the most global of all the manufacturers, in terms of its internal culture.

Toyota and Nissan have perhaps the most obvious future: to continue to prosecute their global expansion and domination strategies, building on their manufacturing and sourcing presence throughout the Triad to extend into local engineering and product design. This organic growth route is laborious but also the least hazardous, for those who can afford it. They will need to exercise some skill and judgement to avoid destructive head-on competition with each other. They still have a good way to go before they can operate as truly global companies – much decision making is still concentrated in Japan. The cultural challenge of achieving this is a serious one for them.

Honda has now taken the decision – albeit forced – to go its own way in Europe. It was the earliest Japanese manufacturer to attempt a major transplant operation. It has manufacturing presence in the UK, although it has done much less well in Europe than in the US, in marketing and market terms. A critical issue may be financial resources as Honda is the only fully independent Japanese player. Honda has now taken its decision and will build its own position in Europe, which makes it revert to a globalization strategy similar to that of its two larger brethren.

Mitsubishi might try to secure its global position by taking control of Volvo and infusing much-needed Japanese know-how into the Swedish as well as the Dutch operations. It may also move closer to Chrysler again.

BMW/Rover could be a future Volvo of the industry – looking for a partner at a time when partners will be scarce indeed. PSA, Renault and VW will be left to jostle for power in Europe. It is likely that PSA and Renault will draw closer together, reverting to the tendency of the 1970s. The cost in rationalization of products and facilities will be high, without solving their common footprint problem. VW must now face the same battles as Renault fought, against entrenched costs, and internal and external resistance to change – starting almost ten years later.

Chrysler will continue along the path towards the virtual VM but is likely to need and to find a partner. Its flexibility may increase its chances of doing so successfully. Hyundai may be on the treadmill to nowhere if it persists in trying to follow in the footsteps of the Japanese, without sufficient differentiation or ultimate resources. A possible outcome might be an attempt to develop in and with China.

# 21

# A global shake-out: the other actors and the future of the industry

## The components sector faces an even greater shake-out than the vehicle manufacturers

The world components industry is doubly exposed to pressures for rationalization because of the competitive pressures on its customers and its own incomplete restructuring. The vehicle industry will continue its march towards global oligopoly, as described above, which will put huge pressure on the smaller, regional competitors. This pressure will be particularly intense in Europe, whose native vehicle industry is fragmented and sub-scale, and coming under increasing pressure from its Japanese competitors, including their growing transplant operations. The components sector itself has historically been fragmented and inefficient. It remains mainly regionally-based, with the exception of a few semi-global players. A few large American and European suppliers span the Atlantic. Some Japanese are established on both sides of the Pacific. Hardly anyone is truly global as yet, although a few come close, such as Bosch, or GKN or some of the larger US groups, such as Allied Signal or TRW. The major Japanese suppliers are still some way behind in this but will surely continue to establish a global presence, through direct investments, joint ventures and alliances.

The whole components sector is still in the process of emerging from a 'dark age', in which the vehicle manufacturers applied a 'divide and rule' hegemony to it. In the face of the increasing opening up and global-ization of their sector, the vehicle manufacturers have been pushing hard to rationalize their supply chains and upgrade the quality of their relationships with their suppliers.

The Western players, however, still have a long way to go before the sharing of responsibility between vehicle and components manufacturers approaches the Japanese balance. Japanese vehicle manufacturers start with far lower levels of vertical integration. While their Western coun-terparts are moving in this direction, they are probably at least five years behind in terms of relationships and behavioural traits. As demonstrated earlier, the results show, in terms of gaps in speed of response, quality and – above all – cost.

The Japanese approach is easy to recognize – and indeed to imitate up to a point – in structural terms. Everyone knows about the concepts of tiering and delegation of responsibility, for both product and process. The problem is that the human relations dimensions are far more difficult to replicate, because the Western and Japanese traditions within the industry are so different. Worse, the Japanese have shown that they can replicate theirs in Western cultures faster than their Western competitors can adapt. The form of the tiering pyramid is less important in reality than the substance of relationships between vehicle manufacturers and suppliers, and between suppliers and suppliers.

There is still a long way to go. Japanese suppliers have at least partially effected their transplantation into North America. The North American components industry has begun to respond. In Europe, the Japanese have created an 'industry within an industry'. Their vehicle manufacturers have neither encouraged a lock-stock-and-barrel transplantation of their domestic suppliers into Europe, nor have they automatically signed up to be supplied by the *élite* of the European components industry. Instead, they have chosen a selected band of suppliers, about 200 strong, not all large, and predominantly based in the UK – a country widely assumed to have died within its automotive industry. It seems that willingness to work together was more important to them than established position or reputation.

The ultimate pattern in the components sector can already be guessed at. A few items – those that are standard, scale- and technology-intensive, and easily transportable – will be globally sourced. The classic example is the electronic chip. Most will be regionally sourced. A few large, complex assemblies will require a relative degree of proximity to the point of end-use, i.e. the vehicle manufacturer's assembly plant – within 300 to 400 km. Highly-sequenced assemblies, such as seats or painted bumpers or complete front-ends, will be put together virtually *in situ*, very close to the final assembly line.

Large, global suppliers will carry the responsibility for the develop-ment and supply of major systems and assemblies. Their R&D will be centrally conducted; customer applications engineering and module assembly will be decentralized, to a degree appropriate to the size, complexity and variability of the item; they may produce scale-driven components for themselves or source them outside from plants normally serving a regional or continental market base. Small, local suppliers will provide local fabrication and other services. The size distribution in the supplier industry will approximate the classical bimodal pattern of very large and very small survivors, with those in the middle trapped in non-competitiveness.

Again, and most importantly, structure, size and scale will not suffice alone. The critical items – whatever one's level in the supply hierarchy – will be:

- possession or at least control of a distinctive technology;
- the capabilities required to apply it effectively and proactively to the solution of customers' problems;
- world-class delivery capabilities, with respect to time, quality and cost;
- the ability to organize one's own sub-suppliers in a similar fashion;
- seeing right through the structures, in order to understand and anticipate requirements.

All this represents a vast set of challenges. In an industry long brought up to work with being told what to do from above, the adaptations will not be easy. We are looking at few survivors among the major proprietary suppliers of systems and components: perhaps 200 or 300 global players. It is the change of culture which will be so hard to achieve.

# An equivalent shake-out is coming in distribution – but when?

If divide-and-rule is henceforth dead upstream of the vehicle manufacturers, then symmetry at least suggests it should disappear downstream also. The distribution, retailing and after-sales support of cars has already been described above as the last frontier for competitive advantage. The inefficiencies and costs of the present arrangements are ultimately not acceptable. In the short term this is clearly going to be the last ditch of irrational resistance. There are too many economic and personal interests at stake in this particular sector for reform to happen readily. One must also be realistic: this remains – and always will remain – a domain in which personal service and individual relationships can go some way to compensate for lack of overall scale.

Nevertheless, in some place, at some time, someone will break ranks. We shall see the emergence of large, powerful, scale-driven service groups, which will act in partnership with the vehicle manufacturers – and, indeed, the suppliers of replacement parts and accessories – but on a basis much closer to equality. The consequences for the industry will be incalculable. But they will also bring it much closer to full maturity.

# The industry's relations with governments will need to be put on a sounder footing

The role of governments in controlling and regulating the industry is likely to increase rather than decrease over the next several years and even decades, and to change in emphasis.

It may be that, with consolidation and rationalization of the industry, opportunities for national governments to protect their national champions will diminish. It may take some time yet for this message to be heard and understood, particularly in developing countries which still believe that an export-based national industry can be created by government encouragement and support.

What is increasingly clear, as discussed in Part One of this book, is that market forces unaided do not produce satisfactory sets of options or choices in the field of transportation. As the demand for personal transport is not likely to decrease radically for quite a while, if ever at all, conflicts between individual options and decisions and the interests of the community are bound to become sharper. All the evidence suggests that the freedom of decision of the individual will become increasingly constrained: by road pricing schemes, more parking restrictions and charges, even automatic guidance of vehicles on highways, if some of the more ambitious research programmes come to fruition.

There is no direct economic or financial motivation, for players on the supply side of the industry, to invest voluntarily in developing safer, lighter, more economical, or less polluting vehicles unless they can see a decisive competitive advantage in doing so. These investments are hardly likely to produce vehicles that cost significantly less than those they would replace. Which is the only ultimate piece of differentiation in a competitive world.

Governments inescapably will have to set the parameters which influence and determine the trade-offs made by manufacturers in designing vehicles, and those made by individuals in purchasing and using them. They will determine construction and use regulations, the taxation of vehicles and fuels for them, what will be provided in the way of highway and informational infrastructures, and what incentives and inducements are offered in favour of alternative means of transportation and communication. They will, in all likelihood, get drawn into the disputes – nominally internal to the industry, but in fact with a much wider, public-interest dimension – around the restructuring of distribution, and the extent to which exclusive franchising arrangements can or cannot be retained.

The industry has a huge opportunity in this area. Historically, it has been generally reactive in its relationships with governments. It has often been defensive when under accusation – whether justified or not. As this book has tried to show, cars are a great boon but they do also have real costs and cause real societal problems. Much of the debate around these points is reduced to opinion because of the lack of an adequate basis of objective fact. There are real options for blending personal and public transportation, for example. They are not easy to define, sell or implement. Much more could be done to establish common ground with governments and other interested parties. There is a very good – but not unlimited – case to be made for the car as part of advanced societies in the twenty-first century.

The industry would do itself a power of good by accepting this fact – and then acting to promote the most acceptable solutions. Simply put, it needs to act less as a set of supply-side actors who use fairly crude marketing hype to maximize the market's uptake of their products. This means taking a wider view of what 'demand' is, and of the stakeholders in it. It means promoting wider transportation solutions, rather than the narrower one of personal vehicles only.

This is certainly not going to be an easy task, given the multiplicity of actors and interests, and the complexities of the automotive and transportation sectors. Nor does the fragmentation of responsibilities on the side of governments help much, either. Nor the industry's own difficulty in defining what can be treated on an open, pre-competitive, collaborative basis, and what cannot. Despite that, there is a real possibility that the product/market segmentation of the industry will change yet again – and in an uncontrollable fashion, if no better-founded dialogue is established with the legislators and regulators. Those who fall behind on this dimension may be putting themselves at risk in the long term. Conversely, those players who develop a superior capability for playing this complex and difficult game may make substantial gains.

# The future of the industry – a conclusion

Beyond the ups and downs of economic and automotive market cycles, the ebbing and waning short-term fortunes of models and marques, the conflicts with suppliers and distributors, some realities of the industry have to be borne in mind when thinking about winners and losers.

### Scale is for real

Despite some brave talk, scale is a fact of life in the industry. Lean production has not flattened scale curves: it has cut out waste and brought costs back down onto the scale curves. The basis through which effective scale is achieved has changed, notably through the new relationships between car manufacturers and their suppliers. Major suppliers will increasingly be the creators, proprietors and purveyors of technology and of the design of sub-systems and components. The vehicle manufacturers will concentrate more on the higher-order strategic roles of market analysis, product positioning, design of vehicle packages, and the management of the innovation and delivery chains of the industry.

### Consolidation is inevitable

In this root-and-branch restructuring, consolidation is inevitable – at the level of both car and component manufacturers. One consequence will be a significant shift in the balance of power, with smaller and less capable car manufacturers attracting much less interest and respect, and thereby eventually becoming product- and cost-disadvantaged.

### Strategic alliances are but way stations

Recent history has graphically demonstrated what should have been obvious: that strategic alliances are dynamically unstable creations which have their uses, need careful managing, and also eventually collapse or fly apart. They are no more than way stations on the painful road to consolidation. The major Japanese car manufacturers appear to have made their opinions about them clear; all are now pursuing globalization via organic development.

### There are no hiding places for the Europeans

It is hard to escape the conclusion that there will be no easy hiding places for the Europeans – unless Europe contrives to shut out the world by act of political will. They have maintained a competitive stalemate within Europe for too long, thereby failing to rationalize the European-owned industry, while surrendering or failing to gain positions overseas.

### There is no escape through new markets

There is no evident means of escape from the consequences through seeking new, growing markets in South East Asia or elsewhere: they are too limited, too well-identified and too heavily-targeted by potent competitors.

This industry faces a very tough future. It is omnipresent – at least in the developed world – important to individuals and economies, and uniquely resilient. It will not disappear or be rapidly superseded. It still has an immense amount to offer. But it will be subject to enormous changes, caused by both external and internal pressures. In the end, for all its size and glamour, it is subject to the same laws of economics, competition and ageing as all others. That is why it is so rich in lessons, along every dimension of industrial, organizational and human behaviour.

# Summary of Part Four

Good strategies are both creative and realistic. In the words of Bruce Henderson, the founder of modern strategy consulting, 'Be brilliantly conceptual – but then stand back and subject your creation to searching critique'. You need to be able both to break the mould in imagination and then to test the new concepts rigourously for self-consistency and good sense. The business world is not forgiving of slackness:

- Good strategies are multi-dimensional and look beyond the existing organization. Companies frequently define strategies that depend on their existing organizational structures, their existing products or an historic market segmentation. Good strategies need to account for the manufacturing and supply options, the distribution network, the opportunities to change the market, to change the products, to change the cost curve. Each part of the value chain can be used to create opportunity.

- Industries tend towards oligopoly, an equilibrium where around four to six suppliers dominate the market – assuming the segmentation has been done right and the boundaries of the business have been correctly defined. Pushing for the creation of these oligopolies can present strategic opportunities and advantage. It is essential to define the borders. Is the oligopoly going to be local, national, regional or global?

- Strategic alliances are but way stations – they are inherently unstable, although valuable in very specific conditions. Strategic options that involve strategic alliances should also include a post-alliance vision of what to do when independence is re-established.

- Within the correctly-defined business, scale is the ultimate source of competitive advantage – not profit or technology or patent or production processes or branding. Scale offers cost reduction and power, power to influence or even drive markets, to change the segmentation and even to change the scale curve itself.

- The idea of a niche producer surviving for long in a global oligopoly industry is a romantic illusion, unless that player has a means of changing the industry's rules to its advantage – and thus of ceasing to be a niche player. If an industry requires global scale for success, being sub-scale means failure. The scale competitor can replicate the niche player's skills more cheaply. Properly led, the big battalions tend to win. Scale is essential for advanced systems and fundamental technology. It also counts heavily in procurement and in securing effective distribution.

# PART FIVE

# Learning from
# the industry

# Managing change: the car industry and the lifecycle

## The maturing car industry

The world car industry is complex, involving as it does lengthy innovation, delivery and marketing chains, that reach from the smallest sub-supplier to the aftermarket customer for service, repair or accessories – perhaps ten years after the vehicle was last produced and 20 or even 25 years after it was first designed. Our whole thesis has been that, wrapped around these already long product lifecycles, is an even longer industry lifecycle. This one is not easy to visualize, on account of its very length and because of all the short- and medium-term events and fluctuations which obscure it. But it is there to be seen – if one takes enough *recul historique*. Which is what every student of business is required to do academically, and which every manager ought to do professionally.

# The lifecycle is present in every facet of the industry

In this book we have discussed eight different aspects of this complex industry. They are summarized in Figure 22.1.

- First, the automobile as a social phenomenon. It has clearly gone through a lifecycle process in this guise: from an exciting novelty; to something one couldn't have enough of ('What's good for GM, etc.'); to an emerging problem; and finally to a moloch to be contained – in the eyes of some, at least.
- Second, the staggering – and then slowing – growth of the volumes produced. From a European curiosity made in dozens; to an American mass product built in hundreds of thousands; to a global production of over 40 million per year; to the limits imposed by its affordability and by market saturation.
- Third, the changes in its end customers: from European and near-European aristocrats and other experimenters; to the motorization of the American farmer; to mass motorization and suburbia; to the cult object; and, finally, to the beginnings of questioning the resulting dependence.
- Fourth, the staggering transformation of the product, within the same basic purpose of providing private transportation: from the craft-assembled, bespoke carriage; to the Model T and its later European and still-later Japanese imitators; to product ranges and variety wars; and – perhaps – back to more standardization again, whether visible or under the skin.
- Fifth, the changes in technology: from hesitating competition between electric, external combustion (steam) and internal combustion; to the dominance of the internal combustion engine; and – possibly – a partial revival of the electric car. From the bolt-on structure

---

- The social phenomenon
- Volume growth
- Changing customer needs
- The product transformation
- Technological change
- Changes in engineering and production
- The supply revolution
- Changes in distribution and support

---

**Figure 22.1**   Elements of the automotive industry lifecycle.

of separate chassis and body; to unitary construction; and perhaps partially back, to spaceframes and hang-on, replaceable panels. From an almost purely mechanical engineering proposition to a hive of electronic controls.

- Sixth, the great adventures in engineering and production: from craft manufacturing; the micro-division of labour and the strictly-timed assembly line; and then back to group work and the pre-assembly of modules. From deeply vertically-integrated mass production of standard designs to a much more project-oriented industry.
- Seventh, the huge changes in supply structures: from the early vehicle manufacturers doing virtually everything (even their own engine oil and tyres, in some cases); through massive vertical integration upstream, as in the case of Ford; to the emergence of powerful independent suppliers. From fragmented and vassalized national suppliers to tiered structures and powerful international supplier groups, with an increasing control over the underlying technology of the vehicle. From the vehicle manufacturer as all-powerful feudal lord to his role as architect of the house, with minimum resources.
- Eighth, the changes in distribution and after-sales support: from the owner being expected to be his own mechanic and adventurer, in a era of frequent breakdowns; to the simplification of the task, as in the Model T; to the emergence of franchised dealer networks and the battles with the independent repair and distribution sector; to – perhaps one day – less conflictual and more rational structures.

Is history over, in this industry? Most assuredly not. The changes – outlined above – have been immense. In its nascent and growth phases, the automobile industry was every bit as dynamic and exciting as today's *Wunderkinder*, such as PCs or telecommunications. Indeed, it was the pioneer of massive industrial change, directly affecting the consumer. The title of 'The Machine that Changed the World' is deserved indeed – within some limits, notably those of the developed world. Change goes on – but no longer in the heady atmosphere of growth. We are well into the phase of maturity and perhaps edging that of decline, even though we may not quite clearly perceive it yet. The future battle will be long – and bitter.

# An imperfectly-structured and image-dependent industry

The conclusions reached at the end of Part Four can be summarized in the terminology of economics: the automotive industry is still imperfect. It is still quite a long way from having reached its ultimate mature structure.

It is still full of redundancies and contradictions. There are still far too many players in it. Most of them only just survive because an image- and price-umbrella is maintained over most market/product segments. The full force of a scale- and cost-advantaged global competitor has not yet been felt. The industry is in a major transition phase, from regional to global oligopoly. The shake-out is in progress at all levels – visibly so for the vehicle manufacturers; invisibly for the components suppliers; and incipient in distribution.

Trade restrictions prevented the Japanese bringing their capabilities to bear fully during their export-based expansion phase. Once they are fully installed in their second-phase transplant strategy and no longer have to face any volumetric quotas, they may resume the aggressive pursuit of market share. Then cost and scale will reappear as the ultimate differentiators. There will not be enough image-conscious, car-lover, price-insensitive niches for weaker competitors to hide in. The vicious circle of product proliferation and marketing hype will be broken. The bubble will burst. The industry shake-out will be all the more brutal for having been so long delayed.

The attempts to delay this through sterilizing distribution will ultimately prove extremely dangerous to the weaker, defending players. The traditional set of franchised distribution arrangements is a strong inertial factor in this industry, which has so far been vehemently opposed to a concentration and liberalization of these arrangements. There is an understandable fear of what has so clearly happened in other sectors where large, strong distributors and retailers have seized an increasing degree of power and control. The difficulty is that here, too, structural costs are considerably in excess of what they might be under more rational and less fragmented structures.

The idea of a general transfer of market power and brand strength from product/producer to outlet/distributor/retailer remains profoundly unpalatable to the industry. Yet this is exactly what has happened in other sectors, and even within some sub-sectors of the automotive industry, such as tyres, exhausts or glass replacement. But this has only generally been true where the economic arguments in favour of the large independent retailer or distributor are overwhelming. In most instances, the industry is still a long way from achieving real partnership relations in its downstream distribution and retailing components. If the analogy of what has happened and continues to happen upstream, in the structures of and relationships with suppliers, has any validity at all, then a great deal is going to change here also.

# Understanding the need for change has always been difficult

At the start of the 1920s, the Model T accounted for around 50% of car sales in the United States. By 1926, it controlled only a third. It was a great car, responsible for the demise of many early competitors through a combination of cost, innovation and standardization. Yet its decline was rapid. Why? Because, like many companies, Ford had become complacent, it had reached a plateau. It is almost as if companies in monopoly positions self-destruct. Henry Ford forgot to take into account changes taking place in the market and at his competitors.

The Model T was a touring, open topped car, available only in black. Competitors had already demonstrated that consumers wanted closed cars and in a choice of colours. Moreover, while the Model T emphasized its low price, competitors had discovered that consumers were willing to pay more for an additional diversified set of products, with additional features. Of course, by the 1980s, the Japanese demonstrated that consumers would be even happier if they could pay less and get a better product.

The experience of Ford's Model T has been repeated many more times. In the 1970s, GM refused to change its products to meet the needs of the market after the oil shock, and lost considerable market share. More recently, Mercedes-Benz believed that its 100-year-old reputation could easily withstand an assault by the upstart Lexus – which it did. For just over two years.

The decline of the Model T offers lessons. Most obviously, it says that you should understand the market and your competitors. It also illustrates that consumers will happily pay a premium for higher quality. But, there is a far more important message about leadership. Leaders of organizations, particularly successful ones, need to have a vision. Ford clearly did. It is tough, however, to develop a new vision once the original objectives have been achieved. It is even tougher to sustain a series of internal revolutions within a large organization – yet this is exactly what top management should do.

Henry Ford achieved his great and epoch-making vision. A low-cost, high-volume car, that made individual mobility a reality. But he found it incredibly difficult to develop an alternative mission once this had been achieved. Ford was not simply being forced to change a product. He was being forced to abandon the Model T, the car that had created personal mobility, that had proved the value of mass production, that had made the Ford Motor Company one of the most significant in the world.

When he eventually accepted that the Model T needed to change, he closed his factories for six months to develop the Model A. That lost momentum and even more market position. Despite loyalty for the Model T, which generated sales in the first year after the Model A was launched, sales began to falter. It seems that even the best leaders of businesses, countries, public bodies and armies have a finite level of energy. Their visions and ambitions, once achieved, can stumble. Henry Ford, as probably the single most significant businessman to have lived, highlights this well.

# Scale is the ultimate differentiator

The car industry illustrates that technology, often seen as a source of differentiation, only offers advantages for a limited time. The upline car producers of the 1980s, Mercedes-Benz, BMW and Jaguar, were seen by the industry as innovators. They held the technological lead at the time and their cars commanded a premium as a consequence. High profits meant that they could spend more on research and development. That meant that they were the originators of technological innovations, the first to fit new features. When electronic fuel injection was developed, it was fitted on the top of the range cars first. It was the same with ABS, with air bags and with air-conditioning. The upline car builders could afford to invest in the research, to develop these products and to fit them because their vehicles were so expensive.

But this equation does not ultimately stand the test of time, or of economies of scale. The following figures are illustrative. If an upline car maker like Mercedes-Benz makes around 450,000 cars a year and each is valued at $50,000, that gives a sales figure of $22bn a year. If 5% of that is spent on research and development, that makes just over $1.1bn a year available. If a Japanese car maker, such as Toyota, produces around 4.7 million vehicles a year, despite a much lower average value, of, say, $15,000 each, its annual turnover is more than $70bn. If it spends the same percentage of its turnover on R&D, it will have more than 3.5 times the budget of Mercedes. Of course it will have a much bigger model range to spend that money on, but there will clearly be economies of scale. The power of scale only becomes obvious, however, if Toyota decides to increase its development expenditure. If it needs another $1bn to develop an upline car, like a Lexus, it need only put aside another 1.4%

of sales. For Mercedes to put aside another $1bn, it would need to double its R&D budget, and would probably wipe out its profits in the process. The same is true of manufacturing technology. Increased scale means more funds are available for investment, for outplaying competition. This is an iron law – all too often obscured in the heady phases of industry launch and growth, but increasingly and painfully obvious in maturity.

## Even profit is secondary

In the US and much of Europe, the conventional approach to business is that profit is the main objective. The stockmarkets measure earnings per share and annual reports concentrate on margins. Of course, a business must make a profit to survive, but if that objective overrides that of growth, it will ultimately fail. Ask any business student, looking at his first corporate strategy case study, what the first objective of a business is and he will say it is to make a profit. Entrepreneurs are in business to make money.

Such a view makes it acceptable for businesses in the West to rationalize, to cut-back, to concentrate on 'core products'. Yet this is short-sighted. If product technology and manufacturing technology need development, the larger company will always be better placed to finance the necessary investment, over the long term. As the example above illustrates, an extra few hundred million dollars of expenditure is a lot less serious for a multi-billion dollar corporation than for a multi-million dollar one. Yet the amount of money each will need to spend to develop a product will be the same. If the development of anti-lock brakes costs $300m and needs 50 full-time engineers, it costs the same to the big company as it does to the small one.

The most important measures of strategic strengths are therefore size and the rate of growth. It is not profitability or earnings per share. Look at many of the Japanese conglomerates. Their rates of profitability are low compared to many companies in the West (Table 22.1). Their rates of growth are much higher. The profitability will come, it may just take 20 years for payback, rather than 18 months.

A comparison of these conclusions can be made with military strategy. Technology, image and even profitability are features that offer short-term advantage. They will not win the war, they may win short-term, tactical skirmishes or battles. Competitors have to keep sight of the long-term objectives, if they want to win the war. In industrial economics, winning is determined by scale. Of course, you have to invest in technology, but it will not allow you to win the war.

The situation is more obvious in such industries as automobiles, cameras or consumer electronics, because the Japanese have not only

**Table 22.1**   Japanese firms go for growth, the others for profitability.

| | Net income/Sales, 1991 % | | Net income/Sales 1991 % |
|---|---|---|---|
| Nissan | 0.7 | British Aerospace (1990) | 2.6 |
| Daihatsu | 0.9 | Hitachi | 2.9 |
| Mitsubishi | 0.9 | Matsushita | 3.7 |
| Suzuki | 0.9 | Toyota | 4.0 |
| Mazda Motor | 1.0 | TRW (1992) | 4.2 |
| NEC | 1.5 | Allied Signal | 4.4 |
| Honda | 1.6 | General Electric | 4.4 |
| Toshiba | 2.4 | Lucas Industries (1990) | 5.6 |
| | | IBM | 6.7 |

| | Sales growth 1988–92 % | Margins % |
|---|---|---|
| Allied Signal | 1.1 | 4.4 |
| General Electric | 17.0 | 4.4 |
| TRW | 19.5 | 4.2 |
| Lucas Industries | 20.2 | 5.6 |
| British Aerospace | 28.7 | 2.6 |
| Suzuki | 29.0 | 0.9 |
| Mitsubishi | 53.7 | 0.9 |
| Daihatsu | 76.6 | 0.9 |

(*Source*: annual reports)

fought and won the tactical battles with the long term in mind – they have defined them. In the past, these industries were very slow moving, with little technical innovation. The Japanese increased the pace of technological development. They brought better processes and accelerated the lifecycles to diffuse new technology more rapidly. Their long-term objective, however, was growth.

It is essential to understand the time horizons of competitors. Are they looking at long-term scale, as the Japanese seem to be in this industry, or are they concentrating on short-term-technology fixes to problems, like much of the pharmaceutical industry?

## But growth doesn't necessarily mean you are doing it right

Having said that, growth is not an indication, in itself, that you are meeting the needs of the market. The car market's move from being product-push to demand-pull in the US also offers lessons. In the 1970s, the traditional suppliers kept pushing the same products out to their customers year after year with minor changes. Each car was individually specified, with a huge range of options. The Japanese entrants offered a cost-effective package, with everything as standard.

It may seem simple, but this illustrates the need to understand the changes that take place in markets over time. Although the volume of vehicles sold was continuing to grow, the nature of demand was changing. Traditional suppliers thought that their continued sales growth indicated a successful and defensible position, a good strategy. They were fooled into thinking that the growth meant that the products on offer were right. Traditional product-push suppliers therefore lost share as consumers became more demanding and moved to new suppliers that offered a more cost-effective and complete product range.

# Image is another historical positional asset – and potentially transient

It's the same with image. Mercedes-Benz' image was its source of differentiation, as much as its technology. It had carefully nurtured its image over many decades until the name commanded a premium. Its reputation was like that of Gucci or Christian Dior. Since Lexus, Mercedes-Benz' position is moving back to normal economics, driven by cost and scale. While the name still commands added respect in most markets it may be losing that premium in California and other parts of the US. That said, it will be a long time until it disappears altogether, unless the company makes a slip. While image was a source of differentiation for Mercedes it now seems to be on a 20-year wane.

# Strengths can become weaknesses

There are two clear examples in this industry of strengths changing to weaknesses. The first is where model variations offered to car consumers by the US vehicle manufacturers in the 1970s became a liability when the Japanese began to standardize. The second is in the 1990s, when the reverse occurred. Standardization became a weakness when the Japanese used improvements in production technology to increase the choice available to consumers without a significant increase in costs. These examples are relevant for any industry, as they illustrate that an over-simplistic view of strengths and weaknesses can lead to trouble. It is too easy to sit and analyse a company's competitive position and assume that strengths can be built off and that weaknesses need to be addressed. It was one-dimensional thinking of this sort that caused the US and European car manufacturers to suffer. The Japanese used their competitors' strengths as weapons against them on both occasions.

Worse, to misquote Oscar Wilde, for the US and European suppliers 'to have been caught out once by this strategy is unfortunate, to have been caught out by it twice seems a little careless'. The strengths and weaknesses of a business are not absolute – they depend entirely on where you are standing. It also highlights the fate of those that do not understand the past. They may be condemned to relive it.

Other examples of strengths that are likely to become weakesses can be seen in retail banking and telecommunications. In retail banking, banks have invested heavily in the development of branches. While customers needed these to carry out their business these were essential assets. Now many banks in the United States and Europe are developing telephone-banking services to meet the needs of their customers. Some banks have been set up without any branches at all. This has changed the economics of retail banking completely as those banks that can provide services without having to maintain an expensive branch network are able to offer lower charges and better rates of interest. For the traditional retail banks what were once their biggest assets are increasingly becoming costly liabilities.

Similarly, the biggest asset of traditional telecommunications suppliers, and the largest barrier to entry for competitors, was the vast network of land-based copper cable pairs and exchanges that they had installed over the last 50 or more years. The emergence of cellular, satellite and optical-fibre-based telecommunications is increasingly making these assets redundant. Once again, what only a few years ago would have been regarded as a major strength, has become a formidable weakness.

# Opportunities can become risks

There are also times when opportunities can become risks. Few industries are exposed to environmental legislation as much as the car industry. This means that while it will create many problems for the industry, it will also create a great many opportunities. Further growth in catalysts is assured, for example. That does not necessarily mean that traditional suppliers to the catalyst industry will benefit.

The main metal used in catalysts today, platinum, is expensive and often sourced from unstable countries. While the number of catalysts in use was low, this was an issue, but not a major one. As the volume of platinum used has grown catalyst manufacturers have found it increasingly worthwhile for them to invest in research into alternative metals. The irony for the platinum industry is that what first appears to be an opportunity, is actually a risk. The increase in demand has changed the economics of researching an alternative.

# Many markets are fragmenting

The car market, like many other consumer sectors, is becoming increasingly fragmented. This is both supply and demand led. The demand side of the equation is explained by the growth of individualism in the West, largely a result of the increase in average levels of wealth.

On the supply side, improvements in production technology have allowed greater flexibility in the manufacturing process without adding enormous additional cost. This means that we can better satisfy the increasingly fragmented demands of consumers. This is not only true in the motor industry but also in financial services where technology has allowed a revolution to take place in the delivery channels. This has allowed more flexibility and a better matching of the product, e.g. a bank account, to the consumer's needs. The same is true in many other sectors, from mountain bikes to television channels to clothing. Increasingly diverse customer demand means that suppliers have to invest in new technology if they are to meet these demands without increasing costs. That does not mean that there are more niches on the supply side. While the demand side may offer opportunities for focus, the underlying economics of the supply side of most consumer businesses remains firmly dependent on scale.

# Environmentalism is here to stay

For many committed environmentalists this may seem a ridiculous statement, of course environmentalism is here to stay. Yet there are many in the car industry, the oil industry the chemicals industry and the consumer-goods industries that believe that environmentalism is a passing, marketing wave. Their arguments are powerful and logical. They say, 'it was only 20 years ago that we were all talking about an impending ice-age and look what happened to that'. Or, more cynically, 'how else can environmental scientists generate funding for their research unless they create a scare that the end of the world is imminent'. Such scepticism may be right.

However, the issue of whether or not environmentalism is here to stay depends on whether its impact is transitory or structural. A look round any supermarket would suggest that it is transitory, given the volume of 'eco-friendly' labels that have emerged in the last few years. It appears to be a marketing bandwagon used to boost sales. We believe that there is evidence to suggest that the growing environmental consciousness is structural.

First, there is a hole in the ozone layer and there are government plans in place to reduce CFC use. More and more species are facing extinction, fish stocks are declining, city atmospheres are deteriorating and carbon dioxide emissions are rising. These are facts, and there are others of a similar nature. So, something bad is actually happening and we, as a race, are trying to address these problems and their effects.

Second, there is a great deal of 'low-level noise' that suggests that a wave of structural change could be growing. There is the legislation in California, the attempt to ban cars in many cities, increasing evidence of a link between skin and respiratory problems and motor vehicles, greater legislation on industrial and sea pollution, the Rio treaty to reduce carbon emissions, more limits on waste disposal and the increasing power of bodies like the Environmental Protection Agency in the US. There are clearly many more examples. Looked at together, they suggest that the pressure for change, for a more environmental perspective is increasing. Clearly, this only applies to the developed world.

The third piece of evidence that the change could be structural is more difficult to quantify. It is that the opinions of our children, those that will make the future leaders of our society, seem radically in favour of environmental protection. Although it is certainly arguable that this generation does not yet understand the economic costs of protecting our environment, the strength of their views is such that this may not matter.

This growth in environmentalism has serious implications for almost every business. For the car industry, it is particularly serious. The motor car is one of the primary targets for environmental attack and unless it is ready to respond the industry may suffer accordingly.

In response to this growing environmentalism, industries and governments face a number of difficult choices. For large multinational industries cost competitiveness is essential for survival. If environmental taxes are imposed in one region of the globe they will simply move production to a less costly region. This was clearly explained to us by the chief executive of a large chemical company: 'If the EU imposes taxes on my emissions or restricts my outflows I will simply move my production to the Third World, where such restrictions do not apply.'

While this may be shocking, it is clearly economically and strategically sound. If he were to remain in Europe his cost base would rise and he would be increasingly uncompetitive with suppliers outside. Even if the EU were to tax chemical imports to account for this variation, the European supplier would remain at a disadvantage. The chemical industry, like the car industry, is global. Being restricted to one region limits the economies of scale available. So a chemical company restricted to the higher costs of the EU could not become global, resulting in a structural disadvantage.

Of course, this only covers the effects of environmentalism from a business perspective. Its impact on governments and countries would be just as serious. The Third World, where labour is cheap and environmental restrictions less stringent, would become a centre for the most polluting industries. To attract and keep these businesses countries in the region would be constrained. They could not impose restrictions on pollutants, unless they all acted together and applied these globally.

The prospect of their acting together is remote. There will always be nations so desperate for substantial inward investment that they are willing to pay almost any price to achieve it.

In contrast, the developed regions of the world would lose the investment and jobs that the migrating business sectors create for them today. Although they may be grateful in the short term, as it solves the problems of pollution, the longer-term implications may be less palatable. While new economic sectors can be developed which create jobs and wealth, without being polluting, the developed nations may have to face the loss of strategically important industries and skills.

Besides, although the developed nations would, at best, be pollution free, the net effect of industries migrating to other areas is that the total pollution generated would remain the same, from a global viewpoint. It may actually increase. All that taxes in one region do is move the pollution elsewhere. They do not solve the problem. And, if legislation in the Third World were already less stringent than in the developed world, then such a migration may actually increase the damage on a global scale.

# Conservatism is a dangerous weakness

Despite its image, the car industry is not very innovative – it applies the technology of others. It is not a very fast moving industry any more, and that can be a weakness. In 1946, John O'Neil, the Pulitzer winning author, predicted the emergence, by the early 1950s, of atomic cars that would be simple and safe. Similarly today, electric cars, mulitplex wiring and navigation systems are all said to be ten years away. The trouble is that they were ten years away in 1985, in 1975 and before that. The technology for future vehicles is largely understood, the industry, however, is very conservative. To be fair, most big industries are the same. Banks, for example, have had the technology to introduce a virtually cashless society for more than 20 years. Yet for one bank to invest in the new technology required is expensive and risky. It may win but, more likely, other banks will ensure that it fails. As Machiavelli said, 'There is nothing more difficult to carry out...than to initiate a new order of things.'

Limiting the pace of change is dangerous. Radical and fundamental change often comes from outside the conventional borders of an industry. Radical change is also easier to achieve if it is directed at a conservative, mature business. The replacement of gas lamps with electric lighting, the eradication of the slide-rule by the calculator, and the demise of the vinyl record, are examples of where mature, complacent and conservative businesses have been knocked sideways by new technologies. It was the same with the horse and carriage when the car came along. The auto industry's conservatism is a weakness – as it is for any industry.

# Industries have ratchets that obstruct needed change

It's not just the car industry that has a ratchet, making change difficult. The same problem exists in many other sectors. Despite the best intentions of companies, new ideas often face structural barriers. In the case of the car industry, the factors which cause radical change to be resisted are:

- The way we live makes motor vehicles essential to lifestyle in the developed world.
- Governments earn considerable revenues from motor vehicles, making them unwilling to promote limitations.
- The industry accounts for a large part of the GNP of developed nations – it generates employment and wealth.
- The political strength of vehicle and fuel suppliers is considerable.
- The investment in traditional roads and support services is huge – throwing away this investment is economically foolish.
- The existing parc will continue to be used for many years – 470 million cars can't be wrong.
- There are no obvious alternative fuel or engine technologies suitable for mass production.
- The opportunities for radical change to vehicle design are limited.

That said, changes are possible, they may simply not be as radical as many would like. Conservatism is an added barrier to change, certainly in this business. Cars can be made safer and less polluting, although this requires co-ordinated effort from legislators and car producers. They can be made lighter and more recyclable through the greater use of plastics. Since 1970 the use of plastics has grown four-fold, mainly in bumpers and interior panels, although a number of vehicles, notably Saturn in the US, have started to use plastic body panels. These offer the opportunity for greater design flexibility and individuality as well as offering less weight and so better fuel consumption.

Manufacturing cars with due regard for the environment is possible. Volkswagen keeps goldfish in its reception at its largest plant in Wolfsburg. The water they swim in has been used in the manufacturing process before being recycled. The VW Group is proud of how it can manage its business and tend to the country's environmental needs simultaneously.

Making emission-free vehicles in a clean way is generally much more expensive. It is difficult to see a business opportunity or increased profitability from an investment in sound environmental management. If this is to happen, government intervention will almost certainly be required.

All these arguments can – and will – be deployed in other industries. They should be scrutinized with equal care. There is no worse threat than that concealed behind an apparently unbreachable barrier to change, which then collapses.

# Dealing with governments is a necessity of life and can be an opportunity for advantage

The industry's relationships with governments will change considerably in the future. Governments have a major impact on the automotive industry. They have a considerable influence on the design and performance standards for products. Indeed, it can be argued that they have contributed a considerable amount to product improvement. They largely set the conditions under which cars can be used, through providing roads, regulating traffic, licensing drivers, and so on. They control the capital and operating cost of the products through taxation. They use the industry as an industrial development tool, through various incentives and inducements. They recognize its large role in overall economic activity. They have sometimes used it as an economic regulator, sometimes with unintended and usually negative consequences for the industry itself.

For the industry, therefore, the message is clear. The power of governments is growing, particularly concerning emissions and the environment. The pressure on them to act, limiting the use and applications of motor vehicles, is also rising. If the industry is to influence these changes, then it should work more closely with government bodies, proposing change, rather than resisting it as it often does today.

There are some things that economics alone won't solve. The development of safer, more fuel-efficient, less polluting vehicles has not been due to *laissez-faire* economic policies. The major steps forward have been because of legislation – on fuel economy, anti-lock brakes, catalytic converters, safety glass, and so on. Free-market economics works against such developments – any vehicle manufacturer choosing to fit a catalyst of his own accord, would be raising his costs unnecessarily. He would lose out. The only way vehicles can become safer, cleaner and more fuel efficient is by government intervention. Similarly, the only way nations can become less dependent on oil is through legislation. While this seems obvious, many governments, particularly in Europe, still fail to accept their role in the development of the car industry.

# Summary of Part Five

Business, like war, is fundamentally dynamic and may be complex. Realizing that change will take place, knowing what form it is likely to take and understanding the factors and events that drive it are fundamental to strategic success:

- The real strategic objective is scale-based dominance in a properly defined and bounded competitive arena. Yet this alone may not suffice for ever, as many apparently stable industries are imperfectly structured internally and therefore liable to undergo major upheaval. Understanding the nature of and the need for change is difficult, especially for industry leaders.

- Profit is not a long-term strategic objective in itself. It is a measure of performance and a result. It can also be a very misleading indicator of future performance. Profits must be reinvested to achieve growth. Moreover, the growth must be of the right sort. There is little to be gained in the long term from a strategy that achieves rapid growth but still leaves the company trailing competitors.

- Image and brands are historically acquired assets of a transient nature, which can be acquired and divested. They can also be made irrelevant by astute competitors. Overreliance on them can be dangerous.

- Environmentalism is here to stay. It is neither a passing fad nor a bureaucratic imposition but part of an underlying long-term change in societal values and attitudes, and therefore in the patterns of demand which affect businesses. Some more than others, obviously.

- Governments and legislators can offer strategic opportunities if they are managed correctly. They can also present major problems if not managed adequately. Most large-scale businesses have to deal with them among their constituents. Doing so, well, can be a major skill and source of competitive advantage.

# Lessons in business analysis

## The wider lessons of the automotive experience

The issues outlined in this book are clearly not unique to the automotive industry. Over-dependence on image-creation and branding is starting to create problems in consumer goods. There has been a spreading opposition to over-branding and over-marketing in pharmaceuticals. Virtually every Western bank thought in the 1980s that it had a unique strategy based on targeting high income and high net worth individuals. The personal computer and software industry is a clear example of excessive product proliferation and too many players – another bubble which will burst painfully, as dominant, cost-advantaged competitors finally emerge to drive the multiple marginal players out. As market and product segments crystallize in their mature form and product costs and prices come down, the value of producer and product brands weakens and the visibility, influence and economic power of distributors increases. The choice and management of channels becomes of paramount importance, particularly in any business that addresses individual consumers.

## The changes that matter to an industry are those that break down the traditional segment structure

The fundamental thesis of this book is that even a very complex, interrelated and entrenched sector, such as the automotive industry, goes through a lifecycle and is therefore subject to major structural change at times. There will be resistance and inertia but the forces of market, economic and competitive rationality are ultimately irresistible. The main forces are:

- Fundamental changes in the nature of demand and of market structures.
- Major changes in the design and performance of products or services, and in the technologies that underpin these.
- The development of a better way of organizing the innovation and delivery chains.

- The emergence of new distribution channels, that provide a better performance-cost compromise for final customers.
- Changes in the balance of power between manufacturers, suppliers and distributors.
- Major geographic realignments, whether coalescence or divergence.

The automotive industry may appear monolithic and stable to the outsider. In fact, it is far from monolithic and is internally very complex. It is in constant internal movement. Yet one must distinguish superficial from fundamental change. A major product launch is an event in the industry and its authors will as often as not try to hail it as a breakthrough. But it is no turning point. In fact, it may be yet another contribution to blowing up a bubble of product proliferation that must ultimately burst. To make that prediction requires a considerable insight into markets and their requirements, into the supply side and its economics and into the nature of competition.

Product (or service) obsession is the hallmark of many industries and businesses – to the point at which the realities of the market are often lost from sight.

# It is absolutely vital to step back from time to time and ask questions about the business you are in

The questions that must be asked are:

- Which people buy this product or service?
- Why do they buy it?
- Are they getting what they really want?
- Are they getting the proper support in its use?
- Are they reached through the proper distribution channels?
- Are the product development and supply structures a rational match to the needs of the end customers and the distribution channels?
- Is vertical integration along the development and supply chains right?
- Is the industry potentially unstable structurally?
- Is it efficiently run?
- Are there major unsatisfied markets, or markets that might quickly shrink?
- How well-structured is the industry competitively?
- Is competition fierce or passive?
- Is someone poised to change the way things are done?
- What are the strengths and weaknesses of the different players?
- What are the opportunities and threats that exist now or may arise in the future?
- What are the roles of governments, legislation and regulation?
- Are they likely to trigger change or inhibit it?
- What are the opportunities for players in the industry to influence its future through this route?

## Some generic lessons apply in looking at any industry

It is essential to be simple yet rigorous when looking at an industry and the position and prospects of a particular enterprise within it. Look carefully at the segmentation. Go through the traditional product/market mapping exercise outlined above. Think how consumers or customers can sensibly be grouped, not as a function of superficial demographic variables, but based on their fundamental needs, preferences and purchasing behaviour, and those of the channels through which they are reached. Group products and services rationally – not in terms of detailed features presented in catalogues and sales literature, but as a function of whether they require different development and supply structures. Determine which combinations of demand-side segments and supply-side structures constitute complete, defensible businesses.

## To analyse a business successfully, one must ask fundamental questions about it

There are six key questions that need to be asked:

(1)    Is this a single business or several?
(2)    What differentiates the business commercially?
   (a)    technology of the products
   (b)    technology of processes
   (c)    application sets and/or customer requirements
   (d)    distribution and marketing channels
   (e)    cost
(3)    How does one gain secure dominance in one or other of the businesses?
   (a)    scale
   (b)    excellence
   (c)    minimum product or market segment coverage
(4)    What drives growth?
   (a)    demand
   (b)    substitution
(5)    Could the barriers between businesses collapse?
   (a)    technological change
   (b)    user changes
   (c)    costs changing with growth
   (d)    within competitors
(6)    Which competitors understand and exploit the business economics?

Once this segmentation framework is set up, even as a first rough-cut, put in some simple numbers on demand volumes and growth, unit price levels and turnovers. Identify the factors which determine competitive success or failure in each business: product performance or cost leadership, distribution capabilities, etc. Position competitors against this framework. Apply the test of reasonableness: does it provide a consistent explanation of how the industry functions, as a market and as a competitive arena? If it does not, what extra information is required to perfect the model?

## The analysis must then be developed further, to probe the competitive patterns and prospect

Again, a series of probing questions needs to be asked:

- Have the structure of the industry and the competitive pattern reached equilibrium?
- Is it still in the development phase, has it reached maturity? Is it in decline?
- Is the segmentation structure stable, so that change is evolutionary and predictable, or are there latent discontinuities – such as those we have suggested for the automotive industry today?
- If so, who is likely to benefit from them and how?
- Is there any room for players other than giants and small, flexible service providers to survive?
- Are niche strategies viable in this business, given the market, technological, economic and competitive realities? The evidence from the automotive and several other global or globalizing industries – such as banking or tele-communications – is that there are few niches left to hide in.

Every time, try to look through the industry's conventional wisdom, get behind the information structured for whatever other purposes – and ask the awkward questions.

# Glossary

| | |
|---|---|
| **4WD** | four-wheel drive |
| **ABS** | anti-lock braking systems |
| **aftermarket** | products, typically parts, sold to car owners to repair or enhance their vehicles |
| **ASEAN** | Association of South East Asian Nations |
| **BRITE/ EURAM** | Basic Research in Industrial Technologies for Europe/European Research on Advanced Materials |
| **CAD** | computer aided design |
| **CAFE** | corporate average fuel economy |
| **CARB** | California Air Resources Board |
| **CFC** | chlorofluorocarbon |
| **CKD** | completed, knocked down |
| **CNC** | computer numerically controlled |
| **CO** | carbon monoxide |
| **CO$_2$** | carbon dioxide |
| **CV** | commercial vehicle |
| **DI** | direct injection |
| **EC** | European Community |
| **ECU** | European currency unit |
| **EDI** | electronic data interchange |
| **EEA** | European Economic Area |
| **EFI/EFi** | electronic fuel injection |
| **EFTA** | European Free Trade Association |
| **ERM** | exchange rate mechanism, in Europe |
| **EU** | European Union |
| **EV** | electric vehicle |
| **GATT** | General Agreement on Tariffs and Trade |
| **GDP** | gross domestic product |
| **GM** | General Motors |
| **GM Europe** | General Motors Europe which includes Opel, Vauxhall and Saab |

| | |
|---|---|
| **GNP** | gross national product |
| **HC** | hydrocarbon |
| **IDI** | indirect injection |
| **IMF** | International Monetary Fund |
| **IMVP** | International Motor Vehicle Programme |
| **JIT** | just-in-time |
| **LCV** | light commercial vehicle |
| **LDC** | less developed country |
| **LEV** | low emission vehicle |
| **Mercosur** | or the **southern cone**, an association of South American countries |
| **MITI** | The Ministry for International Trade and Industry in Japan |
| **MPV** | multi-purpose vehicle |
| **Nafta** | North American Free Trade Agreement |
| **NAPA** | National Automotive Parts Association |
| **NC** | numerically controlled |
| **NIC** | newly industrializing nation |
| **NOx** | oxides of nitrogen |
| **OECD** | Organization for Economic Cooperation and Development |
| **OEM** | original equipment manufacturer |
| **OES** | original equipment supplier |
| **OPEC** | Organization of Petroleum Exporting Countries |
| **parc** | the number of cars in use |
| **PM** | particulate matter (soot) |
| **PSA** | Peugeot SA (Peugeot and Citroën) |
| **SMMT** | Society of Motor Manufacturers and Traders (UK trade organization) |
| **ULEV** | ultra-low emission vehicle |
| **VAG** | Volkswagen AG (includes Seat and Skoda as well as Volkswagen and Audi) |
| **VAT** | value added tax |
| **VM** | vehicle manufacturer |
| **WTO** | World Trade Organization (to succeed GATT) |
| **ZEV** | zero emission vehicles |

# Index